AN INTRODUCTION TO

MATHEMATICAL

PROBABILITY

BY

JULIAN LOWELL COOLIDGE

Late Professor of Mathematics in Harvard University

DOVER PUBLICATIONS, INC.
NEW YORK

Published in the United Kingdom by Constable and Company Limited, 10 Orange Street, London W. C. 2

This new Dover edition, first published in 1962, is an unabridged and corrected republication of the work first published by Oxford University Press in 1925.
This edition is published by special arrangement with Oxford University Press.

Manufactured in the United States of America
Dover Publications, Inc.
180 Varick Street
New York 14, N. Y.

PREFACE

THE present work is based upon the lectures which I have delivered, usually in alternate years, at Harvard University. It is not intended primarily as a contribution to mathematical science, but as a text-book introductory to a branch of mathematics which has assumed an unexpected importance in recent times.

There are plenty of good books dealing with the theory of mathematical probability. In French we have the beautiful treatises of Bertrand * and Poincaré †—the former reads like a romance, the latter has much of the originality and brilliance characteristic of the master—as well as the text of Borel ‡ on the same high level, to say nothing of others of less note. In German there is, first of all, the encyclopaedic but readable text of Czuber,§ the translation of Markhoff, ‖ with its unusual attention to rigour, as well as several others. In Italian there is the recent work of Castelnuovo,¶ careful, critical, and judicious. How is it in English? There is only one recent text-book,** that of Fisher, very full in its treatment of statistics and frequency curves, but omitting many of the most important parts of the subject. The striking book on probability by Keynes †† is purely philosophical in

---

* *Calcul des probabilités*, Paris, 1889.

† *Calcul des probabilités*, 2nd ed., Paris, 1912.

‡ *Éléments de la théorie des probabilités*, Paris, 1908.

§ *Wahrscheinlichkeitsrechnung*, 2nd ed , Leipzig, 1908.

‖ *Wahrscheinlichkeitsrechnung*, Leipzig, 1912.

¶ *Calcolo delle Probabilità*, Rome, 1919.

** *Mathematical Theory of Probabilities*, 2nd ed., New York, 1922.

†† *Treatise on Probability*, London, 1921.

interest, inclining to the thesis that probability is not a mathematical subject anyway.

It would, of course, be far better if every English-speaking reader were a sufficient master of foreign languages to study all of these excellent texts, but such is manifestly not the case. The simple fact is that such readers absolutely will not make the linguistic effort necessary. The need for a brief but comprehensive English text is obvious, if regrettable.

From the purely mathematical point of view, the calculus of probabilities is somewhat unsatisfactory. To begin with, we are forced to use approximate formulae, and it is not always easy to have an exact knowledge of their degree of exactness, at least without arduous calculations. Then certain fundamental laws, like the Gaussian Law of Error, are based on a variety of so-called proofs, each making some very broad assumptions of doubtful validity. And lastly, there is a nasty habit of developing a formula under the assumption that it holds for a very limited range, and then calculating the constants by computing out to infinity. For this reason the mathematician is tempted at times to view the whole subject with distrust. This is a mistake. However the formulae may be derived, they frequently prove remarkably trustworthy in practice. The proper attitude is not to reject laws of doubtful origin, but to scrutinize them with care, with a view to reaching the true principles underneath. It seems to me that, in the last analysis, probability is a statistical, that is to say, an experimental science, and the mathematical problem is to establish rules which yield correct and valuable results.

Perhaps the most characteristic feature of the present work is that the statistical definition of probability is adhered to throughout. This has been done in philosophical discussions, and Castelnuovo comes very near to adopting it, but the usual method is to have several different definitions of probability, and reconcile them *tant bien que mal*.

As a matter of history, the calculus of probability started with the study of games of chance. The present book does the same. Of course, this branch of the subject is not the most important to-day, but in studying any science it is wise to pay some attention to the problems that gave it birth. Moreover, from a didactic point of view, it is doubtful whether the plan of replacing problems in games of chance by problems in life insurance is likely to increase the interest of the beginner. On the other hand, the tendency which some people show of attempting to solve all problems in probability by assimilating them to drawing balls from an urn is fundamentally unsound, as it departs from the facts.

The subjects of mean value and expectation, which have always played a central role in the theory of probabilities, have taken on additional importance in recent years, owing to the idea of dispersion, and its application to statistical series. For that reason they have been given a good deal of prominence. *Per contra*, geometrical probability, which is little more than a plaything, and the probability of causes, which rests on very shaky foundations, are treated briefly. Yet they should not be omitted entirely, for the former is related to statistical mechanics, and the latter gives the only answers we have to certain questions which recur insistently.

The most important part of the theory is that which deals with the distribution of errors of observation. The fundamental question here is what to do with the exponential law of Gauss. I have tried to make it as plausible as I could by basing it on very broad assumptions, even though this adds somewhat to the length of the deduction. I have, however, given the principles of combining observations as far as possible independently of the Gaussian law. The study of errors in two dimensions, which formerly interested few but students of artillery practice, has taken on a new importance through its relation to statistical correlation.

The treatment of least square and indirect observations

follows traditional lines. In studying the application of least squares to curve fitting, I have briefly explained the modern method of moments. I have also included a summary treatment of the applications of probability to such widely divergent topics as the kinetic theory of gases and life insurance.

In general, it has been my idea to give the mathematical basis underlying each of the important applications of probability rather than to write a treatise on games of chance, or errors of observation, or the combination of measurements, or statistics, or statistical mechanics, or insurance.

With a view to adding to the didactic value of the work I have introduced a certain number of exercises for the student. It would be easy to multiply these indefinitely. The few which I have chosen seemed to me particularly interesting, but that, perhaps, is a matter of individual preference. The teacher or student will find little difficulty in adding to the number.

Paragraphs marked ¶ are more difficult than the others, and may well be omitted by the beginner.

There is little need for elaborate bibliographical notes as Czuber's comprehensive report,* though not entirely free from mistakes, covers the ground thoroughly.

J. L. C.

CAMBRIDGE, U.S.A.,
  December 1924.

* *Die Entwickelung der Wahrscheinlichkeitsrechnung und ihrer Anwendungen. Jahresbericht der deutschen Mathematikervereinigung*, Vol. vii, Part 2, Leipzig, 1899.

CONTENTS

CHAPTER I
THE SCOPE AND MEANING OF MATHEMATICAL PROBABILITY

CHAPTER II
ELEMENTARY PRINCIPLES OF PROBABILITY

§ 1. Formulae for Combinations and Arrangements

§ 2. Simple Problems in Total and Compound Probability

§ 3. Expectation

§ 4. Risk

CHAPTER III
BERNOULLI'S THEOREM

§ 1. The Problem of Repeated Trials

§ 2. Stirling's Formula

§ 3. The Probability Integral

CHAPTER IV

MEAN VALUE AND DISPERSION

§ 1. Elementary Theorems in Mean Value

§ 2. Dispersion

CHAPTER V

GEOMETRICAL PROBABILITY

CHAPTER VI

PROBABILITY OF CAUSES

CHAPTER VII

ERRORS OF OBSERVATION

§ 1. Determination of the 'Best Value'

CHAPTER X

THE STATISTICAL THEORY OF GASES

CHAPTER XI

THE PRINCIPLES OF LIFE INSURANCE

CHAPTER I

THE SCOPE AND MEANING OF MATHEMATICAL PROBABILITY

EVERYBODY has a pretty good working knowledge of the meaning of the words 'probable' and 'improbable'. If a man be asked: 'Is it probable that the sun will rise to-morrow?' 'Is it probable that you will be elected next Grand Lama of Tibet?' he knows precisely what the question means, and is able to answer without hesitation. That is because the terms are used in a general sense, without any attempt at the refinement of accuracy needful for mathematical purposes. In exactly the same way, everybody understands the statement that Cap Gris-Nez is the nearest point in France to Great Britain. The trouble comes when we undertake to say what we mean by a mathematical point, and in like manner we encounter serious difficulty when we try to express probability in exact mathematical language. A brilliant contemporary philosopher has defined mathematics as the science where we never know what we are talking about, or what our results mean; the calculus of probability is no exception to this pessimistic definition.

How shall probability be defined as a mathematical term? The first definition which we have to consider, and which is ascribed to James, *alias* Jacob, Bernoulli, is that probability is the measure of the strength of our expectation of a future event. If we feel almost sure that an event is going to happen, we say that it is highly probable; in the contrary case, we call it highly improbable; and if we are so inclined, we may express our expectation in the form of a bet, for or against the arrival of the event. Probability appears as the mathematical measure of our state of expectancy.

The mere statement of such a definition is sufficient to raise a host of objections. If, as the statement suggests, probability is merely a sort of psychological coefficient, the practical application of it should be in the psychological laboratory, where it could be measured in the same way as reaction time, intensity of response to stimulus, persistence of illusion. But no large circle of persons is interested in any such sort of probability as that. Moreover, different persons will assign different degrees of probability to the same future event, and the same person will feel differently about it at different times, according to his mood, or the state of his digestion. In consequence of this, the supporters of such a definition put in a qualifying adjective, saying that probability is the measure of our 'intelligent' expectation of a future event. This raises the question, 'What is intelligent expectation?' The answer would seem to be that it is the expectation of an intelligent person, reasoning on the facts in the case, and not on his own personal hopes and fears. But if all intelligent persons will reach the same degree of expectancy when they reason intelligently on the facts, then the measure of this expectancy must be a function of the facts themselves, and not of the individual; who may thus be left out of account.

A lineal successor of Bernoulli has appeared in very recent times in Keynes, whose remarkable book was referred to in the preface. This writer's main thesis is that probability is not concerned with events, but with judgements or propositions.* This is a question of definition, and his point of view is certainly legitimate. But a science of the probability of judgements can scarcely be made a subject of exact mathematical treatment, and this also is one of Keynes's principal contentions.†   His method is, to use his own words:‡ 'To regard subjective probability as fundamental, and to treat all other relative conceptions as derivative from this.' It is perhaps open to question whether he has entirely answered the difficulties raised against Bernoulli, but in any case

* Loc. cit., p. 5.   † Ibid., p. 34.
‡ Ibid., p. 282.

it is perfectly evident that a line of reasoning which starts from the premiss that a certain subject is non-mathematical, is not a good introduction to a mathematical treatment of that subject.

A second definition, which has the great authority of John Stuart Mill, may be expressed as follows : * Let us suppose that an event depends upon a certain nexus of causes, each of measurable intensity. We measure the total field or extent of variation of these causes, and take this as denominator, while as numerator we take the measure of that field or extent of variation which will produce what we call a *favourable outcome*. The fraction is defined as the *probability* for a favourable result. For instance, if a coin be spun in the air, there is an equal chance that it will turn up head or tail, because the initial angular velocities of spin and translational velocities of the centre of gravity which will cause the coin to show a head, cover one-half the total ranges of angular and translational velocities which need be considered in the particular problem.

The difficulties attending such a definition are so many that it is scarcely worth consideration. What antecedent events are to be classed as causes? Are there not different groups of independent events, each of which might be called the group of causes, and how do we know that the result will be independent of the choice of group? Moreover, it is by no means certain that the calculation will yield in every case the number which the uninitiated would designate as the probability for a favourable outcome. Suppose that in a certain congressional district there were five rock-ribbed Republicans to each three stalwart Democrats. The forces tending to elect a Republican congressman would seem to bear a ratio of five to three to those tending to elect a Democrat, but we should hesitate to say that there were only five chances in eight that the successful candidate would be a Republican.

* *Logic*, 8th ed., vol. ii, p. 72, London, 1872. Mill does not require all probabilities to come under this head, but insists that we have here the real reason for the persistence of statistical ratios.

We now come to the definition of probability which is used in practically all mathematical treatises on the subject, and which can be put into the following words : ' An event can happen in a certain number of ways, which are all equally likely. A certain proportion of these are classed as *favourable*. The ratio of the number of favourable ways to the total number is called the probability that the event will turn out favourably.'

This definition is ever so much more clear-cut than the others, and is capable of immediate application in many cases. Nevertheless there are two objections which may be easily raised. The first is, ' Exactly what is meant by the phrase " equally likely " ? ' This question is of fundamental importance in our subject, and must be treated in detail later. The other criticism, on the strength of which we reject this definition, is that as it stands it excludes many probabilities which are, nevertheless, among the most important. As stated above, it is inapplicable to a large number of cases where the number of ways is infinite; also it excludes the whole field of statistical probability. If we ask the probability that a letter in the lost-letter office contain money, we are asking a concrete and intelligible question, but to base the answer on the number of ways in which money can be put into or left out of a misdirected letter would be the height of absurdity. It is the desire to include all forms of probability under one definition that leads us to the form which we shall now explain.

First empirical assumption.

IF AN EVENT WHICH CAN HAPPEN IN TWO DIFFERENT WAYS BE REPEATED A GREAT NUMBER OF TIMES UNDER THE SAME ESSENTIAL CONDITIONS, THE RATIO OF THE NUMBER OF TIMES THAT IT HAPPENS IN ONE WAY, TO THE TOTAL NUMBER OF TRIALS, WILL APPROACH A DEFINITE LIMIT, AS THE LATTER NUMBER INCREASES INDEFINITELY.

Definition.

The limit described in the first empirical assumption shall

be called the *probability* that the event shall happen in the first way, under those conditions.*

There are quite as many objections to this method of defining probability as to any other, and we must set about defending it as best we can. To begin with, how do we know that the first empirical assumption is true? The only answer is that experience in many fields under all sorts of circumstances has demonstrated its truth. Few laws of nature are so well established as this, and we are not only justified, but compelled, when it appears to be at fault, to examine whether the conditions of experiment have not undergone unnoticed but important alterations. For instance, the forms of inadvertence which cause people to leave their umbrellas in public conveyances are many and various, but the proportion of umbrellas to the total number of travellers in any particular locality is apparently fairly constant. An increase of marked amount would suggest the query as to whether the weather had not been unusually bad; a notable diminution would suggest either good weather or dishonest employees.

The most serious difficulty with the definition is the following: What is meant by 'the same essential conditions'? No two experiments are ever performed under identical conditions. There are always slight changes in temperature, barometric pressure, the state of the experimenter's digestion, the chemical composition of his blood. How can we tell what conditions are essential, and what ones are not? The objection is perfectly valid, and does not admit of any perfect refutation. We must recognize, however, that it does not

* This is essentially the definition used, for the most part, in Mill's *Logic*, and defended in great detail in Venn's *Logic of Chance*, 3rd ed., London, 1888. Neither of these writers, however, draws a sufficiently sharp distinction between a ratio and the limit of a ratio. A much more accurate statement will be found in an article by Von Mises, 'Grundlagen der Wahrscheinlichkeitsrechnung', *Mathematische Zeitschrift*, vol. v, pp. 53 ff. Keynes, loc. cit., part I, ch. viii, attacks it with the utmost vigour. His objections seem to me to fall completely to the ground if one considers that probability has to do with events, not with judgements. He refuses for philosophical reasons to consider the probability of events, he scarcely will acknowledge the existence of such a probability. I am equally sure that the probability of events is the only kind worthy of serious mathematical study.

bear on the present question alone, but on the whole of experimental science. If we seek to determine any physical law by experimental means, we tacitly assume that such changes as occur in the conditions are immaterial to the result. Without some such fundamental postulate all experimental science would be impossible. Shall the psychologist, experimenting on the sensitiveness of a patient to certain faint stimuli, give up all hope of learning the truth because between one experiment and another the earth will have performed a certain number of turns about its axis, and will have travelled a certain distance along its orbit, while the whole solar system will have made a certain progress through space? Evidently the postulate that we can distinguish between essential and unessential conditions lies at the basis of all inductive science, and cannot be charged up to the calculus of probability.

Another criticism which can be levelled against our definition is the following. In making probability merely the limit of a statistical ratio, we exclude the possibility of ever determining a probability except as the result of a long series of experiments, and even then we could only determine it approximately. There are some writers who are frankly willing to accept this limitation,* but our own view is that we need not tie our hands quite to this extent. It is hard to base the probability that a card drawn at random from a pack should be black upon a series of experiments *ad hoc*, when we do not know whether such experiments have really ever been performed. We therefore make our

Second empirical assumption.

IF AN EVENT CAN HAPPEN IN A CERTAIN NUMBER OF WAYS, ALL OF WHICH ARE EQUALLY LIKELY, AND IF A CERTAIN NUMBER OF THESE BE CALLED FAVOURABLE, THEN THE RATIO OF THE NUMBER OF FAVOURABLE WAYS TO THE TOTAL NUMBER IS EQUAL TO THE PROBABILITY THAT THE EVENT WILL TURN OUT FAVOURABLY.

---

* Venn, loc. cit. Mill, on the other hand, looks upon probabilities determined by reasoning as more certain than those determined statistically.

It cannot be too much emphasized that this is an empirical assumption based upon experience, exactly like the other. It tells us that the ratio of favourable outcomes to trials approaches, as a limit, the ratio of the number of favourable ways to total ways. It is sometimes assumed that the one or the other of these assumptions can be proved by Bernoulli's theorem, to be developed in a later chapter. This is pure illusion. No one's theorem, based on *a priori* considerations, can prove that in practice a coin will show heads about one-half the time. Moreover, a few moments' reflection will show that in one guise or another we must have both of these assumptions. Without the second, we could never predict the probability of an outcome from the data; the matter would always have to be put to the test. Without the first assumption, there would be absolutely no connexion between the ratio of favourable to total ways and the statistical ratio determined by practice; a probability defined by the former would be an abstract number, having no practical significance.*

There is one other very important point in this second assumption, which we mentioned above, and which we must now examine carefully. What is meant by ' equally likely ' ? If we say that two ways are equally likely when the number of arrivals either way bears to the number of trials a ratio with the same limit, we are running around in a circle, and saying that if the limit of a certain ratio is the probability of success, why, then the probability of success is the limit of that ratio. No, if our second assumption is to tell us anything at all, we must mean something else by ' equally likely '.

There has been a good deal of debate among philosophers as to just what meaning should be attached to these mystic words, and two sharply divergent views have been expressed, and ably defended. The first of these, which has the great authority of Laplace,† and has been vigorously defended

---

* This is admirably brought out by Cournot, *Théorie des chances*, Paris, 1843, pp. 437 ff.

† See his *Traité analytique des probabilités*, Paris, 1812.

by Stumpf,* is expressed by saying that two results are equally likely when we know that one of them must happen, but have no information leading us to expect the one rather than the other. Everybody will admit that this expresses a necessary condition that two events should be equally likely, the doubt is as to its sufficiency. Assuming that Mars is inhabited, what is the probability that the inhabitants are carnivorous? The most imaginative observer will acknowledge that, as far as our present information goes, we are completely in the dark on this interesting point, there is nothing to guide our opinion. Shall we, therefore, say that the probability that these enterprising engineers are carnivorous is expressed by the fraction $\frac{1}{2}$? And if we say so, shall we go on to the assertion that if future astronomic research revealed to us that a large number of the heavenly bodies were inhabited we might expect to find carnivorous inhabitants in about one-half of them? Such an assumption is the merest juggling with words, and we do not hesitate to pronounce against the sufficiency of this condition.† It is not unnatural, then, that some philosophers have been led to the opposite extreme, and have maintained that we can only say that two events are equally likely if we are acquainted with all the causes tending to produce the one or the other, and know them to be of equal potency. We do not say that a spinning coin is equally likely to turn up head or tail because we know no reason to expect the one rather than the other; we make this affirmation only upon the hypothesis that it is a real coin and not a counterfeit, nearly homogeneous, with the centre of gravity near the middle, while the method of throwing is such that it had no tendency to favour the one face at the expense of the other. This idea was skilfully elaborated by Von Kries ‡ in his theory of 'range', which is essentially Mill's idea of equal field of variation for forces. Two ways in which a thing can

---

* *Ueber den Begriff der mathematischen Wahrscheinlichkeit*, Sitzungsberichte, Royal Bavarian Academy, Philosophical Class, 1892.

† There is a good discussion of this point in Keynes, loc. cit., part I, ch. iv.

‡ *Prinzipien der Wahrscheinlichkeiten*, Freiburg, 1886. The last chapter of this work contains an excellent historical summary of the various theories of probability.

happen may be said to be equally likely when, and only when, we know that the fields of variation or the forces tending to produce the one or the other have equal content.

It is certain that we have here the best possible way for determining whether two events are equally likely or not, when it can be applied; unfortunately in many cases we have no complete information, and are tempted to fall back on the other principle, namely, that we have no reason to believe the range for one set of causes to be greater than that for the other. There is a subsidiary difficulty, which Von Kries himself recognized, and which raises fearful havoc in certain parts of the theory of probability. Suppose that we measure two ranges for a certain variable, and find them equal. We next replace that variable by a function of itself, and measure the corresponding ranges of this new variable. They may be very far from being equal to one another. Consequently two eventualities which seemed to be equally likely when stated in terms of the first variable, might appear far otherwise in terms of the second. For instance, suppose that we know that a certain variable lies between 10 and 1,000, the ranges 10 to 100 and 100 to 1,000 are very different in magnitude, and would not seem to produce equally likely cases for any event dependent on them. But if we found that the natural measurement to make was not the variable itself, but its logarithm; if the variable appeared naturally as the anti-logarithm of a certain number, then the ranges of 1 to 2 and 2 to 3 for the logarithm would seem to produce equally likely cases.

In spite of this difficulty, our own preference is strongly towards the latter form of definition. Not the least of its merits is that it is an objective, not subjective shape, and so harmonizes with our general point of view. We shall say, then, that the words ' equally likely' cannot be used unless the essential conditions governing the result are known, using the word essential in the same sense as in Assumption 1. It is conceivable that some of these essential conditions might tend to favour one outcome, some another. If nothing be known about the relative strength of these diverse tendencies, we cannot go further. But if we can say that the total resultant of the essential conditions does not tend to favour one outcome rather than the other, then the two may be said to be *equally likely*.

Our second empirical assumption enables us to predict probabilities in cases where the number of ways in which an event can happen is finite. We need some corresponding assumption in the case where there are an infinite number of possibilities. What we shall need here is some assumption as to the probability that a group of variables should take values within a small neighbourhood of a given group. We have lurking in the background the same difficulty we saw above in finding two ranges leading to equally likely results; at best we cannot make any very clear-cut hypothesis.

Third empirical assumption.

If AN EVENT DEPEND UPON n INDEPENDENT VARIABLES $X_1 X_2 \ldots X_n$, WHICH CAN VARY CONTINUOUSLY IN AN n-DIMENSIONAL CONTINUOUS MANIFOLD, THERE EXISTS SUCH AN ANALYTIC FUNCTION $F(X_1 X_2 \ldots X_n)$ THAT THE PROBABILITY FOR A RESULT CORRESPONDING TO A GROUP OF VALUES IN THE INFINITESIMAL REGION

$$X_1 \pm \tfrac{1}{2} dX_1, \ X_2 \pm \tfrac{1}{2} dX_2, \ldots X_n \pm \tfrac{1}{2} dX_n$$

DIFFERS BY AN INFINITESIMAL OF HIGHER ORDER FROM

$$F(X_1, X_2, \ldots X_n) \, dX_1 \, dX_2 \ldots dX_n.$$

It must be acknowledged that as long as we are in total ignorance as to what function F may be, this assumption does not lead us very far. The requirement that it should be analytic is unnecessarily strong, but we need a continuous function, and we can approach as near to such a function as we please by an analytic function. Moreover, the assumption is not quite so fruitless as one might fear. Let p be the probability that the event take a form which we shall call favourable, and let this correspond to a region of variation R, then

$$p = \int \ldots \int_R F(X_1, X_2, \ldots X_n) \, dX_1 \, dX_2 \ldots dX_n.$$

If the total field of variation be T, we have

$$1 = \int \ldots \int_T F(X_1, X_2, \ldots X_n)\, dX_1\, dX_2 \ldots dX_n.$$

Now let $x_1 x_2 \ldots x_n$ be such a set of independent variables, functions of the old ones, that regions R and T correspond to regions r and t, and that

$$\frac{\partial(x_1, x_2, \ldots x_n)}{\partial(X_1, X_2, \ldots X_n)} = F(X_1, X_2, \ldots X_n).$$

Then the probability for a set of variables lying in the favourable region is

$$p = \frac{\int \ldots \int_r dx_1\, dx_2 \ldots dx_n}{\int \ldots \int_t dx_1\, dx_2 \ldots dx_n} \tag{1}$$

and this is the ratio of the content of the desired manifold r to the total manifold t, when measured in terms of the variables $x_1 x_2 \ldots x_n$. Or, to put the matter otherwise, the probability of a favourable outcome is the ratio of the content of the favourable range to that of the total range, when the right variables are chosen. In many cases, the mere statement of the problem leads naturally to the right variables; it is only when there is considerable doubt as to which variables these are that the problem is obscure. And of course the correctness of any answer depends upon the correctness of the choice of variables. We shall explain these points in greater detail in a subsequent chapter, that dealing with geometrical probability.

There is one other possible method of defining probability which should receive a passing notice. In modern discussions of the foundations of mathematics, we do not define points or numbers, except in the sense that we make certain independent postulates about them. In the same way, we might say that the probability of an event was a number which was a function of that event, and which obeyed certain formal laws of logic. This method, which we should like to see developed, would be unexceptionable from the point of view of abstract mathematics, but the real importance of the calculus of probability does not lie in any such field as that. We emphasize once more that we are dealing with what is somewhat loosely called an 'applied science', and the fundamental questions do not deal with the abstract philosophical nature of probability, which always seems to remain somewhat obscure and elusive, but rather the meanings of numerical probabilities in specific cases. The purpose of this first chapter has been to develop a general definition for that meaning which should 'make sense' in every case.

CHAPTER II

ELEMENTARY PRINCIPLES OF PROBABILITY

§ 1. Formulae for Combinations and Arrangements.

IF n be a positive integer, we give the name *factorial* n to the product $n \cdot (n-1) \cdot (n-2) \cdots 3 \cdot 2 \cdot 1$, and we have for this a special notation, namely

$$n(n-1)(n-2) \cdots 3 \cdot 2 \cdot 1 = n! \tag{1}$$

It is convenient to extend this equation to the case where $n = 0$

$$(n-1)! = \frac{n!}{n}$$

$$0! = \frac{1!}{1} = 1.$$

The student must not forget that this is a definition, it is not a statement that if 0 be multiplied by the positive integers less than itself, the product is 1.

Suppose that from n distinguishable objects we pick r objects, and arrange them in order; in how many ways can this be done? Evidently we have a choice of n objects for the first place, $n-1$ for the second, &c. The number of arrangements is $n(n-1) \ldots (n-r+1)$.

This is sometimes called the number of permutations of n things taken r at a time, and written P_r^n, but we do not need to burden ourselves either with the name or the symbol.

A more interesting and important number is that which tells us in how many ways r objects can be picked from n objects, regardless of order. If this number be x, and if we subsequently multiply by the number of ways that r objects can be arranged among themselves, the product is the number of arrangements of r objects taken from n objects, thus

$$x \cdot r! = n(n-1) \cdots (n-r+1),$$

$$x = \frac{n(n-1) \cdots (n-r+1)}{r!},$$

$$x = n!/r!(n-r)! \tag{2}$$

It is to be noted here that r and $(n-r)$ appear symmetrically, but that might have been foreseen, for the number of ways that we can pick r things to be taken from n things is the number of ways that we can pick $(n-r)$ to be left. The total number of ways in which *something* can be taken is

$$\sum_{r=1}^{r=n} \frac{n!}{r!(n-r)!}$$

and this may be written, by the aid of the binomial theorem,

$$(1+1)^n - 1 = 2^n - 1.$$

This again might easily have been foreseen, for each individual object may be taken or left, irrespective of the others, but we must exclude the one case where all are left.

Let us return to formula (2). An easy and important extension is found as follows. In how many ways can n objects be divided into a group of a objects, another of b objects, another of c objects, and so on? The first group can be chosen in $n!/a!(n-a)!$ ways. The second group can be taken from the remainder in $(n-a)!/b!(n-a-b)!$ ways, and so on. Multiplying together, we get

$$\frac{n!}{a!\,b!\,c!\dots}. \tag{3}$$

There is one modification of this formula which is easily overlooked. Let $n = rs$, and let us imagine that we have r groups, each of s objects. The formula above will give as the number of ways $n!/(s!)^r$, and this answer is usually right. But in certain cases we may wish to make no distinction between the first group, the second group, &c., so that to get the answer, we should divide this by the number of ways in which the r groups might be arranged in an order of preference, thus getting $n!/(s!)^r\,r!$.

As an example, we see that the number of ways that four

hands can be dealt in such a game as whist or bridge is $52!/(13!)^4$, for the situation of a hand with regard to the dealer is important. But if we ask in how many ways can 52 cards be divided into four indistinguishable piles, the correct answer is $52!/(13!)^4 4!$.

This number is a good deal smaller than the other, but is by no means a small number for all that.

It is time to illustrate these principles with some examples.

Example 1] *In a certain company there are 15 men and 10 women; in how many ways can a committee be picked including 3 men and 2 women?*

The answer is clearly the product of the numbers of ways in which the representatives from the two sexes can be chosen, namely

$$\frac{15!}{12!\,3!} \times \frac{10!}{8!\,2!} = \frac{15 \times 14 \times 13}{1 \times 2 \times 3} \times \frac{10 \times 9}{2 \times 1} = 20{,}475.$$

Example 2] *3 travellers arrive at a town where there are 5 inns; in how many different ways can they be lodged?*

The natural way is to treat each traveller as an independent unit, capable of making 5 choices, thus getting $5^3 = 125$. But if we know further that the travellers have quarrelled on the road, so that no two will lodge at the same inn, the choice is reduced to $5 \times 4 \times 3 = 60$.

Example 3] *In how many ways can all the letters of the word Mississippi be arranged?*

If all of the letters were distinguishable, the number would be, clearly, $11!$, but we must divide this by the number of ways in which the indistinguishable i's can be arranged, the indistinguishable s's, and the p's, getting

$$11!/(4!)^2\,2! = 34{,}650.$$

§ 2.   Simple Problems in Total and Compound Probability.

Example 4]   *6 cards are chosen at random from a pack of 52; what is the probability that 3 will be black and 3 red?*

The words 'at random' here signify that we consider all combinations of 6 equally likely in the sense explained in the last chapter.   We have thus, by our first two empirical axioms, merely to find the ratio of favourable ways to total ways, namely

$$\left[\frac{(26\,!)}{(3\,!)\,(23\,!)} \right]^2 \div \frac{52\,!}{6\,!\,46\,!} = 0{\cdot}324.$$

Example 5]   *A card is chosen at random from each of 6 packs; what is the probability that 3 cards will be black and 3 red.*

In this case the total number of ways is 52^6.   To find the favourable ways we divide the 6 packs into 3 which are to show red, and 3 to show black, and multiply by 26^6; the answer is

$$\frac{6\,!}{(3\,!)^2} \cdot \frac{26^6}{52^6} = \frac{5 \times 4}{2^6} = 0{\cdot}312.$$

It would not have been easy to say off-hand which of these problems would have the larger answer.

There are two general principles which are of fundamental importance in doing simple problems of the present sort; these must now be explained.   Suppose that there are two events which are mutually exclusive, if the one happen the other cannot; and suppose that their respective probabilities are p_1 and p_2.   Let there be a large number N of trials, and

---

Problems.

1. In how many ways can a boat's crew of 8 be chosen from 20 men?

2. In how many different ways can two dice appear?   How many times will each possible sum appear?

3. Prove the 'multinomial theorem', namely,

$$(a+b+c+ \dots l)^n = \sum \frac{n\,!}{\alpha\,!\,\beta\,! \dots \lambda\,!} a^\alpha b^\beta \dots l^\lambda$$

$$\alpha + \beta + \dots + \lambda = n.$$

let the first event happen M_1 times, while the second happens M_2 times. Then by the fundamental definition of probability

$$\operatorname*{Lim}_{N \to \infty} \frac{M_1}{N} = p_1, \quad \operatorname*{Lim}_{N \to \infty} \frac{M_2}{N} = p_2.$$

Now, one of the basic theorems of the infinitesimal calculus tells us that the limit of the sum of two variables dependent upon the same third variable is the sum of their limits, so that

$$\operatorname*{Lim}_{N \to \infty} \left[\frac{M_1 + M_2}{N} \right] = \operatorname*{Lim}_{N \to \infty} \left[\frac{M_1}{N} + \frac{M_2}{N} \right] = p_1 + p_2.$$

But the limit on the left is the probability that the one event or the other shall happen. We may apply this same principle to any number of mutually exclusive events, the probability that one of n mutually exclusive events shall happen is the sum of the probabilities that a specified event shall happen plus the probability that some one of the other $n-1$ shall happen. Proceeding thus by a downward mathematical induction, we reach the

Theorem of total probability, special case.

The probability that one of any number of mutually exclusive events should happen is the sum of the probabilities for the separate events.

(When we have a constantly increasing number of probabilities, each individual one decreasing indefinitely, if their sum approach a definite limit as the number increases indefinitely, that limit will be the probability in the limiting case.)

Example 6] *2 dice are thrown; what is the probability that the sum shown will be 7 or 11?*

The sum 7 can be shown in six different ways, the sum 11 in only two, hence $\frac{6}{36} + \frac{2}{36} = \frac{2}{9} = 0 \cdot 222.$

Here is the second principle. Suppose that we have a compound event which is the result of the combination of two other events. We shall assume that these two are mutually independent. What does that phrase mean? If we take a mechanistic view of the universe, no one event is ever independent of any other, the outcome of any event must have a definite effect on all future history. Nevertheless, the uncorrupted man of common sense has a perfectly definite idea of what he means by saying that two events are mutually independent. His meaning may be expressed by the following:

Definition] *Two events are said to be mutually independent when the probability for either is the same whether the other happen or not.*

We take it as an empirical fact that there are such events in the universe, and that we can tell them when we see them. Suppose, then, that we have two mutually independent events, the first with the probability p_1, the second with the probability p_2, what is the probability p_{12} for the arrival of the compound event which consists in the arrival of both? Let there be a large number N of trials. Let the first one happen M_1 times, the second happen M_2 times, while both happen M_{12} times.

$$p_{12} = \operatorname*{Lim}_{N \to \infty} \frac{M_{12}}{N} = \operatorname*{Lim}_{N \to \infty} \frac{M_{12}}{M_2} \cdot \frac{M_2}{N};$$

$$p_1 = \operatorname*{Lim}_{N \to \infty} \frac{M_1}{N} = \operatorname*{Lim}_{M_2 \to \infty} \frac{M_{12}}{M_2}; \quad p_2 = \operatorname*{Lim}_{N \to \infty} \frac{M_2}{N}.$$

Now the limit of the product of two variables is the product of their limits, hence $p_{12} = p_1 \cdot p_2$.

Theorem of compound probability.

If a compound event consist in the conjunction of any number of independent events, the probability of the compound event is the product of the probabilities for the individual events.

Strictly speaking, we have only proved this in the case of two independent events, but the reader will find that the previous proof by mathematical induction will apply absolutely in this case also.

Example 7] *A die is thrown 12 times; what is the probability that the face 4 will appear just twice?*

There are various ways of showing 2 fours and 10 not fours, all mutually exclusive and equally likely. Hence the answer is the probability of starting with 2 fours, and then running 10 not fours, multiplied by the number of ways that two objects can be chosen from 12, thus

$$\frac{1}{6} \times \frac{1}{6} \times \left(\frac{5}{6}\right)^{10} \times \frac{12 \times 11}{1 \times 2} = \frac{5^{10} \times 11}{6^{11}} = 0.296.$$

Example 8] *A throws 3 coins, B throws 2; what is the chance that A will throw a greater number of heads than B?*

Note the wording of the problem; A is not to throw as many or more heads, but actually a greater number. This can be done in three mutually exclusive ways. We give them, with their chances :

A throws 3 heads $\qquad\qquad \frac{1}{8} \times 1 = \frac{1}{8}.$

A throws 2 heads, B does not $\qquad \frac{3}{8} \times \frac{3}{4} = \frac{9}{32}.$

A throws 1 head, B throws 2 tails $\quad \frac{3}{8} \times \frac{1}{4} = \frac{3}{32}.$

Total probability $\quad \frac{16}{32} = \frac{1}{2}.$

Example 9] *A card is drawn at random from a pack and replaced, then a second drawing is made, and so on. How many drawings must be made in order to have a chance of $\frac{1}{2}$ that the ace of spades shall appear at least once?*

It is assumed that the cards are properly shuffled after each drawing. The different drawings are, thus, independent events, with the same probabilities each time. The chance that the ace of spades will never appear in n drawings is $(\frac{51}{52})^n$.

We desire the contrary of this, namely,

$$1 - (\tfrac{51}{52})^n = \tfrac{1}{2},$$
$$(\tfrac{51}{52})^n = \tfrac{1}{2},$$
$$n = \frac{\log 2}{\log 52 - \log 51} = 36 - .$$

Example 10] *In how many throws with a single die is there an even chance that the number 6 will appear at least once?*

$$(\tfrac{5}{6})^n = \tfrac{1}{2},$$
$$n = \frac{\log 2}{\log 6 - \log 5} = 4 -.$$

Example 11] *2 dice are thrown; in how many turns is there an even chance that double sixes will appear at least once?*

$$(\tfrac{35}{36})^n = \tfrac{1}{2},$$
$$n = \frac{\log 2}{\log 36 - \log 35} = 25 -.$$

These examples are of not a little historical interest. Two dice can appear in six times as many ways as one die; with one die there is more than an even chance to see the six in four throws, while with two dice there is less than an even chance to see double sixes in six times four, or twenty-four throws. This simple fact is known as the 'paradox of Chevalier de Méré', about which Pascal wrote to Fermat : *

'Voilà quel étoit son grand scandale, qui lui faisoit dire hautement que les propositions n'étoient pas constantes, et que l'arithmétique se démentoit.'

Example 12] *Three players A, B, and C play under the following conditions. In each turn the chance for success is the same for each of two contestants. A and B play together the first turn, the winner plays with C, and if he win again he wins the game; if not C plays with the third man and so on until one man has won two turns in succession; what is the chance for each player?*

Let us begin by showing that there is a zero chance that the game will go on for ever. The only way that this could happen would be for the winner of each turn to be other than the man who won the turn before, and the chance for that is

$$\tfrac{1}{2} \times \tfrac{1}{2} \times \ldots = 0.$$

---

* Pascal, *Œuvres*, edition of 1819, vol. iv, p. 367.

A and *B* have equal chances. We first find *C*'s chance, then one-half the difference between that and 1 is the chance of *A* or *B*. *C* might win his first two turns. Or he might win his first, lose his second, and win his third and fourth, after the man who beat him at his first turn has been defeated by the other man, and so on. His chance is thus

$$\frac{1}{2^2} + \frac{1}{2^2} \times \frac{1}{2^3} + \frac{1}{2^2} \times \frac{1}{2^6} + \ldots = \frac{1}{4}\left[1 + \frac{1}{8} + \frac{1}{8^2} + \frac{1}{8^3} + \ldots\right],$$

$$= \tfrac{4}{14} = \tfrac{2}{7}.$$

Chance for *A* or *B* is $\tfrac{5}{14}$.

Tchebycheff's Example] *What is the probability that two integers chosen at random shall be relatively prime?* *

The chance that the first integer shall be divisible by a prime *r*, is the chance that its remainder, when divided by *r*, should be equal to zero. Assuming, then, that all remainders are equally likely, the chance is $1/r$. Hence the chance that *r* is not a common factor of the two is $1 - 1/r^2$.

* Cf. Markoff, loc. cit., p. 148.

Problems.

1. Let *n* dice be thrown. In how many throws is there an even chance that all will appear sixes at least once. Show that this number is not proportional to *n* as Chevalier de Méré supposed.

2. A popular, if unaristocratic game called 'craps' is played as follows. Two dice are thrown, and one of the players will win if (*a*) the sum be 7 or 11, (*b*) if the sum be 4, 5, 6, 8, 9, or 10, and the same sum reappears before 7 is ever seen. What is the chance that this player will win?

3. In 1921 Lieutenant R. S. Hoar, U.S.A., drew five cards from a pack 1,000 times, with the following results. Two were of the same denomination with three scattering 412 times, three were of the same denomination and two scattering 23 times, two were of one denomination, two of another, and the fifth of a third 5 times, three of one denomination and two of another 1 time. Compare these figures with the numbers to be expected by calculation.

Our required probability is, then,

$$p = \left(1 - \frac{1}{2^2}\right)\left(1 - \frac{1}{3^2}\right)\left(1 - \frac{1}{5^2}\right)\cdots$$

$$\frac{1}{p} = \frac{1}{1 - \dfrac{1}{2^2}} \cdot \frac{1}{1 - \dfrac{1}{3^2}} \cdot \frac{1}{1 - \dfrac{1}{5^2}}\cdots$$

= Limit (for all primes)

$$\left[\mathrm{Lim}\left(1 + \frac{1}{2^2} + \frac{1}{2^4}\cdots\right) \times \mathrm{Lim}\left(1 + \frac{1}{3^2} + \frac{1}{3^4} + \ldots\right) \times \ldots\right].$$

These series are absolutely convergent, so that we are allowed to rearrange the order of the terms and change the order of the limits.*

$$\frac{1}{p} = \mathrm{Lim}\left(1 + \frac{1}{2^2} + \frac{1}{3^2} + \frac{1}{4^2} + \ldots\right).$$

Now
$$\int_0^1 x^n \log x\, dx = -\frac{1}{(n+1)^2}$$

as an integration by parts shows, since $\mathrm{Lim}_{x \to 0} x^{n+1} \log x = 0$.

$$\int_0^1 \frac{\log x\, dx}{1-x} = \int_0^1 \log x (1 + x + x^2 + \ldots)\, dx = -\left(1 + \frac{1}{2^2} + \frac{1}{3^2} + \ldots\right).$$

But †
$$\int_0^1 \frac{\log x\, dx}{1-x} = -\frac{\pi^2}{6},$$

$$p = 6/\pi^2 = 0{\cdot}607.$$

In the special case of the theorem of total probability, we calculated the chance that one of a number of mutually exclusive events might occur. Since the events are mutually exclusive, it is the same thing to calculate the probability that one should happen, or that *at least* one should happen. When, however, they are not mutually exclusive, the two probabilities are quite different. It is now time to take up this ' at least one ' question in the general case.

---

* Cf. Tannery, *Théorie des fonctions d'une variable*, 2nd ed., Paris, 1904, vol. i, pp. 152 ff.

† Cf. B. O. Peirce, *Short Table of Integrals*, 2nd revised ed., Boston, 1910, p. 64.

We begin with two events. Let their probabilities be p_1 and p_2, while the probability that both will happen is p_{12}. The probability that at least one will occur is the probability of the arrival of one of three mutually exclusive events, namely, both happen, the first happens and the second fails, the first fails and the second happens. Moreover, the probability that the first happens is the sum of the probabilities that both happen and the probability that the first happens and the second fails; this latter probability will, then, have the value $p_1 - p_{12}$.

The probability that we seek will thus be

$$(p_1 - p_{12}) + (p_2 - p_{12}) + p_{12} = p_1 + p_2 - p_{12}.$$

Let us now assume that when $n-1$ events are concerned, the probability that at least one happens is

$$P_{n-1} = \sum_{i=1}^{i=n-1} p_i - \frac{1}{2} \sum_{i,j=1}^{i,j=n-1} p_{ij} + \frac{1}{3!} \sum_{i,j,k=1}^{i,j,k=n-1} p_{ijk} - \cdots,$$

where in any one term i, j, k, &c. take on distinct values.

By the same process of reasoning, when an nth event is introduced, the probability that this, and at least one other will occur is

$$P_{(n-1)\,n} = \sum_{i=1}^{i=n-1} p_{in} - \frac{1}{2} \sum_{i,j=1}^{i,j=n-1} p_{ijn} + \frac{1}{3!} \sum_{i,j,k=1}^{i,j,k=n-1} p_{ijkn} - \cdots.$$

The probability that at least one of n events will occur is, by the first case,

$$P_n = p_n + P_{n-1} - P_{(n-1)n}$$

$$= \sum_{i=1}^{i=n} p_i - \frac{1}{2} \sum_{i,j=1}^{i,j=n} p_{ij} + \frac{1}{3!} \sum_{i,j,k=1}^{i,j,k=n} p_{ijk} - \cdots. \qquad (4)$$

Problem.

What form does formula (4) take: (*a*) when the events are mutually exclusive, (*b*) when they are independent? Prove your answer in each case.

Theorem of total probability, general case.

*If n different events be under consideration, and if the
probability for the simultaneous occurrence of the ith,
jth, kth, &c. event be $p_{ijk...n}$, then the probability for
the occurrence of at least one of these events is given by
formula (4).*

There are not a great many interesting applications of this
beautiful general formula, largely owing to the difficulty of
calculating the different p's. We shall, however, give two.
The first is an example worked out by De Montmort nearly
two hundred years ago.*

De Montmort's Example] *If n balls in an urn be numbered
1, 2, 3, ...n respectively, and if they be drawn out at
random, one after another, what is the probability that
at least one will appear in the turn corresponding to
its number?*

The probability that a specific set of k balls shall come
out in the right order is $\dfrac{(n-k)!}{n!}$.

The probability that some one set of k will come in order
is this number multiplied by the number of ways that k
objects may be chosen from n objects, namely,

$$\frac{n!}{k!\,(n-k)!} \times \frac{(n-k)!}{n!} = \frac{1}{k!}.$$

Our required probability is, thus,

$$1 - \frac{1}{2!} + \frac{1}{3!} - \ldots + (-1)^{n-1}\frac{1}{n!}.$$

The probability that no ball will come in the right place is

$$1 - \frac{1}{1!} + \frac{1}{2!} - \frac{1}{3!} + \ldots + (-1)^{n}\frac{1}{n!}.$$

These are the first terms of a familiar rapidly converging
series, the difference between the sum written above and the
sum to infinity being less than $1/(n+1)!$, we thus get the
curious

* *Essai d'analyse sur les jeux de hasard*, 2nd ed., Paris, 1713, p. 132.

Theorem] *If any large number of balls be numbered* 1, 2, ...n, *and if they be drawn out one after another from an urn, the probability that no ball will appear in the turn corresponding to its number is very close to* 1/e.

A colleague of the author's once stated the theorem in the following more picturesque language:

'If all of the inhabitants of Chicago should meet together in one place and get extremely drunk, and then try to go home by guess-work, the chances that at least one would get back to his own bed are almost two out of three.'

This is one of those cases where it is fortunate that the probability can be calculated beforehand, and we are not forced to seek it experimentally.

The general theorem of total probability enables us to set a limit, unfortunately not a very close one, to the size of a composite probability, when we know the values of the individual probabilities involved, but do not know to what extent they depend on one another.

Since
$$p_1 + p_2 - p_{12} \leqq 1,$$
$$p_{12} \geqq p_1 + p_2 - 1.$$

Assume
$$p_{12\ldots n-1} \geqq p_1 + p_2 + \ldots + p_{n-1} - (n-2),$$
$$p_{12\ldots n} \geqq p_{12\ldots n-1} + p_n - 1,$$
$$p_{12\ldots n} \geqq p_1 + p_2 + \ldots + p_n - (n-1).$$

§ 3. Expectation.

Definition] If a person have the chance p_1 to receive the positive or negative sum s_1, p_2 to receive s_2, ... p_n to receive the sum s_n, and if these be the only sums he has a chance to receive under the circumstances, then the sum

$$\sum_{i=1}^{i=n} p_i s_i$$

is called his *expectation* under the circumstances.

Problem.

If it be found that 91% of the recruits of an army satisfy the first of three medical requirements, 86% satisfy the second, and 83% satisfy the third, what will be a lower limit for the proportion of those satisfying all three ?

Theorem 1]   *The expectation is the limit of the average sum received as the number of trials increases indefinitely.*

To prove this let us notice that if in N trials, the sum s_1 be received T_1 times, s_2, T_2 times, s_n, T_n times the average amount received is $(T_1 s_1 + T_2 s_2 + \dots T_n S_n)/N$. The limit of this sum is the sum of the limits of the individual terms, and as

$$\underset{N \to \infty}{\text{Lim}} \frac{T_i}{N} = p_i$$

we have our theorem proved.

The subject of expectation is used especially in connexion with games of chance. This branch of the theory of probability has always had a peculiar fascination for a certain type of reader, and was, moreover, the historic basis of the whole science. We shall therefore pay some attention to it both in the present chapter and in subsequent ones, even though at the present time the calculus of probabilities is principally occupied with more serious matters.

Definition]   A turn at a game of chance is said to be *fair* to a prospective player, when his expectation is 0, it shall be called *favourable*, when his expectation is positive, otherwise *unfavourable*. In the same way a whole game shall be called *fair, favourable,* or *unfavourable,* according to the expectations.

Suppose, for instance, that a player stake a sum a, with a chance p of winning his adversary's stake b, while the chance of loss, a tie being excluded, is q. His expectation is

$$pb - qa.$$

If the turn be fair this is 0, and

$$p/q = a/b ; \ p/a = q/b. \tag{1}$$

Theorem 2]   *If a turn be fair to a player, it is fair to his adversary, and the probability of success for each is proportional to his stake.]*

Suppose that a player plays two successive turns; let the probabilities and the stakes be $p_1 q_1 a_1 b_1$ in the first, and $p_2 q_2 {''}_2 b_2$ in the second. Let us find his total expectation.

$$p_1 + q_1 = p_2 + q_2 = 1,$$

$$p_1 p_2 (b_1 + b_2) + p_1 q_2 (b_1 - a_2) + p_2 q_1 (b_2 - a_1) q_1 q_2 (a_1 + a_2)$$
$$= (p_1 b_1 - q_1 a_1) + (p_2 b_2 - q_2 a_2).$$

Evidently we might carry on to any number of turns, by mathematical induction :

Theorem 3] *A player's expectation from a series of turns is the sum of his expectations from the individual turns.*

Theorem 4] *Any succession of fair turns, favourable turns, or unfavourable turns, will constitute a fair game, a favourable game, or an unfavourable game, as the case may be.*

This theorem is vitally important, and shows the utter futility of a player's altering the amount of his stakes in any game, in the hope of improving his chances. We shall discuss this question in greater detail in the next chapter.

Example 13] A *has three pennies*, B *has two. The coins are all thrown, and it is agreed that the player showing the greatest number of heads shall win all; in case of a tie* B *shall win. How is this game from* A's *point of view?*

A can win (*a*) by throwing three heads, for which the chance is $\frac{1}{8}$, (*b*) by throwing two heads to one or no heads, chance $\frac{3}{8} \times \frac{3}{4}$, or by throwing one head against two tails, chance $\frac{3}{8} \times \frac{1}{4}$. His total chance is $\frac{1}{2}$, and his expectation

$$\frac{1}{2} \times 2 - \frac{1}{2} \times 3 = -\frac{1}{2}.$$

The game is, thus, unfavourable to A, a rather surprising result.

¶ Petrograd paradox. A *spins a penny, and agrees to give it to* B *if it come up heads. If it do not come up heads till the second time he will give* B *2 pence, if not till the third time* 4, *if not till the nth* 2^{n-1}. *How*

Problem.

How will the game appear to A if they agree to begin again in case of a tie ?

much should B *pay for the privilege of taking part in this pleasant game?*

The game will be fair if B agree to pay his expectation as an entrance fee, let us therefore calculate this expectation; it is clearly

$$\frac{1}{2}\cdot 1 + \frac{1}{4}\cdot 2 + \frac{1}{8}\cdot 2^2 + \ldots + \frac{1}{2^n}\cdot 2^{n-1} + \ldots = \frac{1}{2}\left[1 + 1 + 1 + \ldots\right].$$

The absurdity of this answer constitutes the paradox which has given rise to a good deal of discussion, serving Daniel Bernoulli as the basis of his theory of moral value.[*]   Theoretically B's expectation is infinite; practically, as Bertrand remarks,[†] any one would be a fool to risk 100 pence at any such game. B's expectation is infinite provided the possibility of an infinite number of turns is admitted, and provided, of course, that he has an infinite fortune to start with.   Neither of these provisos is related to actual life.   Let us see how many times the coin will be spun on an average before heads come up.   This is a problem in mean value of the sort that we shall take up at length in Ch. IV, but it will be sufficient for our present purposes to notice that this number is the expectation of a man who shall receive a penny if heads appear the first time, two, if not till the second, three, if not till the third, &c.   His expectation is, then,

$$\frac{1}{2} + \frac{1}{2^2}\cdot 2 + \frac{1}{2^3}\cdot 3 + \ldots + \frac{1}{2^n}\cdot n$$

$$= \frac{1}{2}\left(\frac{1}{2^0} + \frac{2}{2^1} + \frac{3}{2^2} + \frac{4}{2^3} + \ldots + \frac{n}{2^{n-1}}\right),$$

$$= 2 - \frac{n+2}{2^n}.$$

The average number of turns will not, therefore, exceed two.   Suppose that in the lifetime of A and B it will be

---

[*] 'Specimen Theoriae novae de Mensura Sortis', *Commentarii Academiae Scientiarum Imperialis*, vol. v, p. 175, Petrograd, 1738.   For further references, see Czuber, *Entwicklung*, cit. pp. 122 ff.

[†] loc. cit., p. 63.

possible to play 2^n games. As a further simplification, we suppose that B wins one penny about half the time, two-pence one-quarter of the time, fourpence one-eighth of the time. If he pay an entrance fee of x each time, and if this be a fair fee for 2^n games, we have

$$2^n x = 2^{n-1} \cdot 1 + 2^{n-2} \cdot 2 + 2^{n-3} \cdot 2^2 + \ldots + 1 \cdot 2^{n-1} + A.$$

The reason for the remainder term A is that

$$2^n = 1 + 2^{n-1} + 2^{n-2} + \ldots + 2 + 1,$$

and we do not know what sum to ascribe to the odd turn, but surely $A < 2^n$ $\quad 2^n x = n \, 2^{n-1} + A$

$$x < \frac{n}{2} + 1.$$

Now if 2^n be allowed to increase indefinitely, so will x, but that is not our present hypothesis. Let A and B play 100 turns per hour, working 8 hours a day, 300 days in the year, for 50 years, the number of games would be 12,000,000, which is less than 2^{24}, so that an entrance fee of twelve pence would seem quite sufficient.

¶ Let us interpolate at this point a problem of historical interest which was proposed to Pascal by our old friend the Chevalier de Méré.*

Example 14] *Two players whose chances of winning an individual turn are p and q respectively, a tie being impossible, are forced to break off a game before the end. The first player A is within m turns of victory, while the second player B is within n turns of victory, how should the stakes be divided?*

We must calculate the chance of one player, say A. Here is De Montmort's solution.†

A may win in various ways which are mutually exclusive :

(1) He may win the next m turns, chance $= p^m$.

(2) In the next $m + 1$ turns he may win the last, and some other $m - 1$, chance $= m p^m q$.

* Pascal, *Œuvres*, cit., vol. iv, p. 360.
† loc. cit., p. 244.

(3) In the next $m + 2$ turns he may win the last, and $m - 1$ of the others, chance $= m(m + 1)p^m q^2/2$.

. . .

Hence his chance of winning the game is

$$p^m \left[1 + mq + \frac{m(m+1)}{2} q^2 + \dots \right.$$
$$\left. + \frac{m(m+1)\dots(m+n-2)}{(n-1)!} q^{n-1} \right]. \quad (2)$$

¶ § 4. Risk.

It sometimes happens that we are interested in knowing, not merely the total expectation, but the negative part which is to be feared. For instance, a player who should undertake to play the Petrograd game because of the infinite expectation would do a foolish thing, thanks to the large negative part of the expectation. More generally, a player should not enter a game, no matter how brilliant the prospects, if the expectation of loss be too large a proportion of his fortune.

Definition] *The absolute value of that part of the total expectation which includes the negative terms, and these only, shall be called the* risk.

Suppose that a man has the chances $p_1, p_2 \dots p_n$ to win the positive sums $s_1, s_2 \dots s_n$. He will pay for the privilege of entering a sum equal to his expectation e. Arranging the sums in the decreasing order of magnitude, his expectation of gain is

$$\sum_{i=1}^{i=m} p_i (s_i - e) \qquad s_i > e,$$

while his risk is

$$r = \sum_{i=m+1}^{i=n} p_i (e - s_i) \qquad e > s_i.$$

Suppose that he insures himself against loss by paying this sum to a speculative company which agrees to pay whatever loss he may sustain in the game.

His present expectation of gain is

$$\sum_{i=1}^{i=m'} p_i(s_i-e-r),$$

his present risk is

$$\sum_{m'+1}^{m} p_i(r+e-s_i) + \sum_{i=m+1}^{i=n} p_i r = \sum_{i=m'+1}^{i=m} p_i(e-s_i) + \sum_{m'+1}^{n} p_i r.$$

Now $\qquad r = \sum_{i=1}^{i=n} p_i r; \quad \sum_{i=m'+1}^{i=m} p_i(e-s_i) \lessgtr 0.$

Hence, for both reasons, the risk is less than r the previous risk, but the expectation of gain is reduced by a corresponding figure.

If a man have the chances q_1, $q_2 \dots q_n$ to lose the sums s_1, s_2, $s_3 \dots s_n$, his risk will be $q_1 s_1 + q_2 s_2 + \dots q_n s_n$, which will be a minimum if all the money be placed on the safest chance, but the chance of total loss will, of course, be much greater.

Let us conclude by returning, for a moment, to the question of fair and unfair turns. It sometimes occurs to a player that he will be sure to win a game if he make the resolution, and stick to it, which may be difficult, of stopping play as soon as he has lost a turn. Assuming that his stake is a, his adversary's b, the respective chances (tie excluded) p and q, and that the game is fair, we may change the unit of coinage so that his stake is p, and his adversary's q. His expectation is then $\qquad -pq + p_1(q-p) + p^2 q(2q-p) + \dots$.

The first term, and perhaps some of the subsequent ones, is negative, but we soon find positive terms, so that the risk is small. Evaluating this we get

$$-pq\left[1 + (p-q) + p(p-2q) + \dots\right]$$
$$= -pq\left[1 + (p-\{1-p\}) + p(p-2\{1-q\}) + \dots\right]$$
$$= 0.$$

The resolution to stop after the first loss is unwise, except for a very poor man. It will discontent the adversary, because it seems unsportsmanlike, but will not change a zero expectation into a positive one.

CHAPTER III

BERNOULLI'S THEOREM

§ 1. The Problem of Repeated Trials.

THE celebrated theorem which gives the title to the present chapter is of central importance in the theory of mathematical probability. Certain persons have argued that it gives a proof of our second empirical assumption. This is an error. No mathematical formula can prove this assumption which is deduced from experience of concrete cases. The confusion arises from the fact that the theorem deals with ratios which arise when an experiment is tried a large number of times under identical conditions.

Fundamental example] *The probability for success in a certain trial is p, the contrary probability for failure is $q = 1 - p$. If n trials be made under the same essential conditions, what is the probability for exactly r successes and $n - r$ failures?*

The probability of starting off with r successes, and following with failures thereafter is $p^r q^{n-r}$, and the probability sought is the product of this multiplied by the number of ways in which the n trials can be divided into r successes and $n - r$ failures, namely

$$\frac{n!}{r!\,(n-r)!} p^r q^{n-r}. \tag{1}$$

Before deducing results from this very important formula, we shall give one or two auxiliary results which are of interest.

Example 1] *The probabilities being as above, it is agreed that a man shall receive one dollar for each trial necessary to achieve exactly r successes; what is his expectation?*

This amounts, by theorem 1 of the last chapter, to asking

what will be the average number of trials necessary to achieve r successes. If this number be n we have

$$n = rp^r + (r+1) p^r qr + (r+2) p^r q^2 \frac{(r+1)\, r}{2} + \ldots$$

$$= r \sum_{k=0}^{k=\infty} \frac{(r+k)!}{r!\, k!} p^r q^k$$

$$= rp^r (1-q)^{-(r+1)}$$

$$= r/p. \tag{2}$$

This suggests the idea that since the average value of n, when r is given, is r/p, so the average value of r, when n is given, will be np, and this we shall soon see to be the case.

Example 2] *In n successive trials of an event the probabilities for success being p_1, $p_2 \ldots p_n$ respectively, what is the probability for just r successes?*

Let the equation whose roots are p_1, $p_2 \ldots p_n$ respectively be written

$$(x-p_1)\,(x-p_2) \ldots (x-p_n) = x^n - s_1 x^{n-1} + s_2 x^{n-2} \ldots = 0.$$

The probability sought will be

$$P_r = \sum p_a p_\beta \ldots p_\rho\, (1-p_\sigma) \ldots (1-p_\nu)$$

where the first products give every term of s_r, and the p's in the last factors are those which do not appear in the first ones. Multiplying out we get

$$\pm P_r = s_r - (r+1)\, s_{r+1} + \frac{(r+1)\,(r+2)}{2} s_{r+2} + \ldots. \tag{3}$$

This is known as 'King's formula'.

We now return to our formula (1) and ask the important question, for what value of r will this be a maximum? To find this maximum, we write the ratios of this term to the

---

Problems.

1. Deduce formula (1) as a special case of (3).

2. An event can happen in k mutually exclusive ways, and no others, the respective probabilities being p_1, $p_2 \ldots p_k$. Find the probability that in n trials it will happen in the first way r_1 times, in the second r_2 times, in the kth r_k times.

preceding and to the succeeding ones. The first ratio will be greater than or equal to unity when

$$\frac{n-r+1}{r} \cdot \frac{p}{q} \geqq 1,$$

$$(n+1)\,p - rp \geqq rq,$$

$$(n+1)\,p \geqq r.$$

In the same way, the second ratio will be greater than or equal to unity when

$$\frac{r+1}{n-r}\frac{q}{p} \geqq 1,$$

$$rq + q \geqq np - rp,$$

$$r \geqq np - q.$$

We have, thus, for our largest term

$$np + p \geqq r \geqq np - q.$$

The two limits differ from one another by unity.

Theorem 1] *If the probability for success of an event be p, that for failure q, in n trials the most likely number of successes will be that integer which lies between the limits $np+p$ and $np-q$.*

In practice, it is usual to take np as the maximum value for r, the number

$$d = r - np \qquad (4)$$

is called the *discrepancy*. Let us find its average value, that is to say, the expectation of a man who will receive a sum equal to this discrepancy.

$$\sum_{r=0}^{r=n} (r-np)\frac{n!}{r!\,(n-r)!}p^r q^{n-r}$$

$$= \sum_{r=0}^{r=n} r\,\frac{n!}{r!\,(n-r)!}p^r q^{n-r} - np\,(p+q)^n.$$

Now $\qquad rp^r q^{n-r} = p\dfrac{\partial}{\partial p}p^r q^{n-r};\; p+q = 1.$

Hence we have

$$p\frac{\partial}{\partial p}(p+q)^n - np\,(p+q)^n = np - np$$

$$= 0.$$

This shows that np is not only the most likely value of r, but is also its average value. Let us now find the average value of the square of the discrepancy. This will be

$$\sum_{r=0}^{r=n} (r-np)^2 \frac{n!}{r!\,(n-r)!} p^r q^{n-r}$$

$$= \sum_{r=0}^{r=n} r^2 \frac{n!}{r!\,(n-r)!} p^r q^{n-r}$$

$$- 2np \sum_{r=0}^{r=n} r \frac{n!}{r!\,(n-r)!} p^r q^{n-r} + n^2 p^2 (p+q)^n$$

$$= \sum_{r=0}^{r=n} r^2 \frac{n!}{r!\,(n-r)!} p^r q^{n-r} - n^2 p^2.$$

But $$r^2 p^r q^{n-r} = p \frac{\partial}{\partial p}\Big(p \frac{\partial}{\partial p} p^r q^{n-r}\Big).$$

Hence our first term is

$$p \frac{\partial}{\partial p}\Big[p \frac{\partial}{\partial p}(p+q)^n\Big] = p \frac{\partial}{\partial p}[np\,(p+q)^{n-1}]$$

$$= np\,(p+q)^{n-1} + n\,(n-1)\,p^2\,(p+q)^{n-2}$$

$$= np + n^2 p^2 - np^2.$$

Our average value is thus $np - np^2 = npq.$ (5)

The expression $d/n = r/n - p$ (6)

is called the *relative discrepancy*, for it is the discrepancy between the actual proportion of successes and the average proportion of successes. The average value of its square is

$$pq/n. \tag{7}$$

Let us see what is the probability of a discrepancy not greater numerically than a given positive number D. The number of such discrepancies is $2D+1$ and the probability is less than this number multiplied by the probability of a zero discrepancy. Let us calculate the variation of this latter as n increases indefinitely. We have to find the limit of

$$\frac{n!}{r!\,(n-r)!}\Big(\frac{r}{n}\Big)^r \Big(\frac{n-r}{n}\Big)^{n-r} \quad r = np \quad n \to \infty.$$

Let us first find for what value of r this will be a minimum, n being fixed. Changing r to $r+1$ we get

$$\frac{n!}{(r+1)!\,(n-r-1)!}\Big(\frac{r+1}{n}\Big)^{r+1}\Big(\frac{n-r-1}{n}\Big)^{n-r-1}.$$

†

This divided by the previous expression will be

$$\left(\frac{r+1}{r}\right)^{r}\left(\frac{n-r-1}{n-r}\right)^{n-r-1}.$$

How long will this expression be as great as 1 ? Evidently as long as its logarithm is not negative.

$$r\log\left(1+\frac{1}{r}\right)+(n-r)\log\left(1-\frac{1}{n-r}\right)-\log\left(1-\frac{1}{n-r}\right)\geqq 0.$$

Approximately, if r and n be very large,

$$r\left(\frac{1}{r}-\frac{1}{2r^2}\right)-(n-r)\left[\frac{1}{n-r}+\frac{1}{2(n-r)^2}\right]+\frac{1}{n-r}\geqq 0,$$

$$\frac{1}{2(n-r)}-\frac{1}{2r}\geqq 0,$$

$$n-r\leqq r.$$

Theorem 2] *When the number of trials is given, the probability of a zero discrepancy is minimum when the probability of success for an individual trial is equal to one half.*

It would really be more interesting to know for what value of r this probability would be a maximum, not a minimum, but this problem does not yield to treatment so easily as the other. Instead we shall show that for every value of r, other than n or 0, the probability of a 0 discrepancy approaches 0 as a limit, when n *increases indefinitely*.

The probability for a discrepancy $d=r-np$ is

$$\frac{n!}{(np+d)!\,(nq-d)!}\,p^{np+d}q^{nq-d},$$

and

$$\sum_{d=-np}^{d=nq}\frac{n!}{(np+d)!\,(nq-d)!}\,p^{np+d}q^{nq-d}=1.$$

The greatest term is $\dfrac{n!}{(np)!\,(nq)!}p^{np}q^{nq}.$

Suppose that $pq\neq 0$ and that, contrary to fact, this greatest term is always $>K>0$.

Then $\dfrac{n!}{(np+d)!\,(nq-d)!}\,p^{np+d}q^{nq-d}$

$$=\frac{nq\,(nq-1)\ldots(nq-d+1)}{(np+1)\,(np+2)\ldots(np+d)}\left(\frac{p}{q}\right)^{d}\cdot\frac{n!}{(np)!\,(nq)!}\,p^{np}q^{nq}$$

$$>\frac{nq\,(nq-1)\ldots(nq-d+1)}{(np+1)\,(np+2)\ldots(np+d)}\left(\frac{p}{q}\right)^{d}K.$$

For any fixed d, the limit of this as $n \to \infty$ is K. Now let v be so large that $vK > 1$. Then let n be so large that $np > v$, $nq > v$. The limit of each of the v largest terms is K, hence the limit of their sum is $vK > 1$, which is inconsistent with the fact that the sum of all terms is 1. This proves the falsity of the assumption that the largest term is always greater than K. The probability of a discrepancy will thus approach 0 as a limit. The same is true of $2D+1$ times this probability, a number greater than the probability of a discrepancy numerically not greater than D.

In the case of the relative discrepancy the matter is exactly reversed. We see from (7) that the average value of the square of this decreases indefinitely as n increases, hence the probability that the square should have a value as great as any finite value approaches zero as a limit. We thus get

Bernoulli's complete theorem] *When the number of trials is increased indefinitely, the probability that the discrepancy shall remain numerically less than any given number, and the probability that the relative discrepancy shall remain numerically greater than any given number, will both approach zero as a limit.*

This theorem is always regarded as central in the whole doctrine of probability, and although it emphatically does not tell us anything as to how events have to occur, it is, under the conditions of our first empirical assumption, exceedingly illuminating as to the way that they usually occur. Of course, to such a writer as Keynes, to whom mathematical probability appears but a subsidiary part of the whole subject, Bernoulli's theorem is of secondary importance,* but in any objective treatment it must be fundamental. We shall later suggest another much shorter proof, which depends, unfortunately, upon the use of approximate expressions to be developed presently. The proof given above is, perhaps, new. Bernoulli himself considered only the case of the relative discrepancy, his statement being as follows: †

Sit igitur numerus casuum fertilium ad numerum sterilium vel praecise, vel proxime in ratione r/s adeoque ad

---

* Keynes, loc. cit., pp. 336–45.
† Jacobus Bernoulli, *Ars Conjectandi*, Basle, 1713, p. 236.

numerum omnium in ratione r/r + s seu r/t quam rationem terminent limites r + 1/t, r − 1/t. Ostendendum est, tot posse capi experimenta, ut datis quodlibet (puta c) vicibus, verisimilius evadat numerum fertilium observationum intra hos limites quam extra casuum esse h. e. numerum fertilium ad numerum omnium observationum rationem habituum nec majorem quam r + 1/t nec minorem quam r − 1/t.

§ 2.   Stirling's Formula.

In our formula (1) for repeated trials, as well as in many formulae of an elementary nature, we have to do with factorials. These are easy to write, and not hard to evaluate when the numbers involved are small, but can become exceedingly difficult to estimate when the highest factor is large. It is therefore extremely useful to be able to replace them by approximate values.

What do we mean by an approximate value for an expression? Ordinarily these words signify another expression, differing from the first by a small quantity; so small, in fact, that its presence may be overlooked. Unfortunately we have no such scheme for approximating to factorials. But when a function of a certain argument increases indefinitely with that argument, then a new function bearing to the first a ratio that approaches unity as a limit may be used to replace it in the sense that the error will bear an infinitesimal ratio to the function itself. The difference between the two functions may actually increase indefinitely, but if their ratio approach unity as a limit, then in ratio problems the one may be used safely as an approximate representation of the other. For instance, the difference between the two functions of x, x^2 and $x^2 + x$, increases indefinitely, but their ratio approaches 1 as a limit. A function whose ratio to a given function approaches 1 as a limit, as the two increase indefinitely, is called an *asymptotic expression* for the given function. It is our present task to find such an expression for $n!$. We shall do so by guessing at various factors, till we reach a form where the unknown factor may be treated as a constant.

As a first approximation, let us note that $n!$ has n factors, the largest of which is n. We therefore start with the crude assumption

$$n! = n^n \phi(n),$$
$$(n+1)! = (n+1)^{n+1} \phi(n+1).$$

Dividing $\phi(n)/\phi(n+1) = (1+1/n)^n.$

$$\text{Lim } n \to \infty \quad \frac{\phi(n+1)}{\phi(n)} = e^{-1}.$$

$$\text{Lim } n \to \infty \quad \frac{\phi(n+k)}{\phi(n)} = e^{-k}.$$

This suggests a second factor, and we write

$$n! = n^n e^{-n} \psi(n),$$
$$\frac{\psi(n)}{\psi(n+1)} = e^{-1}\left(1+\frac{1}{n}\right)^n,$$
$$\log \psi(n) - \log \psi(n+1) = -1 + n\left(\frac{1}{n} - \frac{1}{2n^2} + \frac{1}{3n^3} - \cdots\right)$$
$$= -\frac{1}{2n} + \frac{1}{n^2}\left(\frac{1}{3} - \cdots\right),$$
$$\log n^{\frac{1}{2}} - \log(n+1)^{\frac{1}{2}} = -\log\left(1+\frac{1}{n}\right)^{\frac{1}{2}}$$
$$= -\frac{1}{2n} + \frac{1}{n^2}\left(\frac{1}{4} - \cdots\right).$$
$$\text{Lim } n \to \infty \left[\frac{\log \dfrac{\psi(n)}{\psi(n+1)}}{\log\left(\dfrac{n}{n+1}\right)^{\frac{1}{2}}}\right] = 1.$$

This leads to our next approximation

$$n! = n^n e^{-n} n^{\frac{1}{2}} F(n),$$
$$\frac{F(n)}{F(n+1)} = e^{-1}\left(1+\frac{1}{n}\right)^{n+\frac{1}{2}}.$$

Log $F(n) - \log F(n+1)$

$$= -1 + \left(n+\frac{1}{2}\right)\left(\frac{1}{n} - \frac{1}{2n^2} + \frac{1}{3n^3} - \frac{1}{4n^4} + \cdots\right)$$
$$= 1/12n^2 - \cdots.$$

The series on the right is convergent, and is composed of terms which are alternately positive and negative. The sum of a number of terms is alternately greater than or less than the limit. Hence

$$\log F(n) > \log F(n+1) > \log F(n) - 1/12\,n^2,$$

$$\log F(n) > \log F(\infty)$$

$$> \log F(n) - \frac{1}{12}\left(\frac{1}{n^2} + \frac{1}{(n+1)^2} + \frac{1}{(n+2)^2} + \ldots\right)$$

$$\frac{1}{n^2} + \frac{1}{(n+1)^2} + \frac{1}{(n+2)^2} + \ldots$$

$$< \frac{1}{(n-1)\,n} + \frac{1}{n\,(n+1)} + \frac{1}{(n+1)\,(n+2)} + \ldots.$$

The convergent series on the right may be written

$$\left(\frac{1}{n-1} - \frac{1}{n}\right) + \left(\frac{1}{n} - \frac{1}{n+1}\right) + \left(\frac{1}{n+1} - \frac{1}{n+2}\right) \ldots = \frac{1}{n-1}$$

$$\log F(n) > \log F(\infty) > \log F(n) - \frac{1}{12\,(n-1)}.$$

Again $\log\left(1 + \frac{1}{10\,n}\right) > \frac{1}{10\,n} - \frac{1}{200\,n^2} > \frac{1}{12\,(n-1)}$

when $n > 6$. Hence

$$\log F(n) > \log F(\infty) > \log \frac{F(n)}{1 + \dfrac{1}{10\,n}}.$$

If thus, when $n > 6$ we replace $F(n)$ by $F(\infty)$, we have divided by a factor lying between the limits 1 and $1 + \dfrac{1}{10\,n}$. There remains only the task of finding the value of the constant $F(\infty)$. We do this by a roundabout method.

Let $$I(m) = \int_0^{\pi/2} \sin^m x\, dx,$$

$$I(2m) > I(2m+1) > I(2m+2),$$

$$1 > \frac{I(2m+1)}{I(2m)} > \frac{I(2m+2)}{I(2m)}.$$

It will appear in the course of our work that

$$\operatorname{Lim} m \to \infty \; \frac{I(2m+2)}{I(2m)} = 1,$$

$$\int_0^{\pi/2} \sin^n x \, dx$$

$$= -\left[\sin^{n-1} x \cos x\right]_0^{\pi/2} + (n-1)\int_0^{\pi/2} \sin^{n-2} x \cos^2 x \, dx$$

$$= \frac{n-1}{n}\int_0^{\pi/2} \sin^{n-2} x \, dx,$$

$$I(2m) = \frac{2m-1}{2m} \cdot \frac{2m-3}{2(m-1)} \cdot \ldots \cdot \frac{1}{2} \cdot \int_0^{\pi/2} dx$$

$$= \frac{2m-1}{2m} \cdot \frac{2m-3}{2(m-1)} \cdot \ldots \cdot \frac{1}{2} \cdot \frac{\pi}{2},$$

$$I(2m+1) = \frac{2m}{2m+1} \cdot \frac{2(m-1)}{2m-1} \cdot \ldots \cdot \frac{1}{2} \cdot \int_0^{\pi/2} \sin x \, dx$$

$$= \frac{2m}{2m+1} \cdot \frac{2(m-1)}{2m-1} \cdot \ldots \cdot \frac{1}{3} \cdot \frac{1}{1},$$

$$\frac{I(2m+1)}{I(2m)} = \frac{\left[2m \cdot 2(m-1) \cdot \ldots \cdot 1\right]^2}{(2m+1)\left[(2m-1)\cdot(2m-3)\ldots 1\right]^2} \cdot \frac{2}{\pi}$$

$$= \frac{\left[2m \cdot 2(m-1) \cdot \ldots \cdot 1\right]^4}{(2m+1)\left[2m!\right]^2} \cdot \frac{2}{\pi}$$

$$= \frac{2^{4m} m^{4m} e^{-4m} (\sqrt{m})^4 \left[F(m)\right]^4}{(2m+1)(2m)^{4m} (e^{-2m})^2 (\sqrt{2m})^2 \left[F(2m)\right]^2} \cdot \frac{2}{\pi}$$

$$= \frac{m}{(2m+1)\pi} \cdot \frac{\left[F(m)\right]^4}{\left[F(2m)\right]^2}.$$

Passing to the limit
$$1 = \frac{F(\infty)^2}{2\pi},$$

$$F(\infty) = \sqrt{2\pi}.$$

Stirling's formula: *If the expression* $n!$ *be replaced by the expression* $n^n e^{-n} \sqrt{2\pi n}$ *the true value will have been divided by a number lying between* 1 *and* $1 + \dfrac{1}{10\,n}$.*

---

* Stirling, *Methodus differentialis*, &c., London, 1764, p. 135.

A table of the values of $\log e^x$ and $\log e^{-x}$ will be found at the end of the volume.

We shorten this formula by writing the untrue equation

$$n! = n^n e^{-n} \sqrt{2\pi n}. \tag{8}$$

The development above shows that we should be more accurate if we wrote

$$n! = n^n e^{-n} \sqrt{2\pi n}\left(1 + \frac{1}{12\,n}\right).$$

The gain in accuracy is, for most purposes, not worth the additional complication. For instance, we find *

$$10! = 3,628,800 \qquad 10^{10}e^{-10}\sqrt{20\pi} = 3,598,699.$$

Difference $= 30,101$. Ratio $= 1{\cdot}008$.

As an example of the use of Stirling's formula, let us calculate the probability of a zero discrepancy. We have by 1) and 1]

$$\frac{n!}{(np)!\,(nq)!}p^{np}q^{nq} = \frac{n^n e^{-n}\sqrt{2\pi n}}{(np)^{np}(nq)^{nq}e^{-n\,(p+q)}\,2\pi n\sqrt{pq}}p^{np}q^{nq}$$

$$= \frac{1}{\sqrt{2\pi npq}} \tag{9}$$

This expression decreases indefinitely as n increases, which gives an immediate proof of 2] and of Bernoulli's theorem.

§ 3. The Probability Integral.

We have seen, by two different methods, that as n increases, the probability of any one discrepancy, even the most likely, approaches 0 as a limit. In order, therefore, to concern ourselves with probabilities of finite magnitude, it is wise to change our problem, and calculate the probability that the discrepancy shall lie within specified limits. We are imme-

---

* Czuber, *Wahrscheinlichkeitsrechnung*, cit. p. 24.

Problem.

A coin is thrown 100 times; calculate the probability that it will show exactly 50 heads and 50 tails.

diately faced by the question, What will be limits of a reasonable size ? We have seen that the average value of the square of the discrepancy is proportional to n, and this suggests the propriety of calculating the probability of a discrepancy lying between two different constant multiples of $\sqrt{n}$. In particular, let us calculate the probability of a discrepancy lying between $z_1 \sqrt{2\,npq}$ and $z_2 \sqrt{2\,npq}$, including the limits.

We first revert to (1), putting

$$r = np + z\sqrt{2\,npq}, \quad n-r = nq - z\sqrt{2\,npq}.$$

We seek

$$\sum_{z=z_1}^{z=z_2} \frac{n!}{(np+z\sqrt{2\,npq})!\,(nq-z\sqrt{2\,npq})!}\, p^{(np+z\sqrt{2\,npq})}\, q^{(nq-z\sqrt{2\,npq})}.$$

The deficiency increases by 1 each time, and the expression above is the sum of a number of ordinates at unit intervals, and so the sum of the areas of a system of rectangles of unit base and varying altitude. We wish to find the limit of this sum as n increases indefinitely.

The next point to note is that as n increases, instead of imagining the height of each rectangle to decrease toward 0 while the total base length increases indefinitely, we might equally well imagine that the total base $(z_2-z_1)\sqrt{2\,npq}$ remains constant, while the bases of the individual rectangles approach 0 as a limit, so that the sum of the areas of the rectangles approaches the area under a smooth curve as a limit. Our problem is to find the nature of this curve. We have, essentially, an infinite sum of infinitesimal terms, and Duhamel's theorem tells us that we may replace each by another infinitesimal bearing to it a ratio which approaches 1 as a limit.* In fact, it will be wise to split each of the various quantities to be summed into factors and replace each factor in this way. As a first substitution, we replace the various factorials by their equivalents from Stirling's formula (8), getting

---

* This theorem is at the basis of the integral calculus. See e. g. Osgood, *Differential and Integral Calculus*, New York, 1907, p. 164 ; *Annals of Mathematics*, Series 2, vol. iv.

$$\sum_{z=z_1}^{z=z_2} \frac{n^n e^{-n} \sqrt{2\pi n}}{(np + z\sqrt{2\,npq})^{np + z\sqrt{2\,npq}}\,(nq - z\sqrt{2\,npq})^{nq - z\sqrt{2\,npq}}\,2\pi e^{-n}}$$

$$\times \frac{p^{(np + z\sqrt{2\,npq})}\,q^{(nq - z\sqrt{2\,npq})}}{\sqrt{np + z\sqrt{2\,npq}}\,\sqrt{nq - z\sqrt{2\,npq}}}$$

$$= \sum_{z=z_1}^{z=z_2} \sqrt{\frac{n}{2\pi\,(np + z\sqrt{2\,npq})\,(nq - z\sqrt{2\,npq})}}$$

$$\left(\frac{np}{np + z\sqrt{2\,npq}}\right)^{np + z\sqrt{2\,npq}} \left(\frac{nq}{nq - z\sqrt{2\,npq}}\right)^{nq - z\sqrt{2\,npq}}.$$

We next note that as the quantity $z\sqrt{2\,npq}$ increases by unity each time, we may properly say that z has an increment Δz where $$\Delta z = 1/\sqrt{(2\,npq)}.$$

$$\operatorname*{Lim}_{n \to \infty} \sqrt{\frac{n}{2\pi\,(np + z\sqrt{2\,npq})\,(nq - z\sqrt{2\,npq})}} \div \frac{\Delta z}{\sqrt{\pi}} = 1.$$

The ratio approaches 1 *uniformly* as we see by expanding.

$$\log\left(\frac{np + z\sqrt{2\,npq}}{np}\right)^{np + z\sqrt{2\,npq}}$$

$$= (np + z\sqrt{2\,npq})\left(z\sqrt{\frac{2q}{np}} - \frac{z^2 q}{np} + \frac{z^3}{n^{3/2}}\phi(z)\right),$$

$$\log\left(\frac{nq - z\sqrt{2\,npq}}{nq}\right)^{nq - z\sqrt{2\,npq}}$$

$$= (nq - z\sqrt{2\,npq})\left(-z\sqrt{\frac{2p}{nq}} - \frac{z^2 p}{nq} + \frac{z^3}{n^{3/2}}\psi(z)\right),$$

$$\log\left(\frac{np + z\sqrt{2\,npq}}{np}\right)^{np + z\sqrt{2\,npq}} \left(\frac{nq - z\sqrt{2\,npq}}{nq}\right)^{nq - z\sqrt{2\,npq}}$$

$$= z^2 + \frac{1}{\sqrt{n}}\,F(z).$$

Hence

$$\operatorname*{Lim}_{n \to \infty}\left(\frac{np}{np + z\sqrt{2\,npq}}\right)^{np + z\sqrt{2\,npq}} \left(\frac{nq}{np - z\sqrt{2\,npq}}\right)^{nq - z\sqrt{2\,npq}}$$

$$\div\, e^{-z^2} = 1.$$

Since $F(z)$ remains less than a fixed amount, the ratio approaches 1 *uniformly*.

We therefore seek

$$\operatorname*{Lim}_{\Delta z \to 0} \sum_{z = z_1}^{z = z_2} e^{-z^2} \frac{\Delta z}{\sqrt{\pi}}$$

and this, by the fundamental theorem of the integral calculus, is *

$$\frac{1}{\sqrt{\pi}} \int_{z_1}^{z_2} e^{-z^2} dz.$$

This formula may be made slightly more accurate in the following fashion. When a large number of rectangles is replaced by a curve, the number of rectangles is less by one than the number of points where the curve meets an upright side of a rectangle. When we replace

$$\sum_{z = z_1}^{z = z_2} f(z) \, \Delta z \quad \text{by} \quad \int_{z_1}^{z} f(z) \, dz$$

if, as is perfectly legitimate, the value of f be taken for z at the left end of the interval, then the term $f(z_2) \, \Delta z$ is lost in passing to the integral, so that a more accurate form for the probability will be

$$\frac{1}{\sqrt{\pi}} \int_{z_1}^{z_2} e^{-z^2} \, dz + \frac{e^{-z_2^2}}{\sqrt{\pi}} \, \Delta z.$$

The number of consequences deducible from these formulae is very large. Let us first find the probability that the numerical value of the discrepancy shall not exceed d.

$$z_2 \sqrt{2npq} = -z_1 \sqrt{2npq} = d.$$

This gives us

Laplace's theorem †] *If the probability for success be p, and that for failure $q = 1 - p$, then the probability that in n trials the discrepancy will not exceed numerically the number d is nearly equal to*

$$\frac{2}{\sqrt{\pi}} \int_0^{\frac{d}{\sqrt{2npq}}} e^{-z^2} \, dz, \tag{10}$$

---

* Ibid., p. 155.

† Laplace, *Œuvres*, vol. vii, Paris, p. 284. For an estimate of the size of the error committed by using these formulae see Castelnuovo, loc. cit., pp. 83 ff. The development which we have given follows the general lines of Markoff, loc. cit.

and is still more nearly equal to

$$\frac{2}{\sqrt{\pi}}\int_0^{\frac{d}{\sqrt{2npq}}} e^{-z^2}\,dz + \frac{1}{\sqrt{2npq}}\,e^{-d^2/2npq}. \qquad (11)$$

It cannot be too often emphasized that these are merely approximate expressions for the quantities desired. The integrand is an even function, suggesting that equal positive and negative discrepancies are equally likely, and this is not the case. When $p < \frac{1}{2}$, there are positive discrepancies possible which are much greater than any possible negative discrepancies. Let us push this a little further, before we leave the exact formulae for ever. The probabilities for a discrepancy d or $-d$, are by (1)

$$\frac{n!}{(np+d)!\,(nq-d)!}\,p^{np+d}\,q^{nq-d}\,; \quad \frac{n!}{(np-d)!\,(nq+d)!}\,p^{np-d}\,q^{nq+d}.$$

The ratio of the second to the first is

$$\frac{(np+d)!\,(nq-d)!}{(np-d)!\,(nq+d)!}\left(\frac{q}{p}\right)^{2d}$$

$$= \left[\frac{npq+qd}{npq+pd}\right]\left[\frac{npq+q\,(d-1)}{npq+p\,(d-1)}\right]\cdots\left[\frac{npq-q\,(d-1)}{npq-p\,(d-1)}\right].$$

When $p < q$, and $d = 1$, this expression is greater than 1. Further, when we increased by unity, the product of the two factors multiplied in is greater than one, as long as $npq > d\,(d-1)$. Hence the expression is surely greater than one for these values of d, and we get

Theorem 3] *When the probability for success is less than one half, the probability for each small possible positive discrepancy is less than that for the corresponding negative discrepancy; the ratio of the two, however, approaches 1 as a limit as the number of trials increases indefinitely.*

This may also be surmised from the fact that the average discrepancy is zero, and as there are in the present case more possible positive discrepancies than negative ones, it would seem natural that in every case the probability for the positive discrepancy would be less than that for the corresponding negative.*

Let us return definitely to our approximate formulae. The function

$$\Theta\,(x) = \frac{2}{\sqrt{\pi}} \int_0^x e^{-z^2}\,dz \qquad (12)$$

is absolutely fundamental in the theory of probability. A table of the values of this function will be found on pp. 209–13. Let us find its value when $x \to \infty$. We wish to evaluate

$$u = \frac{2}{\sqrt{\pi}} \int_0^\infty e^{-z^2}\,dz.$$

Let $\qquad z = ay,$

$$u = \frac{2\,a}{\sqrt{\pi}} \int_0^\infty e^{-(ay)^2}\,dy,$$

$$\frac{2\,a}{\sqrt{\pi}} \int_0^\infty e^{-(1+x^2)\,a^2}\,dx = u e^{-a^2},$$

$$\frac{4}{\pi} \int_0^\infty a\,da \int_0^\infty e^{-(1+x^2)\,a^2}\,dx = \frac{2}{\sqrt{\pi}}\,u \int_0^\infty e^{-a^2}\,da.$$

We may reverse the order of integrations on the left, hence

$$u^2 = \frac{4}{\pi} \int_0^\infty dx \int_0^\infty e^{-(1+x^2)\,a^2}\,a\,da.$$

The first integral is

$$\left[-\frac{1}{2\,(1+x^2)}\,e^{-(1+x^2)\,a^2} \right]_0^\infty = \frac{1}{2\,(1+x^2)},$$

$$u^2 = \frac{2}{\pi} \int_0^\infty \frac{dx}{1+x^2} = 1,$$

$$\frac{2}{\sqrt{\pi}} \int_0^\infty e^{-z^2}\,dz = 1. \qquad (13)$$

At this point the careless reader might be led into a very grievous mathematical error by supposing that this formula was self-evident. He might say, 'The probability that the discrepancy will take some value between $-\infty$ and ∞ is

* Cf. Simmons, 'A New Theorem in Probability', *Proceedings London Math. Soc.*, vol. xxvi, 1895.

equal to 1. This is the probability obtained from (10) by letting d become infinite, which proves (13) without more ado.' But we must repeat again and again *ad nauseam* that (10) is merely an approximate formula, for the following reasons:

(1) The integrand is an even function, whereas we saw in theorem 3] that, in the general case, equal positive and negative discrepancies are not equally likely.

(2) We started with the assumption that we were seeking the probability for a discrepancy between two limits proportional to the square root of the number of trials. We obtained an approximate formula good for such limits. This formula gives a finite if extremely small probability for a discrepancy of every numerical magnitude, whereas it is physically impossible to have a discrepancy numerically greater than the larger of the two numbers np, nq.

The verification of formula (13) *by means of the approximate formula* (10) *must be looked upon as a fortunate accident.*

Strangely enough there is another such accidental verification which we now proceed to establish. We apply the law of the mean to (10) getting, as the probability for a discrepancy close to x, the expression

$$\frac{1}{\sqrt{2\,npq}}\,e^{-\frac{x^2}{2\,npq}}\,dx \qquad (14)$$

The expectation of a man who will receive a sum equal to the square of the discrepancy, i. e. the limit of the average value of that square *if formula (10) were universally valid*, would be

$$\frac{2}{\sqrt{\pi}}\int_0^\infty \frac{x^2\,e^{-\frac{x^2}{2\,npq}}}{\sqrt{2\,npq}}\,dx = \frac{1}{\sqrt{2\,n\pi pq}}\int_0^\infty 2x^2\,e^{-\frac{x^2}{2\,npq}}\,dx.$$

Let $$\frac{x}{\sqrt{2\,npq}} = t \qquad \frac{dx}{\sqrt{2\,npq}} = dt.$$

Problem.

Prove Bernoulli's Theorem by means of (10) and (13).

Average $= \dfrac{2\,npq}{\sqrt{\pi}} \displaystyle\int_0^\infty 2t^2\,e^{-t^2}\,dt.$

Let $2\,te^{-t^2}\,dt = dv \quad t = u.$

Since te^{-t^2} vanishes at both limits, if we integrate by parts we find :

Average $= \dfrac{2\,npq}{\sqrt{\pi}} \displaystyle\int_0^\infty e^{-t^2}\,dt = npq.$

This, by a fortunate accident, checks exactly with (5).

Let us calculate the expectation of a man who will receive a sum equal to the numerical value of the discrepancy. In this case the exact formula is hard to manipulate; we therefore, emboldened by recent success, take formula (10) *as though it were exact and universally* valid, knowing that it is always near the truth. We have

$$\frac{2}{\sqrt{2\,npq\,\pi}} \int_0^\infty xe^{-\frac{x^2}{2npq}}\,dx = \frac{\sqrt{2\,npq}}{\sqrt{\pi}} \int_0^\infty 2\,te^{-t^2}\,dt$$

$$= \sqrt{\frac{2}{\pi}}\,\sqrt{npq}.$$

What is the value of the numerical discrepancy which there is a half chance of reaching? We have, by (12)

$$\Theta\left(\frac{d}{\sqrt{2\,npq}}\right) = \frac{1}{2}.$$

Now, by our table, p. 209,

$$\Theta\,(0{\cdot}4769) = \tfrac{1}{2}.$$

Hence $d = 0{\cdot}4769\,\sqrt{2}\,\sqrt{npq}$

$$= 0{\cdot}67\overline{45}\,\sqrt{npq}.$$

Let us recapitulate these last results. The square root of the average value of the square of the discrepancy is called the *mean discrepancy* ; its value is

$$\sqrt{npq} \qquad\qquad (15)$$

Problem.

Calculate by the same two methods the average value of the fourth power of the discrepancy.

The average value of the numerical value of the discrepancy is called the *average discrepancy*; its value is

$$0{\cdot}798\sqrt{npq} \tag{16}$$

The positive number which there is a half chance that the numerical value of the discrepancy will not exceed, is called the *probable discrepancy*; its value is

$$0{\cdot}674\sqrt{npq} \tag{17}$$

How accurate has Bernoulli's theorem turned out in practice? There is a good deal of testimony on this point, generally highly unsatisfactory. Karl Pearson made an analysis of a large number of statistics from the roulette games at Monte Carlo, and came to the conclusion that whereas the alternation of red and black was satisfactory, there was an incredible excess of long runs.[*] Exactly opposite conclusions were reached by Marbe,[†] who maintained that, on the contrary, short runs were predominately the rule. Then Grünwald took up Marbe's work and showed, at least to his own satisfaction, that the apparent result was due to faulty grouping of the observations.[‡] By a proper re-grouping, the results showed a very satisfactory proportion. An account of the work of Marbe and Grünwald is given by Czuber;[§] the average reader will strongly suspect that Grünwald was right, and the other two wrong.

Example 3] *The philosopher Buffon* [||] *one day threw a coin* 4,040 *times, and noted that heads arrived* 2,048 *times. Is this remarkable ?*

In this case p and q are both $\frac{1}{2}$, $n = 4{,}040$, $d = 28$. The chance for discrepancy of this size or less is

$$\Theta\left(\frac{28}{\sqrt{2020}}\right) = 0{\cdot}622.$$

---

[*] Pearson, *The Chances of Death*, vol. i, London, 1897.

[†] Marbe, *Naturphilosophische Untersuchungen zur Wahrscheinlichkeitslehre*, Leipzig, 1899.

[‡] Grünwald, *Isolierte Gruppen und die Marbesche Zahl p''*, Würzburg, 1904. I have not been able to verify these two references taken from Czuber.

[§] *Wahrscheinlichkeitsrechnung*, at vol. i, pp. 144 ff.

[||] Bertrand, loc. cit., p. 9.

There are, hence, nearly four chances in ten for a discrepancy numerically larger than the one obtained, and the result must be looked upon as not unnatural. The probability for obtaining exactly this discrepancy is less than that for a discrepancy 0, which latter is

$$\frac{1}{\sqrt{2020\pi}} < \frac{1}{80}.$$

Example 4] *Two men, each with five pistoles, toss a coin. The first player wins if it show heads, the second if it show tails, the loser owing the winner one pistole. This money is not paid immediately, but an account is kept, the balance to be paid at the end of the game. In how many turns will there be an even chance that the loser is more in debt to the winner than he can pay?*

Here, again, the chances are $\frac{1}{2}$ for each. In how many turns will the probable discrepancy be 5? Applying (17) we have
$$0{\cdot}675\sqrt{\tfrac{1}{4}}n = 5,$$
$$n = 220.$$

It should be noted here that, if the loser had paid cash each time, there would be more than a half chance that one player would be ruined before now, for a discrepancy of 5 at the end of 220 turns is compatible with a larger discrepancy at an earlier stage of the game.

Example 5] *How many times must a die be thrown to produce a probability of $\frac{9}{10}$ that the ratio of the number*

Problems.

1. In 1850 the Swiss astronomer Wolff threw two dice 100,000 times. The two showed the same face 16,647 times. Comment on this result.

2. The game of 'craps' was explained in a problem on p. 21. Prof. Bancroft Brown (*American Mathematical Monthly*, vol. xxvi, 1919) has tabulated the results of 9,900 turns, where the two players won 4,871 times and 5,029 times. Is this result surprising?

3. Discuss the results reached by Lieut. Hoar in dealing five cards, as given in the problem p. 21, from the point of view of Bernoulli's theorem.

4. How many times must a coin be thrown in order that there may be 9 chances in 10 that the discrepancy is numerically greater than 5?

5. Two dice are thrown 100 times. What is the probable discrepancy in the number of times that the sum 7 appears?

of 5's shown shall bear to the number of trials a value between $\frac{4}{30}$ and $\frac{6}{30}$?

Here we have a relative discrepancy of $\pm \frac{1}{30}$, hence

$$d = \frac{n}{30}, \quad p = \frac{1}{6}, \quad q = \frac{5}{6}, \quad \Theta\left(\frac{1}{5}\sqrt{\frac{n}{10}}\right) = 0.9, \quad n = 338.$$

§ 4. Games of Chance.*

There is a very real difficulty involved in handling some of the fundamental problems arising in games of chance owing to the presence of a subtle but important psychological element which cannot be well stated in mathematical terms. Gamblers are notoriously superstitious, which means that they are irrational, still more are they unmathematical. For that reason, the assumptions which are made are of a tentative nature, and only partially represent the real facts.

In the games of chance of the type which we shall consider there are two individuals, whom we shall call the 'Player' and the 'Banker' respectively. The former has a considerable freedom in deciding upon the amount that he will stake, but we shall assume that there is an upper limit to this, as, otherwise, a syndicate of players with a large capital might be formed, and this body might keep on doubling the stakes after each loss, till the Banker was ruined. We shall assume that the Player has a fortune A, and that he intends to play until either he has lost this amount, or won the sum B from the Banker. If the player have any wisdom at all, A will be less than his total fortune, and B far less than the sum of the Banker's quick assets; the word 'ruin' has only this technical sense for us.

Let the Player's chance to win an individual turn be p, the Banker's chance $q = 1 - p$, a tie being excluded. Let P be the Player's chance to ruin the Banker, Q the chance that the Banker will ruin the Player. We must begin by showing that the sum of these two is 1, i.e. that there is no finite probability that the game will continue indefinitely. The

---

* The greater part of the present section will be found in an article by the author, 'The Gambler's Ruin', *Annals of Mathematics*, vol. x, Series 2, 1909.

proof is immediate when we remember Bernoulli's theorem, for the only way to avoid the ruin of the one or the other party is for the discrepancy to remain below a certain fixed limit, and we have seen that the chance for this decreases indefinitely towards 0. If each turn be fair, in the sense defined above, i.e. if the Player's expectation be 0 each time, we see by Ch. II, 4] that the Player's total expectation is 0, hence

$$PB - QA = 0, \qquad P + Q = 1,$$
$$P = A/(A + B), \qquad Q = B/(A + B). \qquad (18)$$

From these equations we draw two important conclusions. First, the Player's chance is independent of the amount staked, or the game played, provided, of course, there is no danger that the game will not be finished for lack of time. The wisdom in any player's setting a low figure for B is evident. Second, who is the Player, from the Banker's point of view? Suppose that the Banker is running a public gaming resort, and that the game is one of pure chance, no question of skill coming in. The Banker is supposed to be ready to play against all comers. In most cases, they will take opposite sides, more or less, so that his real adversary is the surplus of those who back one chance over those who back the opposite chance, but there is always the possibility of a large combination of players taking the same side, in which case the unfortunate Banker would be opposed to an adversary of quasi infinite fortune and his ruin would be certain. In consequence of this, all forms of public gambling are somewhat favourable to the Banker, and our next step must be to study the chances in games of that sort. We do this by adopting an ingenious device, due to De Moivre, which consists in making the game fair once more by assigning fictitious values to the coins used.*

Let us assume that the Player has A individual coins marked $\alpha^0, \alpha^1, \ldots \alpha^{A-1}$, while the Banker's coins are marked $\alpha^A, \alpha^{A+1}, \ldots \alpha^{A+B-1}$. It is agreed that at each turn the Player shall stake his a coins of highest mark, while the Banker will reply by staking his b lowest marked coins.

* De Moivre, *Doctrine of Chances*, London, 1756, p. 52.

In this fictitious system the Player's expectation before a turn is

$$p\left(\alpha^{x+a} + \alpha^{x+a+1} + \dots \alpha^{x+a+b-1}\right) - q\left(\alpha^x + \alpha^{x+1} + \dots \alpha^{x+a-1}\right)$$

$$= \alpha^x\left[p\frac{\alpha^{a+b}-\alpha^a}{\alpha-1} - q\frac{\alpha^a-1}{\alpha-1}\right]$$

$$= \frac{\alpha^x}{\alpha-1}\left[p\,\alpha^{a+b} - \alpha^a + q\right].$$

The game being unfavourable to the Player, we have

$$pb - qa < 0.$$

Consider the function

$$f(x) = px^{a+b} - x^a + q,$$
$$f'(x) = x^{a-1}\left[(a+b)\,px^b - a\right].$$

We make a short table of values

$$x = 0, \qquad\qquad\qquad f(x) = q, \qquad f'(x) = 0,$$
$$x = 1, \qquad\qquad\qquad f(x) = 0, \qquad f'(x) = pb - qa < 0,$$
$$x = \left[\frac{a}{p\,(a+b)}\right]^{\frac{1}{b}} > 1, \quad f(x) = -\frac{b}{a+b}x^a + q < 0, \quad f'(x) = 0,$$
$$x = \infty, \qquad\qquad\qquad f(x) = \infty, \qquad f'(x) = \infty.$$

Since we have noted all the real roots of $f'(x)$ and between each two roots of f there is one of f', we have just one real root of f which is > 1. Call this α.

$$p\,\alpha^{a+b} - \alpha^a + q = 0 \quad \alpha > 1 \tag{19}$$

$$p\,\alpha^b + q\,\alpha^{-a} = 1. \tag{20}$$

If α be given this value, we see that the expectation of the Player, as calculated above, is 0 in this fictitious measure. Hence, the Player's chance is the ratio of his fortune, fictitiously calculated, to the sum of the two fortunes in the same measure, namely

$$\frac{\alpha^0 + \alpha^1 + - \dots + \alpha^{A-1}}{\alpha^0 + \alpha^1 + - \dots - \alpha^{A+B-1}} = \frac{\alpha^A - 1}{\alpha^{A+B} - 1}. \tag{21}$$

Suppose, next, that the Player determines to reduce his stake to a/σ for just one turn, the Banker simultaneously reducing to b/σ; after that, all is to go on as before. Has his chance been improved or injured? That chance, under the present hypothesis, is

$$p\frac{(\alpha^{A+b/\sigma}-1)}{\alpha^{A+B}-1} + q\frac{(\alpha^{A-a/\sigma}-1)}{\alpha^{A+B}-1} = \frac{\alpha^A\left[p\alpha^{b/\sigma}+q\alpha^{-a/\sigma}\right]-1}{\alpha^{A+B}-1}.$$

Now since $\sigma > 1 \quad \alpha^{1/\sigma} < \alpha,$

$$f(\alpha^{1/\sigma}) < 0, \quad p\alpha^{b/\sigma}+q\alpha^{-a/\sigma} < 1,$$

the chance is less than that given by (21).

The conclusion to be drawn from all this is moral, highly moral! It is unwise for the Player to reduce his first stake, it would be similarly unwise for him to reduce any subsequent stake. The series of turns is bound to run till the one party or the other is ruined, hence we have the

Fundamental theorem of games of chance] *The Player's best chance of winning a stated sum at an unfavourable game is to stake the sum which will bring that return in one turn. If that be not allowed, he should stake at each turn the largest amount that the Banker will accept.*

The practical gambler (if there be such a person) will probably reply to this:

'The player who stakes his whole fortune on a single turn is a fool, and the science of mathematics cannot prove him to be anything else.'

The answer is immediate:

'The science of mathematics never attempts the impossible, it merely shows that other players are greater fools.'

Let us look into certain special cases of (21). The Banker's chance is

$$(\alpha^{A+B}-\alpha^A)/(\alpha^{A+B}-1). \tag{22}$$

When A and B are equal, i.e. when the Player undertakes to win or lose a certain sum, his chance is

$$1/(\alpha^A+1). \tag{23}$$

Putting $\alpha = 1 + \epsilon$ we see that his chance is less than

$$1/(2+A\epsilon). \tag{24}$$

When $a = b$ we may take each of them equal to 1, we have then

$$\alpha = q/p. \tag{25}$$

As an example of these principles let us examine the game of roulette, as played at Monte Carlo. Our description is taken from Sir Hiram Maxim.*

'The roulette consists of a large circular basin, about 2 feet in diameter, with the outer rim turned inward. The bottom of the basin, which forms the wheel, is of metal, quite separate from the rim or sides, and is nicely balanced on a fine pivot, so that when set in motion, it will spin for a considerable time. The outer edge of the wheel is accurately divided into thirty-seven sections or pockets, eighteen of which are painted red and eighteen black. One is called zero and is neutral in colour. The other pockets are numbered from 1 to 36.'

The wheel is set in motion, and a small ball started rolling around the edge in the opposite direction. The game consists in betting on the colour or number of the division in which the ball comes to rest. There are fourteen different methods of staking; the simplest are, red or black, odd or even, above or below 18. In each of these cases, the Player and Banker put up equal sums. If a player stake upon a single number, the Banker puts up 35 times the amount. The upper limit for a stake on a simple chance, as red or black, is, or was, 6,000 francs, whereas on a single number the limit was 180 francs. When the ball rolls into the zero, the player on a simple chance may either forfeit one half of his stake, or leave it 'en prison' till the next turn. If he be fortunate in this turn, he saves his stake, but gets nothing from the Banker; if he lose, the stake is gone for ever. Those who bet on individual numbers or combinations, lose all when the zero appears.

Let us calculate the probability favourable to the Player. We shall imagine that he is wise enough (and rich enough) to stake 6,000 francs each time. We may also disregard the possibility of zero appearing twice in succession, as this will certainly be very rare. Then in sets of 74 turns each, the average result will be 36 reds, 36 blacks, 1 zero followed by a gain, which does not count, and 1 zero followed by a loss. Hence

$$p = \tfrac{36}{73}; \quad q = \tfrac{37}{73}; \quad a = q/p = \tfrac{37}{36}.$$

* *Monte Carlo Facts and Fancies*, London, 1906, pp. 257 ff.

The Player's chance is

$$((\tfrac{37}{36})^A - 1)/((\tfrac{37}{36})^{A+B} - 1)$$

where A and B are the two fortunes, reckoned in terms of 6,000 francs as a unit. When they are equal, his chance is

$$1/((\tfrac{37}{36})^A + 1).$$

Let us next suppose that the Player stakes on a number. Has he a better or worse chance? Common sense points to the latter, as the zero is now a sure loss, and this anticipation is borne out by calculation. The amount which may be staked is one thirty-third of what it was before, which amounts to assuming that the stake remains, but that the fortunes have been multiplied by 33. The Player's chance will be what it was previously, if the present value of α be the thirty-third root of $(\tfrac{37}{36})$, and will be less, if it be larger than that. The thirty-third root of $(\tfrac{37}{36})$ is 1·00085 ; to find α we put

$$\alpha = 1 + \epsilon, \quad p = \tfrac{1}{37}, \quad q = \tfrac{36}{37},$$

$$(1 + \epsilon)^{36} - 37(1 + \epsilon) + 36 = 0,$$

$$1 + 36\epsilon + 630\epsilon^2 + 7140\epsilon^3 - 37 - 37\epsilon + 36 = 0,$$

$$1 + \epsilon = 1·00155.$$

This method is less favourable to the Player than was the simple chance.

Let us now look at matters from the Banker's point of view. We have not the data available to do this really correctly, but the method of handling a supposititious case will show how a correct solution might be obtained. Let us consider a set of runs, each of 1,200 turns, and inquire into the chance that the Banker should come out the loser in one run. Let us, for simplicity, assume that there are 200 players, each staking an average sum which we take as the unit. As a matter of observation, not all players follow the same system. Some bet on red because they believe it is 'Red's day', others for precisely the same reason bet on black, as they think it is time for black to appear to even things up. Some prospective players will sit for a long time observing the runs, and not betting at all, until they have made up their minds what is happening, or going to happen. These patient watchers are quite as welcome as the rasher players, and quite as unlucky. However, owing to the variety of motives, we shall come near enough to the truth if we assume that the 200 players are divided by lot into those who back red, and those who back black. The game, therefore, amounts to this. When the zero appears, the Banker gets one half of the stakes of all the players. When zero does not turn up, the reds pay the blacks, or the blacks pay the reds, and the Banker receives or makes good the difference. When a coin is thrown 200 times the average numerical discrepancy, as given by (16), is $0 \cdot 798 \sqrt{200 \times \frac{1}{4}} = 6$, so that we may assume that, on the average, the reds and blacks will offset each other, except for six players, with whom the Banker must reckon.

In 1,100 turns there will be, on an average, 30 zeros. When a zero turns up, the Banker will collect a half unit from each player, the average winnings from the zeros will be

$$\tfrac{1}{2} \times 200 \times 30 = 3,000.$$

To come out behind in the run of 1,100 turns, the Banker must have an adverse discrepancy of $\frac{1}{6} \times 3,000 = 500$ turns. The chance for this is

$$\tfrac{1}{2} - \tfrac{1}{2} \Theta \left(\frac{500}{\sqrt{2 \times 1,080 \times \frac{1}{4}}} \right) = \tfrac{1}{2} - \tfrac{1}{2} \Theta \ (22)$$

which is so small as to be utterly negligible.

There is one more problem in ruin which is worth notice. Assuming that $A = ma$, what is the probability that the Player will be ruined exactly on the μth turn? This is the probability, that in the first $\mu - 1$ turns he will win exactly $(\mu - m)/2$ times, and lose exactly $(\mu + m - 2)/2$ times, and that he thereupon loses the μth turn. This will be *

$$\frac{(\mu - 1)\,!}{\left(\dfrac{\mu - m}{2} \right)! \left(\dfrac{\mu + m - 2}{2} \right)}\,!\ p^{(\mu - m)/2}\, q^{(\mu + m)/2}.$$

* Incorrectly given by Bertrand, loc. cit., p. 123.

Problem.

Work out the theory of some other game according to these same principles.

This expression is only correct if we assume that the Banker is so rich that there is no possibility of his being ruined in the interval. The sum to infinity of expressions like this would be the probability of ruin for a player pitted against an adversary of infinite fortune, but that probability we have already seen is 1. Let us rather seek for what value of μ this will be a maximum. It is to be noted that we have here a term of the expression $q\,(p+q)^{\mu-1}$.

We get a similar expression by changing μ to $\mu+2$, and equating the two we get the rather clumsy quadratic equation

$$\frac{4\,\mu\,(\mu+1)}{(\mu+2-m)\,(\mu+m)} \times pq = 1.$$

A root of this equation will give approximately the term desired.

CHAPTER IV

MEAN VALUE AND DISPERSION

§ 1. Elementary Theorems in Mean Value.

IN the course of the last chapter we had frequent occasion
to solve such problems as to find the expectation of a man
who is to receive a sum equal to the square of the discrepancy
in a certain series of trials. Ch. III, 1] showed us how an
expectation is the limit of an average, as the number of trials
increases indefinitely. The reader must have suspected that
this whole question of averages and expectation was capable
of much fuller treatment, and that new definitions would
help to clarify the whole matter. We now proceed to give
our undivided attention to this task.

Definition] *If a variable take the different values $V_1 V_2 \ldots V_n$ with
the respective probabilities $p_1 p_2 \ldots p_n$, and these are all
the possible values for that variable, then the expression*

$$\sum_{i=1}^{i=n} p_i V_i$$

is called the mean value *of that variable.*

Definition] *If V is a function of the parameters $X_1, X_2, \ldots X_n$,
which vary according to the third empirical assump-
tion, then the integral*

$$\int \ldots \int V F \, dX_1 dX_2 \ldots dX_n$$

*extended over the whole range of variation, giving to
the probability a value other than 0, shall be defined as
the* mean value *of the variable.*

We reach at once from Ch. III, 1]

Theorem 1] *The mean value of a variable is the limit of its
average value as the number of trials increases indefinitely.*

Let us note in passing that the mean value of a variable

is the expectation of a man who will receive a sum equal to this variable.

In speaking of variables throughout the present chapter, we shall mean such variables as take mean values. We must give one important definition in connexion with these :

Definition] *Two variables shall be said to be independent if the probability that one lie close to a given value is independent of the value of the other.*

Theorem 2] *The mean value of the sum of two variables is the sum of their mean values.*

Let us first suppose that each can take only a finite number of values. Let the first one take the values $x_1 x_2 \dots x_n$ with the respective probabilities $p_1 p_2 \dots p_n$, while the second takes the values $y_1 y_2 \dots y_m$ with the probabilities $\pi_1 \pi_2 \dots \pi_m$. Let P_{ij} be the probability that the first variable takes the value x_i, while the second takes the value y_j. The mean value of the sum will then be

$$\sum_{i, j = 1}^{i = n, j = m} P_{ij} (x_i + y_j).$$

The total coefficient of y_j is $\sum_{i = 1}^{i = n} P_{ij}$. This is the sum of the

mutually exclusive probabilities that the first variable should take the values $x_1 x_2 \dots x_n$, while the second takes the value y_j. It is therefore π_j. In the same way the total coefficient of x_i is p_i. The expression above is thus

$$\sum_{i = 1}^{i = n} p_i x_i + \sum_{j = 1}^{j = m} \pi_j y_j$$

and this is the sum of the two mean values. When one or the other variable can take an infinite number of values we pass from a finite sum to a definite integral by the sort of device universally used in the integral calculus.

It is especially important to note that in this theorem there is no assumption as to the independence of the variables. In consequence of this, we can use mean values in cases where the search for the actual probabilities is beyond our power. The next theorem has a more restricted scope :

Theorem 3] *The mean value of the product of two indepen-dent variables is the product of their mean values.*

Using the same notation as before, since P_{ij} is the probability for the simultaneous arrival of the values x_i and y_j, we have by our definition above

$$\frac{P_{ij}}{P_{kj}} = \frac{p_i}{p_k}, \quad \frac{P_{kj}}{P_{kl}} = \frac{\pi_j}{\pi_l},$$

$$\frac{P_{ij}}{P_{kl}} = \frac{p_i \pi_j}{p_k \pi_l}, \quad P_{ij} = \rho p_1 \pi_j.$$

But
$$\sum_{i=1}^{i=n} p_i = \sum_{j=1}^{j=m} \pi_j = \sum_{i,j=1}^{i=n,\,j=m} P_{ij} = 1,$$

$$\rho = 1.$$

Mean value is

$$\sum_{i,j=1}^{i=n,\,j=m} p_i \pi_j x_i y_j = \Big(\sum_{i=1}^{i=n} p_i x_i \Big) \Big(\sum_{j=1}^{=m} \pi_j y_j \Big).$$

The extension to the case where the one or the other variable can take an infinite number of values is immediate.

Theorem 4] *The mean value of the square of a variable is not less than the square of its mean value.*

Using our previous notation, we have

$$\sum_{i=1}^{i=n} p_i x_i^2 - \Big[\sum_{i=1}^{i=n} p_i x_i \Big]^2 = \sum_{i=1}^{i=n} p_i x_i^2 \sum_{i=1}^{i=n} p_i - \Big[\sum_{i=1}^{i=n} p_i x_i \Big]^2$$

$$= \tfrac{1}{2} \sum_{i,j=1}^{i,\,j=n} p_{ij} (x_i - x_j)^2,$$

$$\geqslant 0.$$

Problems.

1. Prove that the mean value of the sum of k variables is the sum of their mean values.

2. Prove that the mean value of the product of k independent variables is the product of their mean values.

Theorem 5] *The mean value of the square of the sum of n independent variables, each of which has the mean value 0, is the sum of the mean values of their squares.*

We see, in fact, that when we square our sum, we have squared terms and product terms, and the mean value of each of these latter is 0 by 3]. Let us go a little further in this direction. Still assuming that the mean value of each of our variables $x_1 x_2 \ldots x_n$ is 0, let the mean value of the squares be $A_1 A_2 \ldots A_n$ respectively. We may write

$$\left[x_1 - \frac{\sum\limits_{j=1}^{j=n} x_j}{n} \right]^2 = \left[\frac{(n-1)}{n} x_1 - \frac{1}{n} x_2 - \frac{1}{n} x_3 \ldots - \frac{1}{n} x_n \right]^2$$

and reach :

Theorem 6] *Given n independent variables $x_1 x_2 \ldots x_n$, each with the mean value 0, while the mean values of their respective squares are $A_1 A_2 \ldots A_n$, then the mean value of the expression*

$$\sum_{i=1}^{i=n} \left[x_i - \sum_{j=1}^{j=n} \frac{x_j}{n} \right]^2$$

is

$$\frac{n-1}{n} \sum_{i=1}^{i=n} A_i.$$

Let us next look at variables whose mean values are not 0. Using the same notation as before, let us assume that the n mean values are $a_1 a_2 \ldots a_n$. Since

$$(x_i - a_i)^2 = x_i{}^2 - 2 a_i x_i + a_i{}^2$$

we have :

Theorem 7] *If the mean value of a variable x_i be a_i, while the mean value of its square is A_i, then the mean value of*

is
$$(x_i - a_i)^2$$
$$A_i - a_i{}^2.$$

Theorem 8] *Given n independent variables $x_1 x_2 \ldots x_n$, whose mean values are $a_1 a_2 \ldots a_n$, while the mean values of their squares are $A_1 A_2 \ldots A_n$ respectively, then the mean value of*

$$\sum_{i=1}^{i=n} (x_i - a_i)^2$$

is
$$\sum_{i=1}^{i=n} (A_i - a_i{}^2).$$

In the further discussion of these quantities, let us assume that each can take but a finite number of values. For instance, let x_1 take the values x_{11}, $x_{12} \ldots x_{1n}$ with the respective probabilities $p_{11}, p_{12}, \ldots p_{1n}$. Our theorem 8] may be expressed by the equation

$$\sum_{i,j,k\ldots} (x_{1i} + x_{2j} + x_{3k} + \ldots - a_1 - a_2 - a_3 - \ldots)^2 \, p_{1i} p_{2j} p_{3k} \cdots$$
$$= \sum_{i=1}^{i=n} (A_i - a_i{}^2),$$

$$\frac{\sum_{i,j,k\ldots} t^2 (x_{1i} + x_{2j} + x_{3k} + \ldots - a_1 - a_2 - a_3 - \ldots)^2 \, p_{1i} p_{2j} p_{3k} \cdots}{n \, \Sigma (A_i - a_i{}^2)}$$
$$= \frac{t^2}{n}.$$

On the left, let us leave out all terms where

$$\frac{t^2 (x_{1i} + x_{2j} + x_{3k} + \ldots - a_1 - a_2 - a_3 \ldots)^2}{n (A_i - a_i{}^2)} \leqslant 1$$

and replace this expression by 1 when it is greater than that. We have thus a quantity distinctly less than t^2/n which represents the probability that this expression should be greater than unity. Taking the contrary probability we have:

Tchebycheff's inequality *] *Given n independent variables $x_1 x_2 \ldots x_n$ whose mean values are $a_1 a_2 \ldots a_n$, while the mean values of their squares are $A_1 A_2 \ldots A_n$ respectively, then the probability that the difference between the average of these quantities, and the mean value of this average, which is the average of their mean values, shall differ from 0 by a quantity numerically not greater than* $\frac{1}{t} \sqrt{\dfrac{\Sigma (A_i - a_i{}^2)}{n}}$ *is greater than* $1 - \dfrac{t^2}{n}$.

---

* Tchebycheff, *Œuvres*, Petrograd, 1899, vol. i, p. 687.

In applying this inequality, we note that the expression

$$\sqrt{\frac{\Sigma\,(A_i - a_i{}^2)}{n}}$$

will vary with n only between fixed limits; we may therefore take t so large that the expression

$$\frac{1}{t}\sqrt{\frac{\Sigma\,(A_i - a_i{}^2)}{n}}$$

is as small as we please. Then we may take n so large that the probability is as near to unity as we.wish. In other words, the inequality tells us that by taking enough variables, we are almost certain that the difference between the average and the mean value of this average, which is the average of the mean values, shall be extremely small. The simplest case is where all the mean values are the same, and the inequality tells us that there is a very large probability that the difference between the observed average and the mean value shall be very small, which is, after all, a restatement of Ch. III 1]. It also leads to:

Poisson's Law of Large Numbers *] *If an event be tried repeatedly with the probabilities $p_1 p_2 \ldots$ for success, which may be constant, or may vary with each trial, then if the number of trials increase indefinitely, the probability that the difference between the average probability and the observed ratio of success will differ by less than any assigned quantity approaches 1 as a limit.*

Let each variable take the value 1 when the event succeeds, 0 when it fails. The mean value of the ith variable is thus p_i. Tchebycheff's inequality tells us that we have a probability above $1 - t^2/n$ that

$$\left(\text{average number of successes} - \frac{\Sigma p_i}{n}\right) < \frac{1}{t}\sqrt{\frac{\Sigma p_i}{n} - \frac{\Sigma p_i{}^2}{n}}$$

$$= \frac{1}{t}\sqrt{\frac{\Sigma p_i q_i}{n}},$$

$$p_i + q_i = 1,\ (p_1 - q_i)^2 \geqslant 0,\ p_i q_i \leqslant \tfrac{1}{4}.$$

* Poisson, 'Recherches sur la probabilité des jugements', *Comptes Rendus de l'Academie des Sciences*, vol. ii, 1835. Bertrand (loc. cit., p. xxxii) comments as

Hence we have a probability $> 1 - t^2/n$ that

(average number of successes $- \Sigma p_i/n) < 1/2t$.

No matter how small $1/2t$ may be, we may make t^2/n as small as we please.

§ 2. Dispersion.*

Suppose that we have n measurements of the same object, or different objects $y_1 y_2 \dots y_n$, where

$$y = \frac{\sum\limits_{i=1}^{i=n} y_i}{n}.$$

Then the expression

$$\sqrt{\frac{\sum\limits_{i=1}^{i=n} (y_i - y)^2}{n}} \tag{1}$$

is called their *dispersion* or *standard deviation*. Let us find its mean value. We shall use the previous notation for the mean value of one of our variables and for the mean value of its square, and write also

$$a = \frac{\sum\limits_{i=1}^{i=n} a_i}{n}.$$

The square of the dispersion is

$$\frac{1}{n}\sum_{i=1}^{i=n} (y_i - y)^2 = \frac{1}{n}\sum_{i=1}^{i=n} \{((y_i - a_i) - (y - a)) + [a_i - a]\}^2.$$

The mean value of each large round bracket is 0, as is the mean value of the product of a large round bracket and a square bracket. The mean value of the square of a square bracket is its ostensible value. When it comes to finding

follows: 'Tel est le résumé fait par Poisson lui-même d'une découverte qui se distingue bien peu des lois connues du hasard, et à laquelle il a, à peu près seul, je crois, attaché une grande importance.'

* The first part of the present section will be found in an article by the author, 'On the Dispersion of Observations', *Bulletin American Math. Soc.*, vol. xxvii, 1921.

the mean value of the square of the large round bracket, we
may apply 6] and 7]. This brings us to the

Fundamental Dispersion Theorem] *If n independent quanti-
ties be given $y_1 y_2 \ldots y_n$, whose mean values are $a_1 a_2 \ldots a_n$,
while the mean values of their squares are $A_1 A_2 \ldots A_n$
respectively, and if the averages of the quantities be y,
while the average of the mean values is a, then the mean
value of the square of the dispersion is*

$$\frac{1}{n}\Big[\sum_{i=1}^{i=n} \Big(\frac{n-1}{n}\,(A_i - a_i^2) + (a_i - a)^2 \Big) \Big].$$

In practice we make two approximations. Firstly, when n
is reasonably large we replace $(n-1)/n$ by 1; secondly, in
accordance with Tchebycheff's inequality, since the square of
the dispersion is an average, we replace its mean value by the
observed value, thus getting the *fundamental dispersion
equation*

$$\frac{1}{n} \sum_{i=1}^{i=n} (y_i - y)^2 = \frac{1}{n}\Big[\sum_{i=1}^{i=n} (A_i - a_i^2) + \sum_{i=1}^{i=n} (a_i - a)^2 \Big]. \quad (2)$$

The reader will not forget that this equation is merely an
approximation. No equation connecting observed quantities
with mean values can be exact. Let us make some applications of this. Suppose that we have N sets, each of s
observations

$$x_{11} x_{12} \ldots x_{1s}; \quad \sum_{j=1}^{j=s} x_{1j} = x_1,$$

$$x_{21} x_{22} \ldots x_{2s}; \quad \sum_{j=1}^{j=s} x_{2j} = x_2,$$

$$\cdot \quad \cdot \quad \cdot \quad \cdot \quad \cdot \quad \cdot \quad \cdot$$

$$x_{N1} x_{N2} \ldots x_{Ns}; \quad \sum_{j=1}^{j=s} x_{Nj} = x_N.$$

Let a_{ij} be the mean value of x_{ij}, while A_{ij} is the mean
value of its square.

Let $\quad \sum\limits_{j=1}^{j=s} a_{ij} = a_i; \quad \sum\limits_{i=1}^{i=N} x_i = Nx; \quad \sum\limits_{i=1}^{i=N} a_i = Na;$

$$\sum_{j=1}^{j=s} \left(x_{ij} - \frac{x_i}{s} \right)^2 = \sum_{j=1}^{j=s} (A_{ij} - a_{ij}{}^2) + \sum_{j=1}^{j=s} \left(a_{ij} - \frac{a_i}{s} \right)^2.$$

Summing again:

$$\sum_{i,j=1}^{i=N,\,j=s} \left(x_{ij} - \frac{x_i}{s} \right)^2 = \sum_{i,j=1}^{i=N,\,j=s} (A_{ij} - a_{ij}{}^2) + \sum_{i,j=1}^{i=N,\,j=s} \left(a_{ij} - \frac{a_i}{s} \right)^2.$$

Again $\qquad x_i - a_i = \sum\limits_{j=1}^{j=s} (x_{ij} - a_{ij}).$

Hence by 5] and 8] the mean value of $(x_i - a_i)^2$ is

$$\sum_{j=1}^{j=s} (A_{ij} - a_{ij}{}^2).$$

Mean value of $x_i{}^2$ = mean value of $(x_i - a_i)^2 + a_i{}^2$ since a_i is mean value of x_i.

Applying (2) again:

$$\sum_{i=1}^{i=N} (x_i - x)^2 = \sum_{i,j=1}^{i=N,\,j=s} (A_{ij} - a_{ij}{}^2) + \sum_{i=1}^{i=N} (a_i - a)^2.$$

Eliminating $(A_{ij} - a_{ij}{}^2)$ between this equation and the last one which contained it, we have

$$\sum_{i,j=1}^{i=N,\,j=s} \left[\left(x_{ij} - \frac{x_i}{s} \right)^2 - \left(a_{ij} - \frac{a_i}{s} \right)^2 \right]$$

$$= \sum_{i=1}^{i=N} [(x_i - x)^2 - (a_i - a)^2]. \qquad (3)$$

In practice we recognize three types of groups of observations.

A. Bernoulli series. All of the observations are supposed to bear upon the same quantity, or, at least, the mean values are all the same. The differences of observed values would thus be purely accidental. Here

$$a_{ij} \equiv a_i/s, \quad a_i \equiv a,$$

$$\sum_{i,j=1}^{i=N,\,j=s} \left(x_{ij} - \frac{x_i}{s} \right)^2 = \sum_{i=1}^{i=N} (x_i - x)^2.$$

Such a series is said to have *normal dispersion*.

B. Lexis series. All observations in the same set are supposed to be on the same quantity, but the quantity varies from one set to another.

$$a_{ij} \equiv a_i/s, \quad a_i \not\equiv a,$$

$$\sum_{i,j=1}^{i=N, j=s} \left(x_{ij} - \frac{x_i}{s}\right)^2 < \sum_{i=1}^{i=N} (x_i - x)^2.$$

This series is said to have *supernormal dispersion*.

C. Poisson series. Here we suppose that within a set there is some difference among the objects, but that all sets are comparable

$$a_{ij} \not\equiv a_i/s, \quad a_i \equiv a,$$

$$\sum_{i,j=1}^{i=N, j=s} \left(x_{ij} - \frac{x_i}{s}\right)^2 > \sum_{i=1}^{i=N} (x_i - x)^2.$$

This series is said to have *subnormal dispersion*.

What we can do in practice is this. We calculate the two quantities

$$\sum_{i,j=1}^{i=N, j=s} \left(x_{ij} - \frac{x_i}{s}\right)^2 \text{ and } \sum_{i=1}^{i=N} (x_i - x)^2.$$

If they be virtually equal, we are sure that the members of one set cannot all be the same, unless all the sets are the same, and vice versa. If the first be less than the second, the different sets cannot be all the same. If the first be greater than the second, there must be a variation within a set.

As an example, we give the observations for precipitation in inches by month in New York City—

Year.	Jan.	Feb.	Mar.	Apr.	May	June	July	Aug.	Sept.	Oct.	Nov.	Dec.	x_i	$x_i/12$
'00	4·18	5·16	3·18	2·06	4·08	3·36	4·33	2·69	2·36	4·17	4·26	1·98	41·78	3·48
'01	2·07	0·86	5·18	6·82	7·01	0·94	5·41	6·88	2·33	2·20	1·31	6·05	47·06	3·92
'02	2·28	5·78	4·32	3·51	1·23	5·91	3·12	3·29	3·59	6·66	1·19	6·19	47·07	3·92
'03	3·44	3·83	3·65	2·88	0·33	7·42	3·33	5·96	2·60	1·55	0·90	2·81	48·60	4·05
'04	3·38	2·18	3·44	3·94	1·61	2·70	4·31	7·13	3·18	3·21	2·62	3·87	41·57	3·46
'05	3·93	2·79	3·65	2·45	1·12	4·18	6·01	5·23	7·11	2·67	1·67	3·67	44·48	3·71
'06	2·98	2·57	5·58	5·78	4·67	1·70	3·21	3·68	2·54	4·30	1·28	3·53	41·82	3·49
'07	3·26	1·52	3·80	3·89	4·08	3·29	1·18	2·48	8·00	3·82	5·05	3·91	45·28	3·77
'08	3·84	5·36	2·15	1·82	9·10	1·70	4·33	5·65	1·60	1·92	0·75	3·21	41·43	3·45
'09	3·33	4·31	3·19	5·93	1·72	3·17	1·98	7·94	2·66	0·74	1·58	5·00	41·55	3·46

$$\sum_{i,\,j\,=\,1}^{i\,=\,10,\,j\,=\,12} \left(x_{ij} - \frac{x_i}{12}\right)^2 = 391{\cdot}38,$$

$$\sum_{i\,=\,1}^{i\,=\,10} (x_i - x)^2 = 69{\cdot}47.$$

This has the characteristics of a Poisson series, and we conclude that the rainfall in New York shows a greater tendency to vary month by month than year by year, a rather natural result.

The most frequent applications of these tests are to the observations of probabilities or frequency ratios, to see whether they vary from case to case or from set to set.* Let the generic letter for one of our probabilities be p_{ij} and let this represent the probability that x_{ij} takes the value 1, while in the contrary case it takes the value 0. Then a_i/s is the average probability for the ith set, and we may put

$$sp_i = a_i = \sum_{j\,=\,1}^{j\,=\,s} p_{ij}; \quad Np = \sum_{i\,=\,1}^{i\,=\,N} p_i = \frac{Na}{s}.$$

$A_{ij} - a_{ij}{}^2 =$ mean value of $(x_{ij} - p_{ij})^2 = p_{ij} - p_{ij}{}^2.$

By the equation preceding (3)

$$\sum_{i\,=\,1}^{i\,=\,N} (x_i - x)^2 = \sum_{i,\,j\,=\,1}^{i\,=\,N,\,j\,=\,s} (p_{ij} - p_{ij}{}^2) + s^2 \sum_{i\,=\,1}^{i\,=\,N} (p_i - p)^2,$$

$$\sum_{j\,=\,1}^{j\,=\,s} [p_{ij} - p_i]^2 = \sum_{j\,=\,1}^{j\,=\,s} p_{ij}{}^2 - sp_i{}^2; \quad \sum_{j\,=\,1}^{j\,=\,s} p_{ij}{}^2 = \sum_{j\,=\,1}^{j\,=\,s} [p_{ij} - p_i]^2 + sp_i{}^2.$$

Similarly $$\sum_{i\,=\,1}^{i\,=\,N} p_i{}^2 = \sum_{i\,=\,1}^{i\,=\,N} (p_i - p)^2 + Np^2,$$

$$\sum_{i\,=\,1}^{i\,=\,N} (x_i - x)^2 = \sum_{i\,=\,1}^{i\,=\,N} \left[sp_i - sp_i{}^2 - \sum_{j\,=\,1}^{j\,=\,s} (p_{ij} - p_i)^2 + s^2 (p_i - p)^2 \right]$$

$$= Nsp - Nsp^2 - \sum_{i,\,j\,=\,1}^{i\,=\,N,\,j\,=\,s} (p_{ij} - p_i)^2 + (s^2 - s) \sum_{i\,=\,1}^{i\,=\,N} (p_i - p)^2;$$

---

* See Fisher, loc. cit., pp. 117 ff., also Forsyth, 'Simple Derivation for the Formulas for the dispersion of Statistical Series', *American Math. Monthly*, vol. xxxi, 1924.

$$\frac{1}{N}\sum (x_i-x)^2 = spq - \frac{1}{N}\sum_{i,j=1}^{i=N,j=s}(p_{ij}-p_i)^2 + \frac{s^2-s}{N}\sum_{i=1}^{i=N}(p_i-p)^2.$$

Bernoulli series : $p_{ij} = p_i = p$; $\dfrac{1}{N}\displaystyle\sum_{i=1}^{i=N}(x_i-x)^2 = spq.$

Lexis series : $p_{ij} \equiv p_{ij}\, p_i \not\equiv p$;

$$\frac{1}{N}\sum_{i=1}^{i=N}(x_i-x)^2 = spq + \frac{s^2-s}{N}\sum_{i=1}^{i=N}(p_i-p)^2.$$

Poisson series : $p_{ij} \not\equiv p_i \; p_i \equiv p$;

$$\frac{1}{N}\sum_{i=1}^{i=N}(x_i-x)^2 = spq - \frac{1}{N}\sum_{i,j=1}^{i=N,j=s}(p_{ij}-p)^2.$$

¶ There are cases where a study of the mean value of the squared dispersion or discrepancy brings out the differences between two series of trials which are otherwise seemingly alike. Let us return to our problem of repeated trials, so thoroughly discussed in the last chapter. Let us first have n_1 trials, with a constant probability p_1 of success, then n_2 trials, with a probability p_2, &c. The mean value of the number of successes will be $\sum\limits_{i} n_i p_i.$

The total discrepancy will be

$$(r_1-n_1p_1) + (r_2-n_2p_2) + \ldots.$$

Since the mean value of the product of two of these is 0, the mean value of the square of this discrepancy is the sum of the mean values of the squares of the discrepancies of the individual series, i.e. $\sum\limits_{i} n_i p_i - \sum\limits_{i} n_i p_i^2.$

Suppose, secondly, we take $n = \sum\limits_{i} n_i$ trials of an event, where the probability for success is

$$p = \frac{\sum\limits_{i} n_i p_i}{\sum\limits_{i} n_i}.$$

Problem.

  Work out another set of observations according to this same plan.

The mean value for the number of successes will be as before. The mean value for the square of the discrepancy is

$$np\,(1-p) = \frac{\sum_i n_i \sum_i n_i p_i - (\sum_i n_i p_i)^2}{\sum_i n_i}$$

$$= \sum_i n_i p_i - \sum_i n_i p_i^2 + \frac{\sum_i n_i \sum_i n_i p_i^2 - (\sum_i n_i p_i)^2}{\sum_i n_i}$$

$$= \sum_i n_i p_i - \sum_i n_i p_i^2 + \frac{\sum_{ij} n_i n_j \,(p_i - p_j)^2}{2 \sum_i n_i}\,.$$

We see that in the second case the mean value for the number of successes is the same, but that for the squared discrepancy is greater.

¶ Here is an even more instructive example of the same kind.* The problem of repeated trials may be stated in the following way. An urn contains a large number N of balls, of which Np are white and Nq are black. A ball is taken out *and replaced* n times in succession, what is the probability for seeing just r white and $n-r$ black balls? This problem we have solved completely. We now take up the analogous problem *where the ball extracted is not replaced.* The probability for just r whites and $n-r$ blacks is now

$$\frac{(Np)!}{r!\,(Np-r)!} \cdot \frac{(Nq)!}{(n-r)!\,[Nq-(n-r)]!} \div \frac{N!}{n!\,(N-n)!}\,.$$

This is a maximum with

$$\frac{1}{r!\,(Np-r)!} \cdot \frac{1}{(n-r)!\,[Nq-(n-r)]!}\,.$$

The ratio of this to the next term is

$$\frac{r+1}{Np-r} \cdot \frac{N\,(1-p)-1-(n-r)}{n-r}\,,$$

which is very close to

$$\frac{r}{Np-r} \cdot \frac{Nq-(n-r)}{n-r}\,,$$

and this will be 1 when $r = np$.

The most likely number of white balls will be as before.

* Castelnuovo, loc. cit., p. 41.

Let us find the mean number of white balls. This is the expectation of a man who shall receive one pistole for every white ball that appears, and nothing for a black one, and this is the sum of his expectations from the individual balls drawn, and so is $p + p + p + \ldots = np$, and this is just the mean value for the number of success that we got before. Now let us find the mean value for the square of the discrepancy. X_i take the value 1 if the ith ball be white, 0 if it be black. Then the mean value of $\underset{i}{\sum} X_i$ is the mean value just found. Furthermore, let $Y_i = X_i - p$. We wish to find the mean value of $(\sum Y_i)^2$.

We have the following table of values:

$$Y_i = q \qquad \text{probability} \quad p$$
$$Y_i = -p \qquad\qquad\qquad q$$
$$Y_i^2 = q^2 \qquad\qquad\qquad p$$
$$Y_i^2 = p^2 \qquad\qquad\qquad q$$
$$Y_i Y_j = q^2 \qquad\qquad\qquad p\frac{Np-1}{N-1}$$
$$Y_i Y_j = p^2 \qquad\qquad\qquad q\frac{Np-1}{N-1}$$
$$Y_i Y_j = -pq \qquad\qquad\qquad \frac{Np-Nq}{\frac{1}{2}N(N-1)} = \frac{2Npq}{N-1}.$$

Hence the mean value of $\underset{i}{\sum} Y_i^2$ is

$$npq - \frac{n(n-1)pq}{N-1}.$$

Comparing this experiment with that where the balls are not replaced, we see that the most likely number of white balls, and the mean number, are the same, but the mean value of the square of the discrepancy is decreased, and we should expect to see less dispersion.

CHAPTER V

GEOMETRICAL PROBABILITY

In the third empirical assumption of the first chapter, we assumed that when an event depended upon n independent variables, varying in an n-dimensional continuum, there existed such an analytic function F that the probability that the variables should take values lying in an n-dimensional sub-manifold was expressed by the integral

$$\iint \dots \int_R F \, dX_1 \, dX_2 \dots dX_n$$

extended over that manifold. By a proper change of variables we then saw that this probability might be expressed by the ratio

$$\frac{\displaystyle\iint \dots \int_r dx_1 \, dx_2 \dots dx_n}{\displaystyle\iint \dots \int_t dx_1 \, dx_2 \dots dx_n} \tag{1}$$

where the integration in the numerator is over the corresponding sub-manifold for the new variables, while that in the denominator is over the total field of possible variation.

The great difficulty in handling problems in this continuous or geometrical probability consists in determining which variables to take in order to express the probability in the form (1). This difficulty can be brought out most clearly by one or two specific examples. Here is a variation on one that appeared in the first chapter. Suppose that a number is chosen at random between 1 and 3, what is the probability that it lies between 1 and 2 ? The natural mode of procedure is as follows. All regions of the interval being supposed equally plausible, we take the number itself as the independent variable, which amounts to assuming that the probability that it lies within an interval is proportional to the length of that interval. Thus, for our particular problem, the probability sought is

$$\frac{\int_1^2 dx}{\int_1^2 dx} = \frac{1}{2}.$$

Leaving this answer for a moment, let us next assume that a number is chosen at random between 1 and $\frac{1}{3}$, what is the probability that it lies between 1 and $\frac{1}{2}$? Following the same reasoning as before, we have

$$\frac{\int_{\frac{1}{2}}^1 dx}{\int_{\frac{1}{3}}^1 dx} = \frac{1}{2} \Big/ \frac{2}{3} = \frac{3}{4}.$$

But we must now notice that if a number lie between 1 and $\frac{1}{3}$, its reciprocal lies between 1 and 3, whereas if it lie between 1 and $\frac{1}{2}$, its reciprocal lies between 1 and 2, and the question arises, have we not found two incompatible answers to the same problem?

A neater paradox of the same sort is due to Bertrand.*

Example 1] *A chord is drawn at random across a circle: what is the probability that it is at least as long as a radius?*

First reasoning. The direction of the chord is obviously immaterial, as the circle lies symmetrically about the centre. All depends upon the distance of the chord from the centre of the circle. As we have nothing to guide us here, we assume that all such distances, not greater than a radius, are equally likely. The chord will be as large as a radius if this distance be $\leqq \frac{\sqrt{3}}{2} r$. Our probability is, then, $\frac{\sqrt{3}}{2} = 0.866 +$.

Second reasoning. The position of the first intersection with the circle is immaterial, owing to this same symmetry, all depends upon the second intersection. All positions for this second intersection being equally likely, all angles between the chord and the radius are equally likely. The chord will

---

* Bertrand, loc. cit., p. 4.

be as great as a radius if this angle be not over 60°, and the probability is $\qquad \frac{2}{3} = 0.666 +$.

Which answer is right? Neither, in an absolute sense. It would be easy to try the matter out experimentally in such a way that the frequency approached the one or the other as a limit. If a disk were cut out of cardboard, and were thrown at random on a table ruled with parallel lines a diameter apart, then one and only one of these lines would cross the disk. All distances from the centre would be equally likely, and we should have a ratio approaching the first answer. On the other hand, if the disk were held by a pivot through a point on its edge, which point lay upon a certain straight line, and were then spun with a random velocity about the pivot, the frequency ratio would approach the second value. The best that we can ever do in almost any case is to make the best guess as to the proper independent variable which our common sense can suggest, and calculate a tentative answer therefrom.

¶ It is fair to say in this connexion that there are exceptional problems where the answer is independent of the choice of the independent variables. The following one is due to the genius of Poincaré.* A wheel turning freely about a fixed horizontal axis is divided into a large even number of equal divisions, painted alternately red and black. The wheel is set spinning. What is the probability that when it comes to rest, a fixed point near the periphery will be opposite a red sector? The result, red or black, will depend upon the total angle θ of spin after a marked point on the wheel has passed the fixed point for the first time. Let $f(\theta)\,d\theta$ be the probability that this angle shall be in the interval $\theta \pm \frac{1}{2}d\theta$. This function is strictly unknown, but we may assume that it is continuous, with a continuous first derivative, and that the value of this latter is always numerically $\leq M$. We take θ as an abscissa, and plot the curve $y = f(\theta)$.

An infinite value of θ being impossible, let us suppose that the whole region of variation for θ runs from 0 to $n\epsilon = l$, where ϵ is the size of one angular division of the wheel. Let

* Poincaré, loc. cit., p. 127.

us show that very nearly one half the area under the curve is under those regions, shaded in the accompanying figure, which correspond to the red sectors.   If M_1 and M_2 be the maximum and minimum values for f at points of two adjacent divisions, then the difference in area between the two cannot exceed

$$2\,\epsilon\,(M_1 - M_2).$$

We next note that, by the law of the mean, $M_1 - M_2$ is equal to the difference between the corresponding abscissas, multiplied by the numerical value of the slope of the tangent at some intermediate point, i. e. $(M_1 - M_2) \leqq 2\,\epsilon\,M$.

The difference between succeeding areas is thus $\leq 4\,\epsilon^2 M$, and

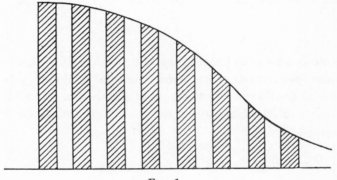

FIG. 1.

the total difference between shaded and unshaded areas, i. e. the total difference between the probability for ending opposite a red or a black sector, is

$$\leqq \frac{n}{2} \times 4\,\epsilon^2 M$$

$$= 2\,\epsilon\,lM.$$

As ϵ decreases indefinitely, l is constant, as is M, our theorem is thus proved.

We have thus seen that the answers given to problems in geometrical probability are subject to considerable suspicion, still it is certainly true that there are quite a number of cases where the choice of the independent variable is clearly dictated by the circumstances, and where, as a matter of fact, the results are found to check up well in practice.   Such problems are also valuable as exercises in the integral calculus, and are, consequently, popular in text-books upon that subject. We shall give a number of the most entertaining.*

Example 2] *A line of given length is divided into three parts: what is the probability that these can be put together to form a triangle?*

Let x be the abscissa of the point which is marked first, x' of that which is marked second. If the point marked first be to the left of that marked second, of which the probability is $\frac{1}{2}$, its abscissa must lie between 0 and $l/2$, where l is the length of the line. The abscissa of the second point must then lie between x and $l/2 + x$. The probability for this is

$$\frac{1}{2l^2} \int_0^{l/2} dx \int_x^{x+l/2} dx' = \frac{1}{8}.$$

There is an equal probability when the point marked first is to the right of the other, hence the total probability is $\frac{1}{4}$.

Here is another solution which is simple and amusing. Let the length of the line be 1, and the lengths of the parts be $x, y,$ and $z,$

$$x + y + z = 1,$$

$$y + z > x, \quad z + x > y, \quad x + y > z.$$

We may take $x, y,$ and z as the distances of a point from the sides of an equilateral triangle whose sides have the lengths $2/\sqrt 3$, the point being within the triangle. The three inequalities will prevent the point from being further from any one side than one half the length of the median thereon. It must therefore lie within the similar triangle- whose vertices are the middle points of the given sides, and this smaller triangle has one-fourth of the area of the larger one.

* The best collection, from which the following problems are taken, is Czuber's *Geometrische Wahrscheinlichkeiten*, Leipzig, 1884.

Problems.

1. Three lengths are taken at random, not greater than three given lengths $a, b,$ and c : what is the probability that they can be combined to form a triangle?

2. Two points are taken at random on a line segment of length a : what is the probability that their distance shall not exceed b ?

¶ Example 3] *Given the quadratic equation*

$$x^2 + 2px + q = 0, \quad -P \le p \le P, \quad -Q \le q \le Q$$

what is the probability that the roots are real?

Let us take q and p as abscissa and ordinate of a point in the plane. The total region is the rectangle whose four corners are the points $(\pm P, \pm Q)$, the area being $4PQ$. The favourable region is not within the parabola $p^2 = q$.

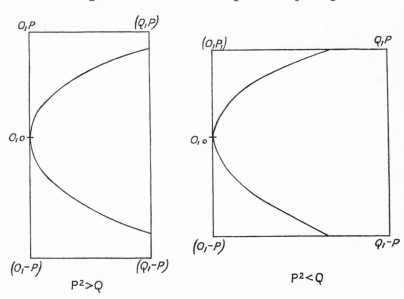

FIG. 2.

In the first case where $P^2 > Q$, the chance for imaginary roots is

$$\frac{2.}{4PQ} \int_0^Q p\,dq = \frac{1}{3} \frac{Q^{\frac{3}{2}}}{PQ} = \frac{1}{3} \frac{\sqrt{Q}}{P}.$$

Favourable chance is

$$1 - \frac{1}{3} \frac{\sqrt{Q}}{P} > \frac{2}{3}.$$

In the second case where $P^2 < Q$, the favourable chance is

$$\frac{1}{2} + \frac{1}{4PQ} \int_{-P}^{P} p^2\,dp = \frac{1}{2} + \frac{P^2}{6Q} < \frac{2}{3}.$$

Example 4] *Two points are taken at random within a circle: what is the probability that the circle through them and the centre of the given circle does not go outside of the latter?*

The radius of the circle being unity, the probability that a given point shall lie at a distance from the centre between x and $x+dx$ is not $dx/1$, as one might hastily assume, but is the ratio of the area of the ring containing all such points to the area of the circle, namely

$$(1/\pi)x\,2\pi x\,dx = 2\,x\,dx.$$

If the circle through P, Q, and O, the given centre, do not go outside the given circle, the point Q must lie within one of the two circles of radius, $\frac{1}{2}$ passing through O and P. The distance between the centres of these is

$$2\left(\frac{1}{4} - \frac{x^2}{4}\right)^{\frac{1}{2}} = (1-x^2)^{\frac{1}{2}}.$$

The common chord subtends at the centre of each angle $2\sin^{-1}x$, the area of the favourable region for Q is

$$\lfloor 2\pi - 2\sin^{-1}x\rfloor \left(\frac{1}{2}\right)^2 + x\left(\frac{1}{4} - \frac{x^2}{4}\right)^{\frac{1}{2}}$$

$$= \frac{1}{2}(\pi - \sin^{-1}x + x\,[1-x^2]^{\frac{1}{2}})\cdot$$

Hence the probability sought is

$$\frac{1}{\pi}\int_0^1 ([\pi - \sin^{-1}x]\,x + x^2\,[1-x^2]^{\frac{1}{2}})\,dx = \frac{7}{16}\cdot$$

We now come to the most famous of all problems in geometrical probability.

Buffon's needle problem.*

A smooth table is ruled with parallel lines separated by a distance d. A needle whose length is l, less than d, is thrown at random on the table. What is the probability that it will cross one of the parallels?

The chance that the distance from the centre of the needle to the nearest parallel should lie between the limits x and $x+dx$ is $2\,dx/d.$

* Buffon, 'Essai d'arithmétique morale'. See his *Œuvres*, ed. 1801 (An. VIII), vol. xxi, pp. 163 ff.

The chance that in this case the needle should cross the nearest parallel is

$$\frac{2}{\pi} \cos^{-1} \frac{2x}{l}.$$

Hence the probability required is

$$\frac{4}{\pi d} \int_0^{\frac{l}{2}} \cos^{-1} \frac{2x}{l} \, dx = \frac{2l}{\pi d} \int_0^1 \cos^{-1} y \, dy = \frac{2l}{\pi d}. \qquad (2)$$

Another simple and ingenious solution was found by Barbier.* The probability of crossing a line is the expectation of a man who shall receive one pistole if the needle cross, and none if it do not. This is the sum of the expectations from the various infinitesimal segments of the needle, and will not be altered if the latter be bent in any way. Assuming, then, that the needle is made of such inferior steel that it can be bent into the form of a circle, of diameter l/π, the probability that the circle shall cross one of our lines is $l/\pi d$; but the expectation is double that, for if it cross once it will cross twice. This gives the same answer as before.

Buffon's needle problem has induced a number of persons to try the experiment of calculating π experimentally in this way. The most elaborate series of experiments was carried out in the year 1901 by Lazzerini,† who made 3,408 trials and got the value $\pi = 3 \cdot 1415929$, an error of $0 \cdot 0000003$.

Let us pause for a moment to discuss this result. The natural method in such cases is to treat the problem as one in relative discrepancy, and find the probability that the latter should be within assigned limits. But here the relative

---

* Barbier, *Liouville's Journal*, Series 2, vol. v, 1860, pp. 273 ff., contains a number of interesting problems.

† Lazzerini, 'Una applicazione del calcolo delle Probabilità', *Periodico di Matematico*, (2) vol. iv, 1901, pp. 140 ff.

Problems.

1. The points P and Q are taken at random in a circle. What is the probability that the circle with P as centre and radius PQ will lie inside?

2. Two points are taken at random within a circle. What is the probability that the perpendicular from the centre on their line does not pass between them?

3. Do Buffon's needle problem when the length of the needle is greater than the distance between the parallels.

discrepancy is so small that the discrepancy in the number of crossings would be less than unity, and the safest plan is to assume that there was no absolute discrepancy at all. The probability for that, according to Ch. III (9), is

$$1/\sqrt{2\,npq\,\pi}.$$

We have no information as to the relative lengths of l and d, but probably shall make no great error in the final conclusion if we make the simple assumption

$$2l = d\,; \quad p = 1/\pi.$$

The probability for finding no discrepancy will then be

$$\frac{1}{\sqrt{6816\left(\dfrac{\pi-1}{\pi}\right)}} = \frac{1}{69}.$$

It is much to be feared that in performing this experiment Lazzerini 'watched his step'.

Barbier's method of solving Buffon's needle problem is easily extended to other cases, and gives an easy solution of the more difficult problem of finding the probability that a line shall cross a closed convex contour or oval. We shall imagine that the experiment is carried out in such a way that we are justified in taking as independent variables the distance of the line from a fixed point, and its angle with a fixed direction. If these numbers be p and θ, and if we slide the origin to the point $x_0 y_0$ and swing through the angle ϕ,

$$p' = x_0 \cos(\theta-\phi) + y_0 \sin(\theta-\phi) + p, \quad \theta' = \theta - \phi,$$

$$\frac{\partial p'}{\partial p} = 1, \quad \frac{\partial p'}{\partial \theta} = -x_0 \sin(\theta-\phi) + y_0 \cos(\theta-\phi),$$

$$\frac{\partial \theta'}{\partial p} = 0, \quad \frac{\partial \theta'}{\partial \theta} = 1,$$

$$\frac{\partial(\theta' p')}{\partial(\theta p)} = 1.$$

Problem.

Captain Fox (*Messenger of Mathematics*, vol. ii, pp. 113, 114) made 1,120 trials of Buffon's needle problem with the resulting value of π, 3.1419. Discuss this result.

Since this Jacobian is equal to 1, the probabilities for an arbitrary line are independent of the point and direction of reference for the normal coordinates, an important point easily overlooked. The probability that a line shall pass between two given points is proportional to the length of their segment, and is independent of the direction of the line when every line passing between them is permissible. The probability that a line shall cross an oval is one half the expectation of a man who shall receive one pistole for each intersection, tangency counting double, and this, in turn, is one half the sum of the expectations for each linear element. It is, therefore, proportional to the perimeter of the oval. If a line cross a certain oval it may, or may not, cross a second oval within the first ; it cannot, however, cross the latter without crossing the former. The probability of crossing the inside oval is, thus, the probability of crossing the first, multiplied by the probability that, having crossed the first, it shall also cross the second. We thus find the latter probability by dividing the probability of crossing the inside oval by that of crossing the outside one, and the factor of proportionality cancels out, giving us :

Theorem 1] *The probability that a line which crosses a given oval shall also cross a second such oval inside the first is the ratio of the perimeters of the two.*

In particular, to solve Buffon's needle problem, we have merely to treat the needle as an extremely thin oval, and glue it on a circular disk of diameter d.

¶ The probability that a line segment should intersect an oval is the expectation of a man who shall receive one pistole if the segment meet the oval once or twice. If the segment be extremely short, the probability of this latter is negligible in comparison with that of the former. The probability that a short segment should meet an oval is proportional to the product of its length and the probability that its line should meet the oval, i. e. proportional to the product of its length multiplied by the perimeter of the oval.

¶ Theorem 2] *The probability that two ovals should intersect is proportional to the product of their perimeters.*

Let us find the probability that a line should intersect two mutually exterior ovals. Let them be connected by direct and transverse common tangents as shown in Fig. 3. The

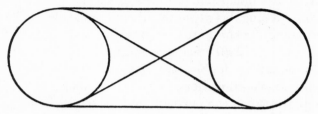

Fig. 3.

probability of meeting the outside contour is the probability of meeting at least one half of the figure ∞. This is proportional to the total perimeter of the ∞ less the probability of meeting both parts of the ∞, which is the probability of meeting both ovals.

¶ Theorem 3] *The probability that a line shall intersect two mutually exterior ovals is proportional to the difference between the perimeter of the figure ∞ formed by the ovals and their transverse common tangents, and the perimeter of the convex figure formed by the ovals and their direct common tangents.*

¶ Example 5] *If a line cross a rectangle of dimensions a and b, what is the probability that it will cross two opposite sides?*

We consider the sides as indefinitely thin ovals, and add the probabilities for each pair.

$$\frac{2\sqrt{a^2+b^2}+2a-2(a+b)}{2(a+b)} + \frac{2\sqrt{a^2+b^2}+2b-2(a+b)}{2(a+b)}$$

$$= \frac{2\sqrt{a^2+b^2}}{a+b} - 1.$$

Let us calculate this probability again, taking as independent variables the positions of the points on the perimeter. The probability that the first intersection should be on a side a, and that the second intersection, which must not be on the same side, should be on the opposite one is

$$\frac{a}{a+b} \cdot \frac{a}{a+2b} = \frac{a^2}{(a+b)(a+2b)}.$$

We have an analogous probability when the first intersection is on a side b, adding the two together we get

$$\frac{1}{a+b}\left[\frac{a^2}{a+2b} + \frac{b^2}{2a+b}\right] = \frac{a^2 - \frac{1}{2}ab + b^2}{a^2 + \frac{5}{2}ab + b^2},$$

and this is somewhat less.

What will be the probability of passing between two ovals? This is clearly the difference between the probabilities of meeting the outside contour and that of meeting at least one oval, whence, by the theorem of total probability general case, we get:

¶ Theorem 4] *The probability that a line will pass between two mutually exterior ovals is proportional to the difference between the perimeter of the ∞ and the sum of their perimeters.*

Example 6] *Two secants are drawn across an oval: what is the probability that they will intersect within the curve?*

Let p be the length of the normal on the first secant, from a chosen origin within the oval, let θ be the angle which this perpendicular makes with a fixed direction, l the length of the chord; the probability that a second secant shall cross this chord is

$$\frac{d\theta}{\pi} \cdot \frac{dp}{L} \cdot \frac{2l}{s}.$$

Here L is the distance between the two tangents parallel to the chord, and s is the perimeter of the curve. Now

$$\int_0^L l\,dp = \text{Area},$$

hence the probability we seek is

$$\frac{2\,\text{Area}}{s}\int_0^\pi \frac{d\theta}{\pi L}.$$

We must find this integral by an indirect method. We see,

in fact, that $1/L$ is the probability that a secant in the given direction, which crosses the given oval, should also cross a circle of diameter 1 within the oval, and by 1]

$$\int_0^\pi \frac{d\theta}{\pi L} = \frac{\pi}{s}.$$

The probability sought is, therefore, $2\pi \text{ Area}/s^2$.

In the case of a circle this is $\frac{1}{2}$. When the area is given, the circumference is a minimum when the oval is a circle. We thus reach a rather curious result:

Theorem 4] *The probability that two random secants of an oval should intersect is equal to one half when the oval is a circle, and less in every other case.*

Problems.

1. Find the analogues in 3 dimensions to Theorems 1-4, and Examples 3-6.

2. A die is thrown on a board ruled with parallel lines whose distance is greater than a diagonal of a face of the die. Find the probability that it will cross a ruling.

3. Find the probability that a line shall intersect two ovals with two common points.

4. Find the probability that a line shall intersect two ovals with four common points.

CHAPTER VI

THE PROBABILITY OF CAUSES

THE form in which we have so far studied problems of probability is not always that in which they present themselves in practice. We have assumed that we knew just which were the equally likely ways in which an event might happen, or the proper independent variables when the number was infinite, and have calculated the probability or frequency ratio from them. But it often happens in practice that what we know is merely an empirical approximation to the frequency ratio from a limited number of cases, and what we wish to find out is the likelihood that the actual probability should lie within certain assigned limits. To put the matter in concrete form, we saw (p. 50) that Buffon threw a coin 4,040 times and saw 2,048 heads. What we wish to know is the likelihood that that series arose from throwing a good coin.

We have already learnt one method of meeting the problem, namely, to assume that the coin is good, and calculate the probability that the discrepancy will be as large as, or larger than, that observed. That does not, however, cover the question entirely. It is one thing to say that if a coin be good the discrepancy will attain a certain figure a certain proportion of the time, it is quite another to say that when a certain discrepancy has been observed a large number of times when a coin of unknown constitution was thrown, a certain proportion of the trials were in all probability made with a good coin. It is the latter fraction, not the former, which answers the question, ' What is the probability that the coin was good ? '

When we have once grasped the real bearing of the question of the likelihood of a good or bad coin, we see immediately that there are two essential elements in the question :

A) The probability that Buffon should pick up a good or bad coin to perform the experiments. Assuming that Buffon's good faith is indubitable, this will depend upon the proportion of coins in circulation at his time which were good, at least for the purposes of such a trial.

B) The probability that if he threw a good coin, he would obtain as large a discrepancy as was observed.

If it were perfectly certain that no bad coins were in circulation at that time, it is clear that the problem would be meaningless, but that is by no means sure. In the same way, if it were absolutely impossible for a good coin to produce an observed result, the problem would have no sense. As both possibilities are open, we are face to face with a real problem.

We shall mean by the *cause* of an event, *any antecedent event whatever.* We mean by the *a priori probability that a certain cause should be operative before the event in question has been observed,* the limit of the number of occasions where the causal event happened to the number of cases where it happened or failed, as this latter number is indefinitely increased. We mean by the *probability that a given cause should produce an observed result,* the limit of the ratio of the number of times where the causal event was followed by the observed result, to the total number of times when the causal event was operative. The reader will not forget that, according to our first empirical axiom, all trials must be made under the same essential conditions. Consequently, in determining the probability that a certain cause should be operative, or that it should produce a certain result, we must assume that no other essential features in the situation have been allowed to vary.

Suppose that there is a certain finite class of causes $C_1 C_2 \ldots C_n$ which might be followed by a certain event, and that they are mutually exclusive, yet one of them must have happened. What is the probability that the actual cause was C_k?

Let the *a priori* probabilities for the various causes be $\pi_1 \pi_2 \ldots \pi_n$, while the respective probabilities that they should be followed by the observed event are $p_1 p_2 \ldots p_n$. Let P be the probability sought.

The probability that cause C_k should occur, and should produce the observed event is $\pi_k p_k$. But this probability may be reckoned otherwise. It is the probability that the event should happen, namely, $\pi_1 p_1 + \pi_2 p_2 + \ldots \pi_n p_n$ multiplied by the probability P that it should arise from the cause in question. This gives

Bayes' Principle *] *If $C_1 C_2 \ldots C_n$ be the total number of mutually exclusive causes of a certain class for an observed event, one of which must have occurred, if $\pi_1 \pi_2 \ldots \pi_n$ be their respective a priori probabilities, while $p_1 p_2 \ldots p_n$ are the various probabilities that they should be followed by the event, then the probability that the operative cause was C_k is*

$$\frac{\pi_k p_k}{\pi_1 p_1 + \pi_2 p_2 + \ldots + \pi_n p_n}. \tag{1}$$

We shall give a statement of this principle in the case of continuous probability, as this will be of use later. We pass to it by the usual process of passing over from a sum to a definite integral.

Bayes' principle for continuous probability] *If all causes of a certain class for an observed event, which are mutually exclusive, yet one of which must have occurred, depend analytically upon n independent variables $z_1 z_2 \ldots z_n$ in such a way that the a priori probability that these variables take values in the infinitesimal interval $z_1 \pm \frac{1}{2} dz_1, z_2 \pm \frac{1}{2} dz_2, \ldots z_n \pm \frac{1}{2} dz_n$ differs by an infinitesimal of higher order from $f(z_1 z_2 \ldots z_n) dz_1 dz_2 \ldots dz_n$, f being an analytic function, while the probability that the observed event shall then follow is $\phi(z_1 z_2 \ldots z_n)$, then the probability that the event was produced by a cause corresponding to variables in a certain region R is*

$$\frac{\iint \ldots \int_R f\phi \, dz_1 dz_2 \ldots dz_n}{\iint \ldots \int_T f\phi \, dz_1 dz_2 \ldots dz_n} \tag{2}$$

---

* Bayes, 'An essay towards solving a problem in the Doctrine of Chances', *Philosophical Transactions Royal Soc.*, vol. liii, 1763, and 'A Demonstration of the Second Rule, &c.', ibid., vol. liv, 1764. Czuber, *Entwickelung der Wahrscheinlichkeitsrechnung*, cit. p. 253, gives the erroneous dates 1764 and 1765.

where the integral in the denominator is taken over the total field of variation of the variables compatible with the problem.

As a first application of Bayes' principle we take a well-known paradox of Bertrand's known as his ' box paradox '.*

Three boxes look exactly alike. Each contains two drawers, and in each drawer is a coin. In the first box there are two gold coins, in the second a gold and a silver coin, in the third two silver coins. A box is chosen at random and a drawer opened : what is the probability that the coin in the other drawer of the same box is of the opposite metal?

First reasoning. This can only happen if we have hit upon the second box, the chance for that is $\frac{1}{3}$.

Second reasoning. There is a $\frac{1}{2}$ chance that the coin first seen shall be gold. When gold has been seen, we know. that we have chosen one of the first two boxes, but we do not know which, they are equally likely, hence the chance for a gold coin followed by a silver is $\frac{1}{4}$. There is an equal chance for a silver coin followed by a gold. Hence the total chance is $\frac{1}{2}$.

It is evident that the first answer is right and the second wrong. The question is, What was wrong with the reasoning in the second case ? Here is the flaw. If a gold coin has been seen, the *a priori* chance for the first or the second box is $\frac{1}{2}$, but whereas the first has a chance 1 of showing a gold coin the first time, the second has only a chance $\frac{1}{2}$ of doing so. The probability that the gold coin is in the second box is

$$\frac{\frac{1}{2} \cdot \frac{1}{2}}{\frac{1}{2} \cdot 1 + \frac{1}{2} \cdot \frac{1}{2}} = \frac{1}{3}$$

and there is a similar probability for a silver coin. This leads to the correct answer again.

Example 1] *An urn contains N balls, black and white, in unknown proportion. A ball is drawn out n times and replaced, the balls being mixed after each drawing, with the result that just r white balls are seen. What is the probability that the urn contains exactly R white balls?*

* Bertrand, loc. cit., p. 2.

Hypothesis 1] All mixtures of white and black are equally likely *a priori*. Then all of the π's are equal and will cancel out, and we have, by (1)

$$\frac{\dfrac{n!}{r!\,(n-r)!}\left(\dfrac{R}{N}\right)^r\left(\dfrac{N-R}{N}\right)^{n-r}}{\displaystyle\sum_{K=0}^{K=N}\dfrac{n!}{r!\,(n-r)!}\left(\dfrac{K}{N}\right)^r\left(\dfrac{N-K}{N}\right)^{n-r}}=\frac{R^r\,(N-R)^{n-r}}{\displaystyle\sum_{K=0}^{K=N}K^r\,(N-K)^{n-r}}\,.$$

What value of R will be the most likely? We obtain a ready and sufficiently accurate answer by equating to 0 the derivative with respect to R of the logarithm. This gives

$$\frac{r}{R}=\frac{n-r}{N-R}=\frac{n}{N}\,.$$

We may, then, say that the most likely mixture is that where the actual proportion of white balls is the observed proportion, and this, indeed, is just what we should expect.

Hypothesis 2] The urn was filled by drawing white and black balls at random from an extremely large number of balls where the two colours were found in equal profusion.*

Here we have

$$\frac{\dfrac{N!}{R!\,(N-R)!}\dfrac{1}{2^R}\dfrac{1}{2^{N-R}}\dfrac{n!}{r!\,(n-r)!}\left(\dfrac{R}{N}\right)^r\left(\dfrac{N-R}{N}\right)^{n-r}}{\displaystyle\sum_{K=0}^{K=N}\dfrac{N!}{K!\,(N-K)!}\dfrac{1}{2^K}\dfrac{1}{2^{N-K}}\dfrac{n!}{r!\,(n-r)!}\left(\dfrac{K}{N}\right)^r\left(\dfrac{N-K}{N}\right)^{n-r}}$$

$$=\frac{\dfrac{R^r\,(N-R)^{n-r}}{R!\,(N-R)!}}{\displaystyle\sum_{K=0}^{K=N}\dfrac{K^r\,(N-K)^{n-r}}{K!\,(N-K)!}}\,.$$

The probability that R should be close to $\dfrac{N}{2}+z\sqrt{\dfrac{N}{2}}$ was found, by the reasoning which led to the probability integral, to be $e^{-z^2}\,\Delta z$.

---

* Bertrand, loc. cit., p. 152.

We wish to maximize

$$e^{-z^2}\left(\frac{N}{2} + z\sqrt{\frac{N}{2}}\right)^r \left(\frac{N}{2} - z\sqrt{\frac{N}{2}}\right)^{n-r},$$

or else

$$e^{-z^2}\left(1 + \frac{z}{\sqrt{\frac{N}{2}}}\right)^r \left(1 - \frac{z}{\sqrt{\frac{N}{2}}}\right)^{n-r}.$$

Equating to zero the derivative of the logarithm

$$\frac{r}{\sqrt{\frac{N}{2}} + z} - \frac{n-r}{\sqrt{\frac{N}{2}} - z} = 2z.$$

Since $z\sqrt{\frac{N}{2}}$ is to be of reasonable size, we may assume $\dfrac{z}{\sqrt{\frac{N}{2}}}$ is negligible, and reject z^2 as compared with $\dfrac{N}{2}$. We get

$$\frac{2r\sqrt{\frac{N}{2}} - n\left(\sqrt{\frac{N}{2}} + z\right)}{\frac{N}{2}} = 2z,$$

$$z = \frac{(2r-n)\sqrt{\frac{N}{2}}}{(N+n)}.$$

The most likely composition is

$$\frac{R}{N} = \frac{1}{2} + \frac{z}{\sqrt{2N}} = \frac{1}{2}\frac{N+2r}{N+n}.$$

This varies between $\frac{1}{2}$ and r/n as we should expect.

This first example leads us naturally to the idea of establishing some general formula for the probability of causes analogous to the Bernoulli formula. Suppose that an event has succeeded np times and failed nq times in n trials. If all probabilities for success be *a priori* equally likely, the most likely probability for success is p. What is the chance that the observed series resulted from the operations of a cause which gave a probability of success lying between

$$p + t_1\sqrt{\frac{2pq}{n}} \text{ and } p + t_2\sqrt{\frac{2pq}{n}} ?$$

The probability is

$$\frac{\displaystyle\sum_{P=p+t_1\sqrt{\frac{2\,pq}{n}}}^{P=p+t_2\sqrt{\frac{2\,pq}{n}}} \frac{n!}{np!\,nq!}\,P^{np}\,(1-P)^{nq}}{\displaystyle\sum_{P=0}^{P=1} \frac{n!}{np!\,nq!}\,P^{np}\,(1-P)^{nq}}.$$

With regard to the summations, which are rather meaningless as they stand, we assume that nP is an integer, so that P increases by $1/n$ each time.

Let us write
$$P = p + z\sqrt{\frac{2\,pq}{n}},$$

$$\Delta z = \frac{1}{\sqrt{2\,npq}}.$$

We multiply every term above and below by this and cancel the factorials, getting

$$\frac{\displaystyle\sum_{z=t_1}^{z=t_2} \left(p+z\sqrt{\frac{2\,pq}{n}}\right)^{np}\left(q-z\sqrt{\frac{2\,pq}{n}}\right)^{nq}\Delta z}{\displaystyle\sum_{z=-\sqrt{\frac{np}{2q}}}^{z=\sqrt{\frac{nq}{2p}}} \left(p+z\sqrt{\frac{2\,pq}{n}}\right)^{np}\left(q-z\sqrt{\frac{2\,pq}{n}}\right)^{nq}\Delta z}.$$

Divide numerator and denominator by $p^{np}q^{nq}$

$$\log\left(1+\frac{z}{p}\sqrt{\frac{2\,pq}{n}}\right)^{np}\left(1-\frac{z}{q}\sqrt{\frac{2\,pq}{n}}\right)^{nq}$$

$$= np\left[\frac{z}{p}\sqrt{\frac{2\,pq}{n}}-\frac{z^2q}{np}+\frac{1}{n^{\frac{3}{2}}}f(z)\right]$$

$$-nq\left[\frac{z}{q}\sqrt{\frac{2\,pq}{n}}+\frac{z^2p}{nq}+\frac{1}{n^{\frac{3}{2}}}\phi(z)\right]$$

$$= -z^2+\frac{1}{n^{\frac{3}{2}}}\psi(z).$$

Our fraction above will approach asymptotically to

$$\frac{\displaystyle\sum_{z=t_1}^{z=t_2} e^{-z^2}\,\Delta z}{\displaystyle\sum_{z=-\sqrt{\frac{np}{2q}}}^{z=\sqrt{\frac{nq}{2p}}} e^{-z^2}\,\Delta z}.$$

The limit of this as n increases indefinitely is

$$\frac{1}{\sqrt{\pi}}\int_{t_1}^{t_2} e^{-z^2}dz = \frac{1}{2}\left[\frac{2}{\sqrt{\pi}}\int_0^{t_2} e^{-z^2}dz - \frac{2}{\sqrt{\pi}}\int_0^{t_1} e^{-z^2}dz\right].$$

We thus get

Theorem 1] *If in a large number n of trials where all probabilities for an individual success are a* priori *equally likely, there be np successes and nq failures, then the probability that the cause is such as to give a probability of success lying between the limits*

$$p+t_1\sqrt{\frac{2\,pq}{n}} \ \ and \ \ p+t_2\sqrt{\frac{2\,pq}{n}}$$

is $\frac{1}{2}\left[\Theta\,(t_2)-\Theta\,(t_1)\right]$ (3)

Converse of Bernoulli's theorem] *Under the conditions of Theorem 1, the probability that the cause is such as to give a probability of success in the limits* $p\pm t\sqrt{\dfrac{2\,pq}{n}}$ *is*

$$\Theta\,(t).   \tag{4}$$

¶ We must now face the possibility that all causes are not equally likely *a priori*. We are thrown back upon our formula (2), which we simplify by the law of the mean

$$\int_{t_1}^{t_2} f(z)\,\phi(z)\,dz = f\left[t_1 + h\,(t_2-t_1)\right]\int_{t_1}^{t_2}\phi(z)\,dz.$$

The most interesting case is to compare the probabilities under the conditions of Theorem 1], except the *a priori* condition, that t should lie in the region between t_1 and t_2, or else between t_1' and t_2'. The ratio will be

$$\frac{f\left[t_1 + h\,(t_2-t_1)\right]}{f\left[t_1' + h'\,(t_2'-t_1')\right]}\cdot\frac{\Theta\,(t_2)-\Theta\,(t_1)}{\Theta\,(t_2')-\Theta\,(t_1')}.   \tag{5}$$

When the regions are both very small, we may put

$$t_1 + t_2 = 2t \; ; \quad t_2 - t_1 = \Delta t \; ; \quad t_1' + t_2' = 2t' \; ; \quad t_2' - t_1' = 2\Delta t' \; ;$$

the ratio then takes the simpler form :

$$\frac{f(t)}{f(t')} \cdot \frac{e^{-t^2}\,\Delta t}{e^{-t'^2}\,\Delta t'} \tag{6}$$

We shall apply this to an amusing problem proposed by Bertrand.*

' The owner of a gaming establishment has· installed a roulette wheel. In 10,000 turns this has shown red 5,300 times, black 4,700 times. The owner refuses to pay for the wheel and claims damages ; his clients have noticed that the wheel seems to favour red. They go to law about it. The owner claims that a good wheel was never known to show such a discrepancy. 300 turns in 10,000 cannot be the result of chance. The chance for red is not $\frac{1}{2}$, as it ought to be. " Never mind the record of the turns so far," says the maker, "you cannot insure against the caprices of fortune. The machine was made by excellent workmen, and was carefully inspected. No part of it is imperfect. There is no bad centring of any wheel, no inequality in the size of the divisions, no error in levelling." The Court calls in an expert; what should he say ? '

According to the maker, the probability for red lies between 0·499 and 0·501 ; according to the owner it lies between 0·529 and 0·531. We have

$$\sqrt{\frac{2\,pq}{n}} = \frac{1}{100}\,\sqrt{0\cdot 53 \times 0\cdot 94},$$

$$= 0\cdot 0070583,$$

$$0\cdot 53 + 0\cdot 0070583\,t_1 = 0\cdot 501,$$

$$t_1 = -4\cdot 10862,$$

$$t_2 = -4\cdot 39197,$$

$$t = -4\cdot 25030,$$

$$\Delta t = 0\cdot 1416,$$

* Bertrand, loc. cit., p. 166.

Problem.

Discuss Buffon's coin and Lazzerini's needle by the methods of the present chapter.

$$0.53 + 0.0070583 t_1' = 0.531,$$
$$t_1' = 0.1416,$$
$$t_2' = -0.1416,$$
$$t' = 0,$$
$$\Delta t' = 0.1416.$$

We thus need to find

$$\frac{f(t)}{f(0)} e^{-(4.2503)^2},$$

and we find from the table on p. 208 that this is

$$\frac{f(t)}{f(0)} \times 0.000000015.$$

Bertrand's solution is simpler. He compares the probabilities under the two hypotheses of getting just this result, namely,

$$\frac{f(t)}{f(0)} \cdot \frac{(0.5)^{5300} (0.5)^{4700}}{(0.53)^{5300} (0.47)^{4700}} = \frac{f(t)}{f(0)} \times 0.000000015.$$

It will readily be granted that if the maker of the wheel be known to be careful and conscientious, $f(t)$ will be many times larger than $f(0)$. It is hard to believe, however, that the ratio of the two would be large enough to bring the product up to respectable size. The expert would doubtless decide against the maker.

There is another point that should be noted in this connexion, which is rather subtle and easily overlooked. We have no right to settle *after the event* what constitutes really a remarkable run. Let us return to Buffon and his coin. It will be noted that the discrepancy was 28, and this is exactly the year of the Christian era when John the Baptist was cast into prison. Let us examine the probability that the coin was so constructed as to show this date when thrown that number of times. It is easy to calculate the probability that a coin giving to heads the probability 507/1010 should show no discrepancy in 4,040 throws, and this is considerably greater than the probability that a good coin should show exactly the discrepancy 28. But the *a priori* probability that a coin should be so constructed as to predict the date of John the Baptist's imprisonment is so microscopic compared with the probability that a coin should be good, that we reject the former hypothesis without more discussion. The reader will find it amusing to apply this type of reasoning to such problems as the probability that the great Pyramid was specially placed by Divine Providence to reveal the value of π, the length of the British inch, and other interesting facts which Piazzi Smyth and others have deduced from its measurements.

Bayes' principle has sometimes been used to deduce the probability for future events. The reader will have no difficulty in proving:

Bayes' principle applied to future events] *If $C_1 C_2 \dots C_n$ be the total number of mutually exclusive causes for an observed event, one of which must have occurred, if $\pi_1 \pi_2 \dots \pi_n$ be their respective a priori probabilities, $p_1 p_2 \dots p_n$ the various probabilities that they should be followed by the observed event, while $P_1 P_2 \dots P_n$ are the respective probabilities that they shall be followed by an expected event, then the probability that the expected event shall take place is*

$$\frac{\sum\limits_{K=1}^{K=n} \pi_K p_K P_K}{\sum\limits_{K=1}^{K=n} \pi_K p_K}. \tag{7}$$

In the same way we may prove:

Bayes' principle for continuous probability applied to future events] *If all causes of a certain class for an observed event, which are mutually exclusive yet one of which must have happened, depend analytically upon n independent variables $z_1 z_2 \dots z_n$ in such a way that the a priori probability that these variables take values in the infinitesimal intervals*

$$z_1 \pm \tfrac{1}{2} dz_1, \; z_2 \pm \tfrac{1}{2} dz_2, \dots z_n \pm \tfrac{1}{2} dz_n$$

differs by an infinitesimal of higher order from

$$f(z_1 z_2 \dots z_n) \, dz_1 dz_2 \dots dz_n,$$

while the probability that the observed event shall then

follow is $\phi(z_1 z_2 \ldots z_n)$ *and the probability for a future event is* $\psi(z_1 z_2 \ldots z_n)$, *then the total probability for the occurrence of the future event is*

$$\frac{\iint \ldots \int_t f\phi\psi \, dz_1 dz_2 \ldots dz_n}{\iint \ldots \int_t f\phi \, dz_1 dz_2 \ldots dz_n} \tag{8}$$

each integral being taken over the whole field of possible values.

Example 2] *If in n trials of an event for which all probabilities are equally likely a priori, there have been just r successes, what is the probability that there will be just R in a further series of N trials?*

If x be the probability for success, the probability will be, by (8)

$$\frac{\dfrac{N!}{R!\,(N-R)!}\displaystyle\int_0^1 x^{r+R}(1-x)^{n+N-(r+R)}\,dx}{\displaystyle\int_0^1 x^r (1-x)^{n-r}\,dx}.$$

Now $\qquad \displaystyle\int_0^1 x^l (1-x)^m \, dx = \frac{l!\,m!}{(l+m+1)!}.$

Hence our desired probability is

$$\frac{N!}{R!\,(N-R)!} \cdot \frac{(R+r)!\,(N+n-(R+r))!}{(N+n+1)!} \frac{(n+1)!}{r!\,(n-r)!}. \tag{9}$$

When all the numbers are large we may apply Stirling's formula, getting

$$\frac{1}{\sqrt{2\pi}} \frac{N^{(N+\frac{1}{2})}(R+r)^{R+r+\frac{1}{2}}(N+n-(R+r))^{N+n-(R+r)+\frac{1}{2}}(n+1)^{N+\frac{3}{2}}}{R^{R+\frac{1}{2}}(N-R)^{N-R+\frac{1}{2}}(N+n+1)^{N+n+\frac{3}{2}}r^{r+\frac{1}{2}}(n-r)^{n-r+\frac{1}{2}}}. \tag{10}$$

When we are interested in only one further trial,

$$N = R = 1$$

and (9) becomes

$$\frac{(r+1)!\,(n-r)!\,(n+1)!}{(n+2)!\,r!\,(n-r)!} = \frac{r+1}{n+2}. \tag{11}$$

When the event has never failed so far, $r = n$ and we have

$$(n+1)/(n+2). \tag{12}$$

The most absurd consequences have, in the past, been deduced from this formula. Putting n equal to the number of times the sun has risen, it has been used to estimate the probability that it will rise the next day. Nothing could be more grotesque. The rising of the sun is not a statistical event whose cause is obscure, but a mechanical necessity which will continue as long as present astronomical conditions do, and will then cease. To use formula (12) we should have to assume that all possible cosmogonies were equally likely. What such a phrase may mean is utterly beyond our comprehension: it undoubtedly means nothing whatsoever.

The probability that exactly the same proportion of success will appear in a second series of n trials as appeared in a first series will be found from (9) by putting $N = n$, $R = r$.

$$\frac{n+1}{2n+1}\left[\frac{n!}{r!\,(n-r)!}\right]^2\left[\frac{(2r)!\,(2n-2r)!}{2n!}\right].$$

Replacing the first factor by $\frac{1}{2}$, approximating to the rest by Stirling's formula, we have

$$\left(\frac{n}{4\pi r\,(n-r)}\right)^{\frac{1}{2}}.$$

On the other hand, if we surely knew that the probability for success was r/n, the probability for exactly r success is given by the last formula of Ch. III, § 2, namely

$$\left(\frac{n}{2\pi r\,(n-r)}\right)^{\frac{1}{2}}.$$

The difference between the two arises from the fact that in one case we are sure of the probability of success; in the other, we only surmise it.*

It is perfectly evident that Bayes' principle is open to very grave question, and should only be used with the greatest caution. The difficulty lies with the *a priori* probabilities. We generally have no real line on them, so take them all equal. Suppose that n balls have been drawn at random

* This interesting comparison is taken from Czuber, *Wahrscheinlichkeits-rechnung*, cit. p. 200.

from an urn having white and black balls in unknown mixture, and that a white ball has been drawn just r times. What is the probability of drawing a white ball the next time? We should like to use formula (11). When is it safe to do so?

That formula was derived on the hypothesis that all mixtures were, *a priori*, equally likely. That does not mean that when we know nothing at all about an urn all mixtures are equally likely. We have already discussed that meaning of equally likely in Ch. I. What it does mean is this: * Imagine an immense number of urns containing black and white balls in varying proportions, but with a fixed number of urns with each mixture. Then if an urn be drawn at random and n drawings, with replacement, be made therefrom, showing just r white balls, the probability that the next ball will be white is accurately given by (11). It is only when we can give a really precise statement of this sort that Bayes' principle can be used with perfect confidence, and the cases are rare.

Why not, then, reject the formula outright? Because, defective as it is, Bayes' formula is the only thing we have to answer certain important questions which do arise in the calculus of probability. The question as to the likelihood that a coin which showed a given succession of heads and tails should be bad is real and insistent. To say what might reasonably have been expected from a good coin under the circumstances does not, by any means, cover the case. Therefore we use Bayes' formula with a sigh, as the only thing available under the circumstances:

'Steyning tuk him for the reason the thief tuk the hot stove—bekaze there was nothing else that season.' †

* Cf. Castelnuovo, loc. cit., p. 170.
† Kipling, *Captains Courageous*, ch. vi.

CHAPTER VII

ERRORS OF OBSERVATION

§ 1. Determination of the 'Best Value'

THERE is no such thing as a perfect physical measurement. Absolute accuracy is a fiction, and is never attained in practice. What is meant by an 'exact value' is a value which is sufficiently exact for purposes of a certain class. In fact it is not always possible to say what is meant by the 'true value' of any quantity. What is the true length of a bar of iron? That will depend on the temperature of the iron; perhaps on the direction and velocity of its motion through space, if the recent theories of relativity be correct. But if there be room for doubt as to what the true value really is, there will be infinitely more about any attempts to measure it. Suppose that we say that two towns are exactly three and one-half miles apart, what do we really mean? Different persons will mean different things by these same words. A careless person might mean that some point within a few rods of the post office in one is exactly three and one-half miles from some point within a few rods of the jail in the other, but such a statement would never do for a surveyor. If he said that the towns were exactly three and one-half miles apart he would mean that some landmark, as a milestone, in one was separated from a similar landmark in the other by a distance within a few inches of three and one-half miles. The geographical meridian of Paris runs from a mark in the middle of a doorway on the south side of the Observatory to a short vertical iron rod in the middle of a hole in a stone column erected in the park of Mont Souris. This extreme topological accuracy would be counted the height of carelessness in a machine shop where lengths were measured to the nearest thousandth of an inch, and machine-shop accuracy is nowhere near sufficient for work in optics, where we think in terms of wave lengths of light.

A true theory of physical measurements must therefore start from the assumption that they always contain errors. To what are these errors due? A few moments' reflection shows that they fall into two general classes:

A) Constant errors. These are due to inherent imperfections in the instruments of observation, and in the observer, but do not vary from one observation to another one bearing on the same object. We measure distances with a scale whose indicated lengths are too short. We observe the altitude of the sun with a sextant whose 0 is wrongly placed. We measure a time interval with a chronograph which gains at a constant rate. We note the transit of a star across the hair-line when our personal equation causes us to record the phenomenon too soon. Errors of this general sort are inseparable from any sort of physical observation. Neither the instrument nor the observer can be perfected to such an extent as to eliminate them completely. All that we can do is to estimate them as accurately as possible by measuring quantities of known value, or by other means.

B) Accidental errors. These are supposed to arise from minute causes which vary from one observation to another; they are fluctuating variations in the observer, the instruments, and the quantity observed. To run through the same list as before, the coefficient of expansion of the scale may be different from that of the quantity measured, and the temperature may be somewhat above or below the mean. In reading the vernier of a sextant, the lines nearest coincidence will differ by a fraction of a hair's breadth, one way or the other. The chronograph is not perfectly sealed from the outer air, and is influenced by variations of temperature and atmospheric pressure. The observer's nervous reaction is slightly faster or slower than usual, causing a variation in the rapidity of perceiving the passage of a star across the spider line.

The fundamental problem with which we shall be occupied in the present chapter is to formulate a general mathematical theory of these accidental errors. At the outset it must be understood, beyond all possibility of misconception, that any such law will represent merely an approximation to the truth. There is no answer to the question, 'Why should accidental errors in different sorts of observations obey the same law?' There is no reason why they should, and undoubtedly they do not. The real question is: Can an approximate law be found which is sufficiently accurate for the purposes for which it is needed? The ultimate test for such a law will be 'how well does it work out in practice?' If it work well, it is a good law, even if founded on assumptions of doubtful validity. If it work badly, then it is of little importance, even though the mathematical deduction be highly instructive. The problem is to make the broadest and most plausible assumptions which will lead to a definite formula, and then to test that formula in practice.

Assumption 1] *The mean value of an accidental error is zero.*

It must be understood that this is just an arbitrary assumption, like those on which elementary geometry is based. That it is a plausible one is seen from considering the opposite case. For if this mean value were positive or negative, there would be a constant tendency towards errors of the one sort or the other, and this would count in with the constant errors.

Assumption 2] *The probability of an accidental error decreases as the numerical magnitude of that error increases.*

There is a so-called proof of this principle which, in reality, is based upon an assumption far less obvious than the assumption in question. The idea is that each accidental error is the result of an accumulation of atomic errors called 'fundamental errors', arising from small independent causes. These fundamental errors are supposed to be of the same size, and each has an equal chance of being positive or negative. The error actually committed represents the excess of positive over negative fundamental errors, or, vice versa, it is proportional to the discrepancy in a series of trials where there is a half chance of heads or tails, and we know already that the chance for a discrepancy is less and less as the latter increases numerically. The reason why we do not favour this method of treating the subject is that, in reality, it seems likely that these fundamental errors are a pure fiction, and that the actual errors committed do not arise in any such way.

We now suppose that we have a set of discordant observations of the same quantity, after all constant errors have been eliminated or accounted for. The obvious fundamental question is this : What value shall we take as our best estimate of the quantity? We shall answer this question by making certain plausible mathematical assumptions about a quantity which we shall call the *best value,* and show how this latter can then be found. It must be understood that these assumptions are nothing but definitions of what the words ' best value ' mean. This method of procedure seems to have been first developed by the Italian astronomer Schiaparelli.* We shall do our best to motivate our assumptions as we go along.

Postulate 1] *When a number of discordant measures have been made on the same magnitude, and constant errors have been eliminated, the best value is a continuous function of the measures, which possesses first partial derivatives with respect to all the arguments.*

The obvious objection has been made to this postulate that it was not at all evident why this function should be differentiable. Schimmack reached the same function by somewhat different postulates which did not include differentiability,† and his postulates have been shown by Beetle to be completely independent.‡ But Schimmack makes the assumption that the best value for $n + 1$ observations is what

---

* Schiaparelli, 'Sul principio della media aritmetica', *Rendiconti del R. Istituto Lombardo,* Series 2, vol. ii, 1868, and ' Sur le principe de la moyenne arithmétique ', *Astronomische Nachrichten,* vol. lxxxvii, 1876 (Czuber, *Entwickelung,* cit., gives for this the erroneous date of 1895). This last is a refutation of a priority claim put forth in the same number by Stone, and based upon his paper, ' On the most probable result which can be deduced from a number of direct determinations of assumed equal values ', *Monthly Notices Royal Astronomical Soc.,* vol. xxxiii, 1873.

† Schimmack, ' Der Satz vom arithmetischen Mittel ', *Math. Annalen,* vol. lxviii, 1909.

‡ Beetle, ' On the Complete Independence of Schimmack's Postulates ', ibid., vol. lxxvi, 1915.

it would be if each of the first n were replaced by the best value for those n, and this does not seem at all self-evident either.   It is certainly hard to believe that the best value is not a continuous function, and, if continuous, we can approach to it with any degree of accuracy we desire by means of differentiable functions, so that the inclusion of differentiability does not add much ' to the load '.

Suppose that for one reason or another we decide, in the course of our observations, to change the scale or unit.   We should naturally expect to produce thereby a corresponding change in our best value.   This leads to

Postulate 2] *If all the observed values be multiplied by the same constant factor, the best value will be multiplied thereby.*

We naturally look upon the best value as intrinsic in the observations, and independent of the origin whence measurements are made.   This leads to

Postulate 3] *If the same constant be added to each of the observed values, that constant will be added to the best value.*

If the best value be a function only of the observations, the order in which they are taken must not affect the latter. This gives

Postulate 4] *When all the measures are equally trustworthy, the best value is a symmetric function of them.*

With these postulates, it is easy to determine what sort of a function the best value is.   Let the observed values, after constant errors have been eliminated, be x_1, x_2, ... x_n.   The best value shall be $f(x_1,\ x_2,\ ...\ x_n)$.   Since it is certainly possible that all the observed values should be equal, the function cannot become singular for every set of values x_1, x_2, ... x_n.   Hence, by change of origin we may assume that the function and its derivatives all exist for the set of values $0,\ 0,\ ...\ 0$.   By the law of the mean we have

$$kf(x_1,\ x_2,\ ...\ x_n) = f(kx_1,\ kx_2,\ ...\ kx_n)$$

$$= f(0,\ 0,\ ...\ 0) + \sum_{i=1}^{i=n} kx_i \frac{\partial f}{\partial y_i}.$$

Where $0 \leqslant y_i \leqslant kx_i$ or $0 \geqslant y_i \geqslant kx_i$.

Putting $k = 0$ $f(0, 0, \ldots 0) = 0$.

Dividing by k

$$f(x_1, x_2, \ldots x_n) = \sum x_i \frac{\partial f}{\partial y_i}.$$

Since the left side is independent of k, on the right we may put $k = 0$, and $y_i = 0$.

If $\dfrac{\partial f}{\partial x_i} = a_i$ when $x_i = 0$

$$f(x_1, x_2, \ldots x_n) \equiv \sum_{i=1}^{i=n} a_i x_i.$$

Changing x_i to $x_i + d$, and applying postulate 3]

$$\Sigma a_i = 1.$$

It is better to replace the coefficients a_i by numbers proportional to them and write the best value

$$f(x_1, x_2, \ldots x_n) \equiv \frac{p_1 x_1 + p_2 x_2 + \ldots + p_n x_n}{p_1 + p_2 + \ldots + p_n} = \bar{x}. \qquad (1)$$

Theorem 1] *If a set of discordant measurements be taken of the same object, the best value to take, after constant errors have been eliminated, is a homogeneous linear function of the measures, where the sum of the coefficients is equal to unity.*

We find immediately from postulate 4]

Theorem 2] *When all of the measurements are equally trustworthy, the best value is their average.*

The coefficients are called *weights*, and it is evident in formula (1) that we are not primarily concerned with their actual values, but with their ratios. We shall also, hereafter, refer to the 'best value' as the *weighted mean*. Suppose, further, that x_1 was found as the average of n_1 standard observations, x_2 as the average of n_2 of them, and x_n as the average of n_n. The weighted mean of all of the standard observations would be the expression (1) where the letter p_i was replaced by the corresponding letter n_i.

Theorem 3] *If it be possible to express each measurement as the average of a certain number of standard observations, then the weights in the weighted mean are proportional to the number of standard observations in each case.*

We must now give a number of definitions which will be of frequent use in what follows.

Definition] *The positive square root of the mean value of the square of an error which may occur in a series of like observations is called the* mean error.

Definition] *The mean value of the numerical measure of the error is called the* average error.*

Definition] *The positive number which there is a half chance that the numerical value of the error will not exceed is called the* probable error.

The reader should compare these definitions with those of mean, average, and probable discrepancies on pp. 49, 50. We shall see later that when the errors are distributed according to the exponential law of Gauss, these three are constant multiples one of another.

Let the real unknown value of the quantity we are measuring be x. The error of the weighted mean is

$$\frac{\sum\limits_{i=1}^{i=n} p_i (x_i - x)}{\sum\limits_{i=1}^{i=n} p_i}.$$

It is a little more convenient to write this in the form

$$\sum_{i=1}^{i=n} a_i (x_i - x) ; \quad \sum_{i=1}^{i=n} a_i = 1.$$

The mean value of each of these terms is, by Assumption 1], equal to 0.

---

* There is no complete agreement as to these definitions. Some books use the term ' mean error ' for that which we have called ' average error '. Others call our mean error, which is really rather ill-named, ' root mean square ', a ponderous title.

Let us assume that the unknown mean error of the measurement x_i is

$$\frac{1}{k_i \sqrt{2}}.$$

The reasons for writing this clumsy expression will appear in the sequel. We wish to find the mean error of the weighted mean. We may apply Ch. IV, 5] and write for this the value

$$\frac{1}{K\sqrt{2}} = \sqrt{\sum_{i=1}^{i=n} \frac{a_i^2}{2k_i^2}}; \quad \sum_{i=1}^{i=n} a_i = 1. \tag{2}$$

When all of the measures are equally trustworthy, each a_i is $1/n$, so that the mean error of the weighted mean is

$$\frac{1}{K\sqrt{2}} = \frac{1}{k_i \sqrt{2n}}.$$

Theorem 4] *The mean error of the average of a number of equally trustworthy measurements is the mean error of a single measurement, divided by the square root of the number of measurements.*

Let us see what values of the coefficients a_i will minimize the mean error of the weighted mean. We must minimize

$$\sum_{i=1}^{i=n} \frac{a_i^2}{2k_i^2}; \quad \sum_{i=1}^{i=n} a_i = 1.$$

This amounts to minimizing

$$\sum_{i=1}^{i=n} \left(\frac{a_i^2}{2k_i^2} - \rho \left(a_i - \frac{1}{n} \right) \right);$$

equating to 0 the partial derivative to a we have

$$a_i = \frac{p_i}{\sum\limits_{i=1}^{i=n} p_i} = \rho k_i^2.$$

When we are in the case where x_i is the average of n_i standard measurements this amounts to putting

$$2k_i^2 = 2k^2 n_i; \quad p_i = \sigma n_i,$$

and gives the system of weighting already found. It is

natural, then, to make the minimizing of this mean value a general principle, and state:

Postulate 5] *The weights in the weighted mean are those coefficients which will make the mean error of this expression a minimum.*

Theorem 5] *The weights in the weighted mean are inversely proportional to the squares of the mean errors of the individual measurements.*

The trouble with all of this work with the mean errors is that we do not really know anything at all about the errors actually committed. If we did, we should know the true value sought. The best we can do is to manipulate certain observed quantities nearly equal to the errors.

Definition] *The difference between a measurement and the weighted mean is called a* residual error, *or, more briefly, a* residual.

The residual corresponding to the measurement x_i is

$$\epsilon_i = x_i - \bar{x},$$
$$= (x_i - x) - (\bar{x} - x),$$
$$= (x_i - x) - \sum_{i=1}^{i=n} a_i (x_i - x).$$

Theorem 6] *The mean value of a residual is* 0.

The quantity in which we are particularly interested is

$$\sum_{i=1}^{i=n} p_i \epsilon_i^2 \Big/ \sum_{i=1}^{i=n} p_i. \tag{3}$$

When we are under the hypothesis of 3] this is the average of certain observed quantities, and by Tchebycheff's inequality, may then safely be replaced by its mean value. This leads naturally to:

Assumption 3] *The mean value of expression* (3) *may be replaced by its observed value.*

Let us calculate this mean value.

$$\epsilon_i = x_i - \bar{x}$$

$$= \frac{\sum'_j p_j x_i - \sum'_j p_j x_j}{\sum_j p_j},$$

$$= \frac{\sum'_j p_j (x_i - x) - \sum'_j p_j (x_j - x)}{\sum_j p_j}.$$

The notation Σ' means that the term with subscript i is lacking. The mean value of each individual term is 0; hence the mean value of ϵ_i^2 is

$$\frac{(\sum'_j p_j)^2 \dfrac{1}{2k_i^2} + \sum'_j \dfrac{p_j^2}{2k_j^2}}{(\sum_j p_j)^2}.$$

Now, by theorem 5]

$$\frac{1}{2k_i^2} = \frac{1}{p_i} \cdot \frac{1}{2k^2}.$$

Hence the mean value of ϵ_i^2 is

$$\frac{\sum'_j p_j \left[(\sum'_j p_j) \dfrac{1}{p_i} + 1 \right] \dfrac{1}{2k^2}}{(\sum_j p_j)^2}$$

$$= \frac{\dfrac{1}{p_i} (\sum'_j p_j) \dfrac{1}{2k^2}}{\sum_j p_j},$$

$$= \frac{\sum'_j p_j}{2k_i^2 \sum_j p_j}.$$

Equating the mean value of (3) to its observed value,

$$\frac{1}{\sum\limits_{i=1}^{i=n} p_i} \frac{n-1}{2k^2} = \frac{\sum\limits_{i=1}^{i=n} p_i \epsilon_i^2}{\sum\limits_{i=1}^{i=n} p_i}.$$

$$\frac{1}{k\sqrt{2}} = \left(\frac{\sum\limits_{i=1}^{i=n} p_i \epsilon_i^2}{n-1} \right)^{\frac{1}{2}},$$

$$\frac{1}{k_i\sqrt{2}} = \left(\frac{\sum\limits_{i=1}^{i=n} p_i \epsilon_i^2}{p_i(n-1)} \right)^{\frac{1}{2}}.$$

We thus get from (2)

Theorem **7**] *The mean error of the weighted mean of a set of measurements whose weights are* $p_1, p_2, \ldots p_n$, *while the corresponding residuals are* $\epsilon_1, \epsilon_2, \ldots \epsilon_n$, *is*

$$\frac{1}{K\sqrt{2}} = \left(\frac{\sum\limits_{i=1}^{i=n} p_i \epsilon_i^2}{(n-1)\,\Sigma p_i} \right)^{\frac{1}{2}}. \tag{4}$$

Theorem **8**] *The mean error of a measure of weight* p_i *under the same circumstances is*

$$\frac{1}{k_i\sqrt{2}} = \left(\frac{\sum\limits_{i=1}^{i=n} p_i \epsilon_i^2}{(n-1)p_i} \right)^{\frac{1}{2}}. \tag{5}$$

Theorem **9**] *When each weighted observation is the average of a number of standard measures, the mean error of a standard measurement is*

$$\frac{1}{k\sqrt{2}} = \left(\frac{\sum\limits_{i=1}^{i=n} p_i \epsilon_i^2}{(n-1)} \right)^{\frac{1}{2}}. \tag{6}$$

¶ We saw in the work which led up to postulate **4**] that when the given observations are equally trustworthy, the average is that weighted mean which will have the least mean error. Moreover, the sum of the squares of the actual errors

$$\sum_{i=1}^{i=n} (x_i - x)^2$$

will be a minimum if

$$x = \frac{\sum\limits_{i=1}^{i=n} x_i}{n},$$

and this gives additional reason to choose the average as the best value. At the same time, there arise cases where the observed values group themselves somewhat asymmetrically about the average, and the question arises whether it be not well to take a best value which will minimize some other function of the observed measurements. For instance, what value will minimize the sum of the numerical values of the errors?

¶ If an assumed value lie between two observed values, the sum of the numerical values of its divergences from the two is equal to their numerical divergence. If it do not lie between the two, this sum increases as the observed value recedes from the observed values, for it is equal to their numerical difference, plus the divergence from the nearest one. Let the observed values be $x_0, x_1, x_2, \ldots x_n$ arranged in ascending order of magnitude, and let

$$x_k - x_{k-1} = r_k.$$

Suppose that we take a value x where

$$x_{k-1} < x \leqslant x_k ; \ 2k < n.$$

The sum of the numerical divergences of x from the different observed values will be

$$(r_1 + r_n) + 2(r_2 + r_{n-1}) + 3(r_3 + r_{n-2}) \ldots$$
$$+ k(r_k + r_{n-k+1}) + (k+1) r_{n-k} + \ldots + (n - 2k + 1)(x_k - x).$$

The value x_k is that value of the interval in question which will make this a minimum. In the same way, if $2k > n$ the sum would be a minimum if $x_{k-1} = x$.

If x lie in the middle interval, the sum will be the same throughout.

Definition] *The middle term in order of magnitude of an odd number of terms and the average of the middle*

Problems.

1. An angle was measured by a theodolite (mean error 46·5″) to be 29° 13′ 40″, and by a transit (mean error 25·3″) to be 29° 13′ 24″. Find best value and its mean error.

2. A distance was measured as follows :

A) with steel tape   741·17 ;   741·09 ;   741·22 ;   741·12 ;   741·01.
B) with chain   741·2 ;   741·4 ;   741·0 ;   741·3 ;   741·1.

Find best value and mean error.

terms of an even number of terms is called the median *of the series.*

We thus have a theorem due, apparently, to Fechner.*

¶ Theorem 10] *The sum of the numerical values of the divergences of a number from a given series of numbers will be a minimum if the number in question be the median.*

Another value occasionally used, especially in statistical work, is the *mode*, which is the point of accumulation of the given set of measures.

§ 2.   The Law of Error.

We saw at the beginning of the present chapter that the title of the present section is essentially a misnomer.   There is no such thing in Nature as a law of error, i.e. a fixed principle according to which accidental errors are always distributed.   For mathematical purposes we desire a continuous function, with a certain number of continuous derivatives, which will express the probability for an error of given magnitude, but in fact there is a certain number which represents the maximum possible numerical error.   The probability for an error very close to this will be finite, the probability for any numerically greater error is rigorously zero.   Consequently no analytic function whose argument runs from $-\infty$ to ∞ can fit the case for all values of that argument.

We mean, then, by the *law of error* a mathematical formula, reached by plausible reasoning, which in practice will give approximately the proportion of accidental errors in any appropriate interval.   To make the law as plausible as possible, we shall start from the broadest assumptions that will give what we want, a set considerably broader than that usually taken, but the acid test will lie in the question : do observed errors conform with any reasonable degree of closeness to the law which has been deduced ?

* Fechner, 'Ueber den Ausgangswerth der kleinsten Abweichungen', *Sitzungsberichte der K. Akademie der Wissenschaft zu Leipzig*, vol. xi, 1874, p. 29.

Assumption 4] *The* a priori *probability that a quantity to be observed shall have a value in the infinitesimal interval* $x \pm \frac{1}{2} dx$, *x being in a certain continuous region S, will differ by an infinitesimal of higher order from* $f(x) \, dx$, *where f is a function, single-valued and analytic, throughout the whole reach of possible values.*

Assumption 5] *The probability that a quantity whose true value is X should under specified conditions be observed to have after the removal of constant errors a value in the infinitesimal region* $x \pm \frac{1}{2} dx$, *where x is a point of S, will differ by an infinitesimal of higher order from* $\Phi(X, x) \, dx$ *where the function* Φ *and its partial derivatives of the first two orders are continuous, and where its value is independent of the choice of origin.*

Assumption 6] *If the infinitesimal increment dx be sufficiently small the probability that the true value lies in the region* $x \pm \frac{1}{2} dx$ *is a maximum when x is the weighted average of the observed values.*

It is evident that these assumptions have not absolutely axiomatic force, yet all are reasonably plausible. To assume that the function Φ is independent of the origin is natural, for we expect that accidental errors will arise from physical causes, and not from the position of the 0 on the recording instrument. As for the last assumption, our continuous function must have a maximum somewhere in the region, and the weighted average seems as likely to give that maximum as any other number we could naturally think of.

Let us proceed to deduce our law from these assumptions. Since Φ is independent of the origin

$$\Phi(X + k, x + k) = \Phi(X, x).$$

Putting $$k = -X,$$

$$\Phi(X, x) = \Phi(0, x - X) = \phi(x - X) = \phi(\epsilon).$$

It appears, therefore, that Φ is a function of the error alone. This fact, which is sometimes assumed in so many words, has given rise to criticism, yet it follows at once from our plausible assumption about the independence of the origin.* As matter of notation, let us write

Observed values $x_1, x_2, \ldots x_n$.

Weights $p_1, p_2, \ldots p_n$.

Weighted average $\bar{x} = \Sigma p_i x_i / \Sigma p_i$.

True value X.

Observed errors $\xi_i = x_i - X$.

Residual errors $\delta_i = x_i - \bar{x}$,

$$= \xi_i - \frac{\Sigma p_i \xi_i}{\Sigma p_i}.$$

The probability that these observations arose from a quantity whose true value is X is given by Bayes' formula for continuous probability, developed in Ch. VI, p. 98,

$$\frac{f(x)\,\phi\,(x_1-x)\,\phi\,(x_2-x)\,\ldots\,\phi\,(x_n-x)}{\int f(x)\,\phi\,(x_1-x)\,\phi\,(x_2-x)\,\ldots\,\phi\,(x_n-x)\,dx}. \tag{7}$$

The integration in the denominator is supposed to be extended throughout the whole of the region S. This expression will be a maximum with the logarithm of the numerator. Equating the logarithmic derivative to 0,

$$-\frac{d\log f}{dx} + \frac{d\log\phi\,(\xi_1)}{d\xi_1} + \frac{d\log\phi\,(\xi_2)}{d\xi_2} + \ldots + \frac{d\log\phi\,(\xi_n)}{d\xi_n} = 0 \tag{8}$$

$$p_1\xi_1 + p_2\xi_2 + \ldots + p_n\xi_n = 0. \tag{9}$$

The first term is independent of the observed values. Suppose that we are so lucky as to get exactly the right value each time, an allowable case,

$$-\frac{d\log f}{dx} + n\frac{d\log\phi}{d\xi} = 0,$$

$$\xi = 0.$$

Now the function f is independent of n, hence

$$\frac{d\log f}{dx} = 0, \quad f = \text{const.} \tag{10}$$

We have thus removed the troublesome *a priori* probabilities from our path.

* Bertrand, loc. cit., p. 177; Poincaré, loc. cit., p. 152.

Going back to the general case, assume that $\bar{x}$ remains fixed, while x_1, x_2, ... x_n take infinitesimal increments.

$$\frac{d}{d\xi_1}\left[\frac{d\log\phi(\xi_1)}{d\xi_1}\right]d\xi_1 + \frac{d}{d\xi_2}\left[\frac{d\log\phi(\xi_2)}{d\xi_2}\right]d\xi_2 \cdots$$
$$+ \frac{d}{d\xi_n}\left[\frac{d\log\phi(\xi_n)}{d\xi_n}\right]d\xi_n = 0. \qquad (11)$$

$$p_1 d\xi_1 + p_2 d\xi_2 + \ldots + p_n d\xi_n = 0. \qquad (12)$$

One of these equations in the variables $d\xi_1$, $d\xi_2$ ... holds whenever the other does, hence

$$\frac{d}{d\xi_i}\left[\frac{d\log\phi(\xi_i)}{d\xi_i}\right] = -2lp_i.$$

Integrating once

$$\frac{d\log\phi(\xi_i)}{d\xi_i} = -2lp_i\xi_i + H,$$

and the constant H is seen to be 0 by (8) and (9).

Integrating again

$$\phi(\xi_i) = re^{-lp_i\xi_i^2}. \qquad (13)$$

It is evident, on the face of things, that this formula cannot be strictly correct outside of certain definite limits, for it gives a finite probability for an obviously impossible error. It is also clear that the statement that f is constant could not hold from infinity to infinity, as that would involve the ridiculous conclusion that $\int_{-\infty}^{\infty} cdx = 1$. We note, however, that: 1) it seems plausible to assume that f is constant throughout a certain region, and drops to zero rapidly outside; 2) expression (13) becomes rapidly very small. The effect called for by the first of these will be sensibly produced by assuming (13) to hold everywhere.

Assumption 7] *For the purpose of calculating constants formula* (13) *may be assumed universally true.*

Assumption 8] *For the purpose of calculating constants, when the observations are all of equal weight, the mean value of* $\delta_i^2 = \frac{n-1}{n} M.V. \epsilon_i^2$ *may be replaced by the observed average.*

Replacing this latter by the familiar expression $1/2\,k_i^2$,

$$r\int_{-\infty}^{\infty} e^{-lp_i\xi_i^2}\,d\xi_i = 1, \quad r\int_{-\infty}^{\infty} \xi_i^2 e^{-lp_i\xi_i^2} = \frac{1}{2\,k_i^2}.$$

Putting
$$\xi_i\sqrt{lp_i} = t,$$

$$\frac{2r}{\sqrt{lp_i}}\int_0^{\infty} e^{-t^2}\,dt = 1, \quad \frac{2r}{(lp_i)^{\frac{3}{2}}}\int_0^{\infty} t^2 e^{-t^2}\,dt = \frac{1}{2\,k_i^2},$$

$$\frac{r\sqrt{\pi}}{\sqrt{lp_i}} = 1, \quad \frac{r\sqrt{\pi}}{(lp_i)^{\frac{3}{2}}} = \frac{1}{k_i^2},$$

$$lp_i = k_i^2, \quad r = \frac{k_i}{\sqrt{\pi}}.$$

Dropping the subscript, we have finally:

Gauss's Exponential Law of Error.* *The probability, under Assumptions 1–6, that the observed measurement of a quantity shall have an accidental error in the infinitesimal region $\xi \pm \frac{1}{2}d\xi$ differs by an infinitesimal of higher order from the expression*

$$\frac{k}{\sqrt{\pi}}\,e^{-k^2\xi^2}\,d\xi, \tag{14}$$

where the mean error of a single observation is

$$\frac{1}{k\sqrt{2}}. \tag{15}$$

¶ It is evident that of all of our assumptions, the least plausible is 6]. It has been suggested that it would be more natural, not to assume that the weighted mean gave the greatest possible probability to the observed series, but that it was the *mean* of all possible *values*, in view of the ones that had been observed. This can be carried through, but the calculation is long.†

The form of the probability function is not in the least surprising. We saw in discussing Assumption 2] that if we

* We have given essentially Gauss's first deduction, which appears in all text-books on Least Squares. The original is in his 'Theoria Motus Corporum Coelestium'. See his Collected Works, vol. vii, Hamburg, 1809, p. 232. But Gauss assumes explicitly that Φ is a function of the error alone, and that f is a constant.

† Poincaré, loc. cit., p. 156.

assumed that the actual accidental error committed was the surplus of positive over negative elementary errors, or vice versa, that this assumption would be fulfilled. The error would be the discrepancy in a series of trials where there was an even chance for success or failure, and our present formula (14) is merely a restatement of formula (10) of Ch. III. This method of reaching the probability function is beyond a peradventure much the simplest,* the only trouble is, as we have already seen, there is no real reason to believe that such things as elementary errors really exist in practice.

The fundamental constant k that appears in the formula is called the *precision*. It is inversely proportional to the mean error of a single observation, and directly proportional to the square root of the weight that should be attached to that observation in combining it with others. In actual practice, however, especially in the United States, it is more customary to give the probable error than the mean error or the precision. To find the probable error p we put

$$\frac{2k}{\sqrt{\pi}}\int_0^p e^{-k^2\xi^2}\,d\xi = \tfrac{1}{2}.$$

Let
$$k\xi = t,$$
$$\Theta\,(kp) = \tfrac{1}{2},$$
$$kp = 0\cdot4769,$$
$$p = 0\cdot4769\left(\frac{1}{k}\right). \tag{16}$$

Again, to find the average error, since positive and negative errors are equally likely, we have

$$\text{Av. error} = \frac{2k}{\sqrt{\pi}}\int_0^\infty \xi e^{-k^2\xi^2}\,d\xi$$

$$= \frac{2}{k\sqrt{\pi}}\int_0^\infty t e^{-t^2}\,dt,$$

$$\text{Av. error} = \frac{1}{k}\cdot\frac{1}{\sqrt{\pi}}\cdot \tag{17}$$

* This method of deduction is apparently due to Hagen, *Grundzüge der Wahrscheinlichkeitsrechnung*, Berlin, 1837.

Theorem 11] *If a set of measurements follow the Law of Gauss, the mean error, probable error, and average error are constant multiples one of another.*

Suppose that we have two independent quantities x_1 and x_2 of such a nature that the measurements of each follow the law of Gauss, their respective precisions being k_1 and k_2. What will be the law of error for the expression

$$x_1' = a_1 x_1 + a_2 x_2,$$
$$X_1' = a_1 X_1 + a_2 X_2,$$
$$\xi_1' = a_1 \xi_1 + a_2 \xi_2.$$

The probability that ξ_1' should be in a given infinitesimal region differs by an infinitesimal of higher order from

$$\frac{k_1 k_2}{\pi} \int e^{-k_1^2 \xi_1^2} \, d\xi_1 \int e^{-k_2^2 \xi_2^2} \, d\xi_2 = \frac{k_1 k_2}{\pi} \int \int e^{-(k_1^2 \xi_1^2 + k_2^2 \xi_2^2)} \, d\xi_1 \, d\xi_2.$$

This integral is extended over so much of the ξ_1, ξ_2 plane as will make ξ_1' lie in the infinitesimal region demanded. We proceed to change variables in this integral, putting

$$\xi_1' = a_1 \xi_1 + a_2 \xi_2,$$
$$\xi_2' = b_1 \xi_1 + b_2 \xi_2.$$

We will choose b_1 and b_2 in such a way that when

$$k_1^2 \xi_1^2 + k_2^2 \xi_2^2$$

is expressed in terms of ξ_1' and ξ_2', there will be no product term. This gives

$$k_1^2 b_2 a_2 + k_2^2 b_1 a_1 = 0,$$
$$\xi_1' = a_1 \xi_1 + a_2 \xi_2,$$
$$\xi_2' = -k_1^2 a_2 \xi_1 + k_2^2 a_1 \xi_2,$$
$$k_1^2 \xi_1^2 + k_2^2 \xi_2^2 = \frac{k_1^2 k_2^2 (\xi_1')^2 + (\xi_2')^2}{k_1^2 a_2^2 + k_2^2 a_1^2},$$
$$\frac{\partial (\xi_1 \xi_2)}{\partial (\xi_1' \xi_2')} = \frac{1}{k_1^2 a_2^2 + k_2^2 a_1^2}.$$

Hence our integral above is

$$\frac{k_1 k_2}{\pi (k_1^2 a_2^2 + k_2^2 a_1^2)} \int_{\xi_1'}^{\xi_1' + d\xi_1'} e^{-\frac{k_1^2 k_2^2 (\xi_1')^2}{k_1^2 a_2^2 + k_2^2 a_1^2}} \, d\xi_1'$$

$$\int_{-\infty}^{\infty} e^{-\frac{\xi_2'^2}{k_1^2 a_2^2 + k_2^2 a}} \, d\xi_2 = \frac{k_1 k_2}{\sqrt{\pi} \sqrt{k_1^2 a_2^2 + k_2^2 a_1^2}} e^{-\frac{k_1^2 k_2^2}{k_1^2 a_2^2 + k_2^2 a_1^2}} \, d\xi_1'.$$

Putting
$$\frac{1}{k_1'^2} = \frac{a_1^2}{k_1^2} + \frac{a_2^2}{k_2^2},$$

we get
$$\frac{k_1'}{\sqrt{\pi}} e^{-(k_1')^2(\xi_1')^2} d\xi_1'.$$

Our new series of observations follow the law of Gauss with the precision k_1'. We thus reach, by mathematical induction,

Theorem 12] *If x_1, x_2, ... x_n be n independent quantities whose measures follow the law of Gauss with the respective precisions k_1, k_2, ... k_n, the quantity*

$$a_1 x_1 + a_2 x_2 + ... a_n x_n$$

obeys the same law with the precision k' where

$$\frac{1}{(k')^2} = \frac{a_1^2}{k_1^2} + \frac{a_2^2}{k_2^2} + ... \frac{a_n^2}{k_n^2}. \tag{18}$$

Where the quantity under observation is the weighted mean we have
$$a_i = \frac{p_i}{\sum_j p_j} = \frac{k_i^2}{\sum_j k_j^2}.$$

Theorem 13] *If a series of observations obey the law of Gauss with the precisions k_1, k_2, ... k_n respectively, their weighted mean will obey the same law with a precision K, where*
$$K = \sqrt{\sum_j k_j^2}. \tag{19}$$

A residual is an observation which is linear in the given system of observations. Its mean value and its true value are 0 by 6]. If ϵ_i be the ith residual,

$$\epsilon_i = x_i - \frac{\sum_j p_j x_j}{\sum_j p_j}$$

$$= \frac{(\sum_j p_j - p_i) x_i - p_j x_j - p_k x_k ...}{\sum_j p_j}$$

$$= \frac{(\sum_j k_j^2 - k_i^2) x_i - k_j^2 x_j - k_k^2 x_k ...}{\sum k_j^2}.$$

For the precision k_i' we have

$$\frac{1}{(k_i')^2} = \frac{1}{k_i^2} - \frac{1}{\sum\limits_j k_j^2}.$$

Theorem 14] *If a set of measurements follow the law of Gauss with the respective precisions k_1, k_2, ... k_n, the ith residual follows that law with the precision k_i' where*

$$\frac{1}{(k_i')^2} = \frac{1}{k_i^2} - \frac{1}{\sum\limits_j k_j^2}. \tag{20}$$

Theorem 15] *The precision of a residual of n observations of precision k is*

$$k' = k\left(\frac{n}{n-1}\right)^{\frac{1}{2}}. \tag{21}$$

To find k' replace $(n-1)$ by n and (6).

For convenient reference, let us make a table of the results of (4), (5), (6), (16), and (17).

TABLE.

Given n observations of weights p_1, p_2, ... p_n.
Let the corresponding residuals be ϵ_1, ϵ_2, ... ϵ_n.

	Standard obs.	Average of n.	Obs. weight p_i.	Weighted mean.
Precision	$k = \sqrt{\dfrac{n-1}{2\sum\limits_j \epsilon_j^2}}$	$K = \sqrt{\dfrac{n(n-1)}{2\sum\limits_j \epsilon_j^2}}$	$k_i = \sqrt{\dfrac{(n-1)p_i}{2\sum\limits_j p_j \epsilon_j^2}}$	$K = \sqrt{\dfrac{(n-1)\sum\limits_j p_j}{2\sum\limits_j p_j \epsilon_j^2}}$
Mean error	$\sqrt{\dfrac{\sum\limits_j \epsilon_j^2}{n-1}}$	$\sqrt{\dfrac{\sum\limits_j \epsilon_j^2}{n(n-1)}}$	$\sqrt{\dfrac{\sum\limits_j p_j \epsilon_j^2}{(n-1)p_i}}$	$\sqrt{\dfrac{\sum\limits_j p_j \epsilon_j^2}{(n-1)\sum p_j}}$
Probable error	$0.6745\sqrt{\dfrac{\sum\limits_j \epsilon_j^2}{n-1}}$	$0.6745\sqrt{\dfrac{\sum\limits_j \epsilon_j^2}{n(n-1)}}$	$0.6745\sqrt{\dfrac{\sum\limits_j p_j \epsilon_j^2}{(n-1)p_i}}$	$0.6745\sqrt{\dfrac{\sum\limits_j p_j \epsilon_j^2}{(n-1)\sum\limits_j p_j}}$
Average error	$0.798\sqrt{\dfrac{\sum\limits_j \epsilon_j^2}{n-1}}$	$0.798\sqrt{\dfrac{\sum\limits_j \epsilon_j^2}{n(n-1)}}$	$0.798\sqrt{\dfrac{\sum\limits_j p_j \epsilon_j^2}{(n-1)p_i}}$	$0.798\sqrt{\dfrac{\sum\limits_j p_j \epsilon_j^2}{(n-1)\sum p_j}}$

When it comes to making these various summations, there are one or two simple expedients which will materially lighten the labour of a computer not provided with an adding machine. The latter is practically indispensable when the mass of data is large. Let the observed values, as usual, be $x_1, x_2, \dots x_n$. Arrange these in order of magnitude. Let the weighted mean be

$$\frac{p_1 x_1 + p_2 x_2 + \dots + p_n x_n}{p_1 + p_2 + \dots + p_n} = \bar{x}.$$

Choose any convenient number x_0, either the numerically smallest, or the median, or any that may seem helpful.

$$\epsilon_j = x_j - \bar{x} = (x_j - x_0) + (x_0 - \bar{x}),$$

$$\epsilon_j^2 = (x_j - \bar{x})^2 = (x_j - x_0)^2 + 2(x_j - x_0)(x_0 - \bar{x}) + (x_0 - \bar{x})^2,$$

$$\bar{x} = x_0 + \frac{\sum_j p_j (x_j - x_0)}{\sum_j p_j} \,. \tag{22}$$

$$\frac{\sum_j p_j \epsilon_j^2}{\sum_j p_j} = \frac{\sum_j p_j (x_j - x_0)^2}{\sum_j p_j} - (x_0 - \bar{x})^2. \tag{23}$$

Let the reader prove the following formula, of use later,

$$\frac{\sum_j p_j (x_j - \bar{x})(y_j - \bar{y})}{\sum_j p_j} = \frac{\sum_j p_j (x_j - x_0)(y_j - y_0)}{\sum_j p_j} - (x_0 - \bar{x})(y_0 - \bar{y}).$$

These devices are particularly useful when the observations and weights are integers, but the weighted mean is not.

¶ The labour of calculation may be further reduced as follows. Let us first recall Tchebycheff's principle whereby an average will probably be close to its mean value. Then the expression

$$\frac{\sum_j p_j |\xi_j|}{\sum p_j \sqrt{(n-1)}}$$

will be close to the average error, and the expression

$$\left(\frac{\sum_j p_j \xi_j^2}{(n-1)\sum p_j}\right)^{\frac{1}{2}} = \frac{0 \cdot 6745}{0 \cdot 798} \frac{\sum_j p_j |\xi_j|}{\sum_j p_j \sqrt{(n-1)}}$$

will be close to the probable error. Replacing the unknown ξ_j's by the residuals we get:

Approximate formula for probable error of weighted mean

$$0 \cdot 845 \, \frac{\underset{j}{\Sigma} p_j \, | \, \epsilon_j \, |}{\underset{j}{\Sigma} p_j \, \sqrt{(n-1)}} \, . \qquad (24)$$

The other probable errors may be easily calculated from this. The approximate precision will be found from the equation

$$\frac{1}{K} = 1 \cdot 77 \, \frac{\Sigma p_j \, | \, \epsilon_j \, |}{\sqrt{n-1} \, \Sigma p_j} \, . \qquad (25)$$

When all of the measurements have the same weight, the precision of the average will be given by

$$\frac{1}{K} = 1 \cdot 77 \, \frac{\Sigma \, | \, \epsilon_j \, |}{n \, \sqrt{n-1}} \, . \qquad (26)$$

The precision of a single observation will be k_1 where

$$\frac{1}{k_1} = 1 \cdot 77 \, \frac{\Sigma \, | \, \epsilon_j \, |}{\sqrt{n \, (n-1)}} \, , \qquad (27)$$

and the precision of a residual will be k' where

$$\frac{1}{k'} = 1 \cdot 77 \, \frac{\Sigma \, | \, \epsilon_j \, |}{n} \, . \qquad (28)$$

The way to test in practice whether a series of observations conform to the Gauss law is as follows. Calculate the precision of a residual by the general formula in the table, and (21), or by approximate formula (28). The number of observations having a residual nnmerically not above e should be close to

$$n \, \Theta \, (ke). \qquad (29)$$

As a quick check, note whether nearly one-half the measures have a residual not greater than the probable error. Here is an example.*

Example] *In the years 1904 and 1905, 104 tests were made*
    of the atomic weight of iodine in the Chemical Labora-

---

* I owe this example to Messrs. William Eldredge and Denning Miller.

tory of Harvard University. Taking as a first approximation $x_0 = 126 \cdot 980$ and multiplying the residuals by 1000 we get

$10^3 (x - x_0)$	$10^3 (x - \bar{x})$	$10^6 (x - \bar{x})^2$	$10^3 (x - x_0)$	$10^3 (x - \bar{x})$	$10^6 (x - \bar{x})^2$
13	11	121	3	1	1
13	11	121	3	1	1
11	9	81	2	0	0
11	9	81	1	1	1
10	8	64	0	2	4
10	8	64	0	2	4
9	7	49	0	2	4
8	6	36	−1	3	9
8	6	36	−1	3	9
8	6	36	··1	3	9
7	5	25	−3	5	25
7	5	25	−3	5	25
7	5	25	−3	5	25
7	5	25	−3	5	25
6	4	16	−4	6	36
6	4	16	−4	6	36
6	4	16	−5	7	49
5	3	9	−5	7	49
5	3	9	−6	8	64
5	3	9	−7	9	81
5	3	9	−7	9	81
5	3	9	−7	9	81
4	2	4	−8	10	100
4	2	4	−11	13	169
3	1	1	−11	13	169
3	1	1	−13	15	225
206	134	892	−94	150	1,282

$$\bar{x}x = 126 \cdot 982.$$

$\dfrac{1}{k'} = 0 \cdot 0092$ [by table]. $\dfrac{1}{k'} = 0 \cdot 0096$ [by (28)].

Errors less than	Observed.	Calculated.
0·001	6	6·3
0·002	11	12.5
3·003	19	18·8
0·004	22	24.5
0·005	30	29
0·006	35	33.4

The discrepancy is never greater than 4 per cent., generally less. On the other hand, the residuals are not symmetrically distributed above and below.

Problem.

Work out a similar table.

¶ § 3. Doubtful Observations.

It will frequently occur that when a large number of measurements have been taken of the same quantity, there will be one or more that differ very sharply from all of the others. These observations create a strong suspicion that in their cases there were additional causes of disturbance at work that did not apply in the case of the other measurements, and that, in consequence, these exceptional values should be rejected in making a calculation of the probable error or precision. This question, as we shall see, is exceedingly delicate, but it is insistent, and there can be no doubt that many observers reject some of their observations by pure guess-work or common sense.

Bertrand has pointed out by an ingenious analysis * that if we assume all of our measures to be equally trustworthy, and reject the worst ones, we shall decrease the probable error of the weighted mean. The reasoning is as follows :

Suppose that we reject those observations whose errors are so large numerically that the chance is less than $1 - p$ of committing them. We have as a limit of error

$$p = \frac{2}{\sqrt{\pi}} \int_0^{k\lambda} e^{-t^2} dt = \Theta\,(k\lambda). \qquad (30)$$

Let $\xi_1, \xi_2, \xi_3, \ldots \xi_m$ be the errors of the observations $x_1, x_2, \ldots x_m$ which are retained. Assuming all measures of equal weight, let us find the square of the mean error of our new average

$$\frac{x_1 + x_2 + \ldots x_m}{m}.$$

This will not be $1/2\,mk^2$ as the reader might suppose, for some observations, the worst, have been rejected, but will be

$$\frac{1}{m}\,[\text{mean value of } \xi^2],$$

when we mean by mean value of ξ^2, the mean value under the present circumstances when the worst measurements have been rejected.

If we examine statistically into the probability that an

* Bertrand, loc. cit., p. 211.

error shall take a particular value numerically less than λ, that probability will be greater than it was before, for the numerator is the same, but the denominator has been reduced as the errors numerically above λ have been rejected. We shall have, approximately, $m = np$.

The mean value of the square of an error less than λ numerically will now be

$$\frac{2k}{p\sqrt{\pi}}\int_0^p \xi^2 e^{-k^2\xi^2} d\xi.$$

Integrating by parts, and remembering (30), we have

$$\frac{-2k}{p\sqrt{\pi}}\Big(\xi\frac{e^{-k^2\xi^2}}{2k^2}\Big)_0^\lambda + \int_0^\lambda \frac{2k}{p\sqrt{\pi}}\Big(\frac{e^{-k^2\xi^2}}{2k^2}\Big) d\xi$$

$$= \frac{1}{2k^2}\Big[1 - \frac{2k\lambda e^{-k^2\lambda^2}}{p\sqrt{\pi}}\Big].$$

Dividing by m, or rather np, we have for the square of the mean error of the new mean

$$\frac{1}{2nk^2}\left[\frac{\Theta(k\lambda) - \frac{2k\lambda}{\sqrt{\pi}}e^{-k^2\lambda^2}}{[\Theta(k\lambda)]^2}\right]. \tag{31}$$

This is less than the square of the mean error of the old mean by the second factor. Unfortunately we have no one to tell us which observations we ought certainly to reject.

A more natural proceeding is to assume that in a few cases there has been at work a disturbing cause, not usually present. The first writer to attack the question from this point of view was Benjamin Peirce.* He set himself the following general problem. Given N observations, and a proposed number to be rejected n, what is the numerical limit of error that makes it more likely that the n observations whose residuals exceed this arose from a disturbing cause than from the operation of the natural laws at work in the other cases? Peirce's solution is highly attractive. He frames two hypotheses, first that there was no disturbing cause, second that there was one. For the first hypothesis he-calculates

* Peirce, 'Criterion for the Rejection of Doubtful Observations', *Astronomical Journal*, vol. ii, 1852.

the probability that n observations should give errors as large as the suspicious ones, and that the other observations should give just the errors committed, multiplying the two probabilities together. For the second hypothesis he rejects these observations *in toto*, recalculates his precision, and the probability of making just the other errors. This he multiplies by the *a priori* probability that n observations should be disturbed and the others should not.

Peirce's paper aroused a good deal of discussion. It was attacked by Airy * on the ground that no judgement should be made as to errors *a posteriori*, but to this Winlock † truthfully replied that the whole theory of errors was based on just this ground. Other criticisms have been made, but the real fault was never laid bare until many years later when Stewart ‡ showed the absurdity of starting with a totally unknown *a priori* probability, and calculating it by assuming that it took its maximum.

A simpler rule than Peirce's was devised by Chauvenet.§ The number of observations being N, if the probability of an error numerically greater than e be p, then Np will be about the number of errors numerically above e. If we set this equal to $\frac{1}{2}$, and calculate e, we are unlikely to have an error as large as that numerically, and larger errors should be rejected. There are various possible objections to this, one obvious one being that the calculus of probability deals with ratios, not with actual numbers. The number of errors of a given size will not be Np, but $Np \pm d$, where d is an unknown number, small compared with N.

A totally different method of attack was devised by Stone.‖ His idea was that each observer erred grossly in a certain proportion of his observations. If the probability that the error of an observation should be as large as a certain number be less than the probability that one of the N observation

---

* Airy, 'Remarks on Peirce's Criterion', *Astronomical Journal*, vol. iv, 1856.

† Winlock, 'Airy's Objections to Peirce's Criterion', ibid.

‡ Stewart, 'Peirce's Criterion', *Popular Astronomy*, vol. xxviii, 1920.

§ Chauvenet, *Astronomy*, vol. i, 1863, p. 558.

‖ Stone, 'Rejection of Discordant Observations', *Monthly Notices R. Astr. Soc.*, vol. xxviii, 1868, xxxiv, 1874, and xxxv, 1875.

should be affected by the observer's personal idiosyncrasy, the observation should be rejected. There are two convincing objections to this method of procedure. One is that we have no exact knowledge of just how often an individual will err in this way. The other is that, after we have calculated the limit of acceptable observations for a series of N, and find that perhaps one observation should be rejected, we might, instead of rejecting this observation, keep on, and observe N more times, with no worse result. On the basis of the $2N$ the observation which was suspicious before, may now be acceptable.

Stone's proposal led him into rather an unedifying dispute with Glaisher, who proposed a method of his own.* His idea was to weight the various observations, deducing their weights by a method of successive approximations. Start in the usual way, and calculate the precision. Assuming the Gaussian law of error, this enables us to calculate the respective probabilities that the given series resulted from a true value equal to the first, the second ... the last of the given values. We next give to each observation a weight proportional to the square of the corresponding probability, find the new weighted mean and corresponding precision, and begin over again. Glaisher assumes that eventually this process will approach to a definite limit. It might well be very long. Moreover, it seems to involve a certain *petitio principii*. For the weight attached to an observation is proportional to the square of the probability that the series arose from this true value when all the observations are equally trustworthy, and is a meaningless coefficient if they be otherwise.

A number of critics have maintained that, *a priori*, it is quite inadmissible to reject any one of a set of observations when all are carried out with the same care. Our own view is that such caution is excessive. It is all a question in the probability of causes. Here is an observation, far away from the mean of the others. It may have arisen from the same

* Glaisher, 'On the Rejection of Discordant Observations', ibid., xxxiii and xxxiv.

causes which were operative in the other cases, there may have been a disturbing cause. Let π_1 be the *a priori* probability that all was as usual when this observation was taken, π_2 the *a priori* probability that there was a disturbing element, tending to favour this result. We do not know the value of either of these, but may safely assume that the first is considerably the larger. Let p_1 be the probability that the particular measurement would be made in the natural course, p_2 that the special disturbing element might produce it. This latter we do not know, but may assume it large. p_1 we can calculate. To compare the two hypotheses by Bayes' principle we must look at the fraction

$$\frac{\pi_1 p_1}{\pi_2 p_2}.$$

If p_1 be infinitesimally small, in spite of the likelihood that π_1 is considerably larger than π_2, there is much reason to suspect that the fraction is small, and the observation should be rejected. It is the same principle we discussed in Ch. VI, p. 95, in discussing the lawsuit over a roulette wheel.

The delicate point is the probability p_1. The safest plan is to calculate $1 - p_1$, the probability that no one of the n observations should vary so widely as the most suspicious observation made. If this be as large as a fixed large probability P, there will be strong grounds for the belief that the worst observation did not arise in the natural course, and that it should, consequently, be rejected. Analytically, the probability that no error will be numerically above re, where e is the probable error, is

$$[\Theta\,(0\cdot4769)]^n = p.$$

Given $\qquad\qquad\quad p = 0\cdot99, \qquad n = 30.$

We get $\qquad\qquad\qquad r = 5.$

A residual 5 times the probable error is, here, suspicious.

CHAPTER VIII

ERRORS IN MANY VARIABLES

§ 1. The Law of Error.*

In all of the work done so far, we have tacitly assumed that we were studying errors in the observation of a single variable quantity. There are, however, cases where it is interesting and important to observe groups of quantities, and the corresponding groups of errors, in other words, error in measurements involving many independent variables. Our present task is to establish a plausible rule for the distribution of accidental errors in such cases.

We must say, by way of preface, a word or two on the matter of notation. The strictly scientific method would be to use a system of double subscripts, the one to indicate the quantity, the other the observation. The resulting formulae would be compact, but would lack clearness. We assume, therefore, that we have n sets of measurements of m independent variables

$$(x_1, y_1, z_1, \ldots) (x_2, y_2, z_2, \ldots) \ldots (x_n, y_n, z_n, \ldots).$$

The true values shall be $X, Y, Z, \ldots$. The true errors shall be

$$(\xi_1, \eta_1, \zeta_1, \ldots) (\xi_2, \eta_2, \zeta_2, \ldots) \ldots (\xi_n, \eta_n, \zeta_n, \ldots).$$

Assumption 1] *The mean value of an individual accidental error is zero.*

This is certainly plausible, for a contrary assumption would

---

* The present section, in so far as it deals with any number of variables, is taken direct from an article by the Author, ' The Gaussian Law of Error for Any Number of Variables', *Transactions American Math. Soc.*, 1923. Apparently the only other treatment is that of Von Mises, ' Fundamental-sätze der Wahrscheinlichkeitsrechnung ', *Math. Zeitschrift*, vol. iv, 1919, and ' Grundlagen der W.', ibid., vol. v, 1920. See also Dodd, ' Functions of Measurements ', *Sartryck ur Skandinavisk Aktuarietidskrift*, Upsala, 1922.

involve a tendency towards a positive or negative error, which should be classed with the constant errors.

Postulate 1] *The Postulates* 1]–5] *for the best value of a single observed quantity hold for each quantity of the group.*

We have for each of our quantities, exactly the assumptions for one quantity which were set up in the last chapter. We may thus write our best values in the form:

$$\bar{x} = \frac{\Sigma p_i x_i}{\Sigma p_i}, \quad \bar{y} = \frac{\Sigma q_i y_i}{\Sigma q_i}, \quad \bar{z} = \frac{\Sigma r_i z_i}{\Sigma r_i}. \tag{1}$$

Theorem 1] *When a set of observations are made under the conditions of Assumptions 1–3, the best value for each quantity is a weighted mean.*

Theorem 2] *When all observations of one quantity are equally trustworthy, the best value is their average.*

We shall, in future, use the words *weighted mean* in place of best value, the coefficients being the weights.

Theorem 3] *If it be possible to express each measurement as an average of a certain number of standard observations, then the weights in the weighted mean are proportional to the numbers of standard observations in each case.*

Theorem 4] *If the mean error for the observation* x_i *be* $1/k_i\sqrt{2}$, *the mean error for the weighted mean will be*

$$\left(\frac{\sum_i \frac{p_i}{2k_i^2}}{\sum_i p_i} \right)^{\frac{1}{2}}. \tag{2}$$

Theorem 5] *The weights in the weighted mean are inversely proportional to the squares of the corresponding mean errors.*

Let the residuals corresponding to the true errors ξ, η, ζ ... be δ, ϵ ....

Assumption 2] *When the number of observations is large, the mean value of each of the expressions such as*

$$\frac{\Sigma p_i \delta_i^2}{\Sigma p_i}, \quad \frac{\Sigma p_i \epsilon_i^2}{\Sigma p_i}, \quad \frac{\Sigma p_i \delta_i \epsilon_i}{\Sigma p_i} \tag{3}$$

may be replaced by its observed value.

Theorem 6] *The mean errors of the weighted means $\bar{x}, \bar{y}, \bar{z} \dots$ are*

$$\sqrt{\frac{1}{2\,K^2}} = \sqrt{\frac{\Sigma p_i \delta_i^2}{(n-1)\,\Sigma p_i}}; \quad \sqrt{\frac{1}{2\,L^2}} = \sqrt{\frac{\Sigma p_i \delta_i^2}{(n-1)\,\Sigma p_i}},$$

respectively.

Theorem 7] *The mean errors of the individual observations $x_i, y_i, \dots$ are*

$$\sqrt{\frac{1}{2\,k_i^2}} = \sqrt{\frac{\Sigma p_k \delta_k^2}{(n-1)\,p_i}}; \quad \sqrt{\frac{1}{2\,l_j^2}} = \sqrt{\frac{\Sigma p_k \epsilon_k^2}{(n-1)\,p_k}}.$$

Theorem 8] *When x_i is the average of p_i standard observations, the mean error of one of these is*

$$\sqrt{\frac{1}{2\,k^2}} = \sqrt{\frac{p_k \delta_k^2}{n-1}}.$$

We must now try to develop a law of error for our groups of observations. For the sake of simplicity, we shall assume all groups are equally trustworthy, so that all are weighted alike.

Assumption 3] *The a priori probability that a group of quantities to be measured should take values in the infinitesimal region*

$$X \pm \tfrac{1}{2}dX; \;\; Y \pm \tfrac{1}{2}dY; \;\; Z \pm \tfrac{1}{2}dZ \dots,$$

where the point $X, Y, Z, \dots$ lies in a continuous m dimensional region S, will differ by an infinitesimal of higher order from

$$f(X, Y, Z, \dots)\, dX\, dY\, dZ \dots$$

where the function f is continuous, with continuous first derivatives in S.

Assumption 4] *The probability that a group of quantities whose true values are X, Y, Z, ... in S, should be observed, after the removal of constant errors, to have values in the infinitesimal region of S*

$$x \pm \tfrac{1}{2}dx, \; y \pm \tfrac{1}{2}dy, \; z \pm \tfrac{1}{2}dz...,$$

will differ by an infinitesimal of higher order from

$$\Phi (X, Y, Z, ... x, y, z ...) \, dx \, dy \, dz ...$$

where Φ is a function continuous in all of its arguments, and with continuous first and second partial derivatives, and is independent of the origin.

Assumption 5] *If the infinitesimal increments be sufficiently small, the probability that the true values lie in the infinitesimal region*

$$\bar{x} \pm \tfrac{1}{2}dX, \; \bar{y} \pm \tfrac{1}{2}dY, \; \bar{z} \pm \tfrac{1}{2}dZ ...$$

is greater than that they lie in any other such region.

We have now a sufficient number of assumptions to determine the form of our function. The fact that f is independent of the origin, enables us to write

$$\Phi (X, Y, Z, ... x, y, z, ...) = \phi (\xi, \eta, \zeta, ...).$$

Let us further write

$$\phi (\xi_i, \eta_i, \zeta_i ...) \equiv \phi_i.$$

The probability that the observations were made on a group with the true values $X, Y, Z, ...$ will be

$$\frac{f(X, Y, Z, ...) \phi_1 \phi_2 ... \phi_n \, dX \, dY \, dZ...}{\int ... \int f(X, Y, Z, ...) \phi_1 \phi_2 ... \phi_n \, dX \, dY \, dZ...}. \tag{4}$$

This will be a maximum with the logarithm of the numerator. Taking the partial derivatives

$$-\frac{1}{f}\frac{\partial f}{\partial X} + \frac{\partial \log \phi_1}{\partial \xi_1} + ... + \frac{\partial \log \phi_n}{\partial \xi_n} = 0,$$

$$-\frac{1}{f}\frac{\partial f}{\partial Y_1} + \frac{\partial \log \phi}{\partial \eta_1} + ... + \frac{\partial \log \phi_n}{\partial \eta_n} = 0. \tag{5}$$

. . .

Since f is independent of the observations, in the particular case where each set is exactly right

$$-\frac{1}{f}\frac{\partial f}{\partial X} + n\frac{\partial \log \phi}{\partial \xi} = 0,$$

$$-\frac{1}{f}\frac{\partial f}{\partial Y} + n\frac{\partial \log \phi}{\partial \eta} = 0. \tag{6}$$

Hence

$$\frac{\partial f}{\partial X} = \frac{\partial f}{\partial Y} = \frac{\partial f}{\partial Z} = \ldots = 0,$$

$$f = \text{const.}$$

$$\frac{1}{\phi_1}\frac{\partial \phi_1}{\partial \xi_1} + \frac{1}{\phi_2}\frac{\partial \phi_2}{\partial \xi_2} + \ldots + \frac{1}{\phi_n}\frac{\partial \phi_n}{\partial \xi_n} = 0,$$

$$\frac{1}{\phi_1}\frac{\partial \phi_1}{\partial \eta_1} + \frac{1}{\phi_2}\frac{\partial \phi_2}{\partial \eta_2} + \ldots + \frac{1}{\phi_u}\frac{\partial \phi_n}{\partial \eta_n} = 0. \tag{7}$$

. . .

These equations exist when

$$\bar{x} = X; \quad \bar{y} = Y; \quad \bar{z} = Z, \&c.$$

$$p_1\epsilon_1 + p_2\epsilon_2 + \ldots + p_n\epsilon_n = 0,$$

$$q_1\eta_1 + q_2\eta_2 + \ldots + q_n\eta_n = 0,$$

$$r_1\zeta_1 + r_2\zeta_2 + \ldots + r_n\zeta_n = 0.$$

. . .

Now let x_1, x_2, $\ldots x_n$ take infinitesimal increments, subject to (1). We have

$$\frac{\partial}{\partial \xi_1}\left[\frac{1}{\phi_1}\frac{\partial \phi_1}{\partial \xi_1}\right]d\xi_1 + \frac{\partial}{\partial \xi_2}\left[\frac{1}{\phi_2}\frac{\partial \phi_2}{\partial \xi_2}\right]d\xi_2 + \ldots + \frac{\partial}{\partial \xi_n}\left[\frac{1}{\phi_n}\frac{\partial \phi_n}{\partial \xi_n}\right]\partial \xi_n = 0,$$

$$\frac{\partial}{\partial \xi_1}\left[\frac{1}{\phi_1}\frac{\partial \phi_1}{\partial \eta_1}\right]d\xi_1 + \frac{\partial}{\partial \xi_2}\left[\frac{1}{\phi_2}\frac{\partial \phi_2}{\partial \eta_2}\right]d\xi_2 + \ldots + \frac{\partial}{\partial \xi_n}\left[\frac{1}{\phi_n}\frac{\partial \phi_n}{\partial \eta_n}\right]\partial \xi_n = 0.$$

. . .

$$p_1 d\xi_1 + p_2 d\xi_2 + \ldots + p_n d\xi_n = 0.$$

Since those which precede the last must hold whenever the last does,

$$\frac{1}{p_i}\frac{\partial}{\partial \xi_i}\left[\frac{1}{\phi_i}\frac{\partial \phi_i}{\partial \xi_i}\right] = a \quad (i = 1, 2, \ldots n),$$

$$\frac{1}{p_i}\frac{\partial}{\partial \xi_i}\left[\frac{1}{\phi_i}\frac{\partial \phi_i}{\partial \eta_i}\right] = \frac{1}{p_i}\frac{\partial}{\partial \eta_i}\left[\frac{1}{\phi_i}\frac{\partial \phi_i}{\partial \xi_i}\right] = b.$$

. . .

$$\frac{\partial \log \phi}{\partial \xi} = a\xi + b\eta + \dots,$$

$$\frac{\partial \log \phi}{\partial \eta} = a'\xi + b'\eta + \dots.$$

. . .

$$\phi = e^{-\psi^2\,(\xi,\,\eta,\,\zeta,\,\dots)}. \tag{8}$$

Here ψ^2 is a quadratic function, necessarily homogeneous, for we have already seen that the partial derivatives vanish when the arguments are all zero. Moreover, its discriminant is not zero, for if it were, the partial derivatives would be linearly dependent, and vanish for an infinite number of real sets of the variables, and this is in direct conflict with our assumption that the maximum arises only from taking all the values equal to zero. Moreover, since this is known to be a maximum, this form must be definite and positive, since otherwise the maximum would be attained at infinity:

The homogeneous quadratic form ψ^2 is definite and positive with a non-vanishing discriminant.

We next notice that all the work done so far has been in a certain region S. We have found the probability that an observation in S should lie in a certain infinitesimal sub-region. What is the region S? It could not be the whole of space, as the assumption that f is everywhere a constant will lead to the absurd conclusion

$$\int_{-\infty}^{\infty}\dots\int_{-\infty}^{\infty} f(XYZ\dots)\,dX\,dY\,dZ\dots = 1.$$

On further consideration two more facts appear. First, it seems plausible to assume that f is constant throughout a certain region, and drops away very rapidly outside of it. Second, the expression (8) is extremely small outside of a very restricted part of space. As this will produce a result like that produced by the disappearance of f, the error in calculating the constants will be small if we allow S to extend throughout all space.

Assumption 6] *For the sake of calculating constants, formula (8) may be assumed true everywhere.*

We have also at our disposal Assumption 2], and this with 6] will be enough to solve the problem. As, however, the solution is rather long, we shall begin with the case of two z variables, and assume that all observations are equally trustworthy. Suppose that the law of error is expressed by the equation

$$\phi = Re^{-(a\xi^2 + 2b\xi\eta + c\eta^2)}. \tag{9}$$

The curves $\qquad a\xi^2 + 2b\xi\eta + c\eta^2 = \text{const.}$

are curves of like probability, and cannot run off to infinity by Assumption 2]. Hence these curves must be ellipses and

$$b^2 - ac < 0.$$

By a rotation of the ξ, η plane about the origin, these ellipses may be written

$$a'\xi'^2 + c'\eta'^2 = \text{const.}$$

The theory of invariants for conics shows us that

$$a + c = a' + c'; \quad b^2 - ac = -a'c'. \tag{10}$$

Since the sum of all probabilities is unity

$$1 = R\int_{-\infty}^{\infty} d\xi \int_{-\infty}^{\infty} e^{-(a\xi^2 + 2b\xi\eta + c\eta^2)}\, d\eta$$

$$= R\int_{-\infty}^{\infty} e^{-a'\xi'^2}\, d\xi' \int_{-\infty}^{\infty} e^{-c'\eta'^2}\, d\eta',$$

$$R = \frac{\sqrt{(a'c')}}{\pi} = \frac{\sqrt{(ac - b^2)}}{\pi}.$$

We find, by Assumption 2],

$$\frac{\sqrt{(ac - b^2)}}{\pi} \int_{-\infty}^{\infty} \xi^2 d\xi \int_{-\infty}^{\infty} e^{-(a\xi^2 + 2b\xi\eta + c\eta^2)}\, d\eta = \frac{\Sigma \delta_i^2}{n-1},$$

$$\frac{\sqrt{(ac - b^2)}}{\pi} \int_{-\infty}^{\infty} \eta^2 d\eta \int_{-\infty}^{\infty} e^{-(a\xi^2 + 2b\xi\eta + c\eta^2)}\, d\xi = \frac{\Sigma \epsilon_i^2}{n-1},$$

$$\frac{\sqrt{(ac - b^2)}}{\pi} \int_{-\infty}^{\infty} \xi d\xi \int_{-\infty}^{\infty} \eta\, e^{-(a\xi^2 + 2b\xi\eta + c\eta^2)}\, d\eta = \frac{\Sigma \delta_i \epsilon_i}{n-1},$$

To solve the first of these, we write

$$a\xi^2 + 2b\xi\eta + c\eta^2 = \frac{ac - b^2}{c}\xi^2 + \left(\frac{b}{\sqrt{c}}\xi + \sqrt{c}\eta\right)^2,$$

$$\xi' = \xi,$$

$$\eta' = \frac{b}{\sqrt{c}}\xi + \sqrt{c}\eta,$$

$$\frac{\partial(\xi', \eta')}{\partial(\xi, \eta)} = \sqrt{c}, \quad \frac{\partial(\xi, \eta)}{\partial(\xi', \eta')} = \frac{1}{\sqrt{c}}.$$

Changing variables, we have

$$\frac{\sqrt{(ac - b^2)}}{\pi\sqrt{c}}\int_{-\infty}^{\infty}\xi^2 e^{-\frac{(ac - b^2)}{c}\xi^2}\,d\xi\int_{-\infty}^{\infty}e^{-\eta'^2}\,d\eta'$$

$$= \frac{\sqrt{(ac - b^2)}}{\sqrt{\pi}\sqrt{c}}\int_{-\infty}^{\infty}\xi^2 e^{-\frac{(ac - b^2)}{c}\xi^2}\,d\xi,$$

$$= \frac{c}{2(ac - b^2)}.$$

Similarly

$$\frac{\sqrt{(ac - b^2)}}{\pi}\int_{-\infty}^{\infty}\eta^2\,d\eta\int_{-\infty}^{\infty}e^{-(a\xi^2 + 2b\xi\eta + c\eta^2)}\,d\xi = \frac{a}{2(ac - b^2)}.$$

There remains

$$\frac{\sqrt{(ac - b^2)}}{\pi}\int_{-\infty}^{\infty}\xi\,d\xi\int_{-\infty}^{\infty}\eta e^{-(a\xi^2 + 2b\xi\eta + c\eta^2)}\,d\eta.$$

Putting, as before,

$$\xi' = \xi,$$

$$\eta' = \frac{b}{\sqrt{c}}\xi + \sqrt{c}\eta,$$

$$\eta = \frac{\eta'}{c} - \frac{b}{c}\xi.$$

Since

$$\int_{-\infty}^{\infty}\eta' e^{-\eta'^2}\,d\eta' = 0.$$

We have

$$- \frac{b\sqrt{(ac-b^2)}}{c\sqrt{(c\pi)}} \int_{-\infty}^{\infty} \xi^2 e^{-\left(\frac{ac-b^2}{c}\right)\xi^2} d\xi = \frac{-b}{2(ac-b^2)},$$

$$\frac{c}{2(ac-b^2)} = \frac{\Sigma \delta_i^2}{n-1},$$

$$\frac{a}{2(ac-b^2)} = \frac{\Sigma \epsilon_i^2}{n-1},$$

$$\frac{-b}{2(ac-b^2)} = \frac{\Sigma \delta_i \epsilon_i}{n-1},$$

$$c:a:b = \Sigma \delta_i^2 : \Sigma \epsilon_i^2 : -\Sigma \delta_i \epsilon_i.$$

$$a = \frac{\Sigma \epsilon_i^2 (n-1)}{2\left[\Sigma \delta_i^2 \Sigma \epsilon_i^2 - (\Sigma \delta_i \epsilon_i)^2\right]},$$

$$b = \frac{-\Sigma \delta_i \epsilon_i (n-1)}{2\left[\Sigma \delta_i^2 \Sigma \epsilon_i^2 - (\Sigma \delta_i \epsilon_i)^2\right]}, \tag{11}$$

$$c = \frac{\Sigma \delta_i^2 (n-1)}{2\left[\Sigma \delta_i^2 \Sigma \epsilon_i^2 - (\Sigma \delta_i \epsilon_i)^2\right]},$$

$$R = \frac{n-1}{2\pi \left(\Sigma \delta_i^2 \Sigma \epsilon_i^2 - (\Sigma \delta_i \epsilon_i)^2\right)^{\frac{1}{2}}},$$

$$\phi = Re^{-(a\xi^2 + 2b\xi\eta + c\eta^2)}. \tag{9}$$

¶ The problem of finding the actual coefficients in the general case * does not seem to lend itself to an analogous method. We therefore take up the question from the start; the theoretical importance of the problem seems sufficient to warrant the labour involved. We shall begin by a change of notation in order to use forms which are frequent in the study of linear transformations. Let us write

$$\xi = x_1, \ \eta = x_2, \ \zeta = x_3 \ldots$$

so that (8) becomes

$$\phi = Re^{-\sum_{i,j=1}^{i,j=n} a_{ij} x_i x_j} \qquad a_{ij} = a_{ji}. \tag{12}$$

* Cf. Greiner, *Zeitschrift für Mathematik und Physik*, vol. lvii, p. 226; and Pearson, *Philosophical Transactions*, vol. clxxxvii, p. 299 ff.

We must first consider the discriminant

$$| a_{11} a_{22} \dots a_{nn} | \equiv | a_{ij} |.$$

Since the quadratic form is definite, this discriminant is not 0, and we may find such a linear transformation

$$x_i = \sum_{k=1}^{k=m} c_{ik} x_k', \quad | c_{ij} | \neq 0, \tag{13}$$

that

$$\sum_{i,j} a_{ij} x_i x_j \equiv \sum_{i,j,k,l=1}^{i,j,k,l=m} a_{ij} c_{ik} c_{jl} x_k' x_l'$$

$$\equiv \sum_{r=1}^{r=m} b_r x_r'^2, \quad b_r \neq 0.$$

Hence

$$\sum_{i,j=1}^{i,j=m} a_{ij} c_{ik} c_{jl} = 0, \quad k \neq l, \tag{14}$$

$$\sum_{i,j=1}^{i,j=m} a_{ij} c_{ir} c_{jr} = b_r,$$

$$b_1 b_2 \dots b_m = | c_{ij} |^2 \cdot | a_{ij} |.$$

The inverse of the substitution contragredient to (13) is

$$u_k' = \sum_{i=1}^{i=m} c_{ik} u_i,$$

$$u_k'^2 = \sum_{i,j=1}^{i,j=m} c_{ik} c_{jk} u_i u_j.$$

The hyperquadric in $(n-1)$ dimensional space

$$\sum_{i,j=1}^{i,j=n} a_{ij} x_i x_j = 0,$$

has the tangential equation

$$\sum_{i,j=1}^{i,j=n} A_{ij} u_i u_j = 0, \quad A_{ij} = \frac{\partial | a_{ij} |}{\partial a_{ij}}.$$

In the new variables the point equation

$$\sum_{k=1}^{k=m} b_k x_k'^2 = 0$$

corresponds to the tangential equation

$$\sum_{k=1}^{k=m} \frac{u_k'^2}{b_k} = 0,$$

$$(b_1, b_2, \ldots b_m) \sum_{k=1}^{k=m} \frac{u_k'^2}{b_k} \equiv |c_{ij}|^2 \sum_{i,j=1}^{i,j=m} A_{ij} u_i u_j,$$

$$|a_{ij}| \sum_{k=1}^{k=m} \frac{c_{ik} c_{jk}}{b_k} = A_{ij}. \qquad (15)$$

As a second step in our development, let us consider the residuals

$$\delta_{11}, \delta_{12}, \ldots \delta_{1m}; \; \delta_{21}, \delta_{22}, \ldots \delta_{2m}; \; \ldots ; \; \delta_{n1}, \delta_{n2}, \ldots \delta_{nm}.$$

We write for brevity

$$p_{ij} = \frac{\sum_{k=1}^{k=n} \delta_{ki} \delta_{kj}}{n-1}. \qquad (16)$$

We get from Assumption 2]

$$p_{ij} = R \int_{-\infty}^{\infty} \ldots \int_{-\infty}^{\infty} x_i x_j e^{-\Sigma a_{ij} x_i x_j} dx_1 \ldots dx_m. \qquad (17)$$

Let us change variables, remembering that the Jacobian is $|c_{ij}|$,

$$p_{ij} = R |c_{ij}| \int_{-\infty}^{\infty} \ldots \int_{-\infty}^{\infty} \sum_{k,l=1}^{k,l=m} c_{ik} c_{jl} x_k' x_l' e^{-\Sigma_r b_r x_r'^2} dx_1' \ldots dx_m'.$$

Now, when $k \neq l$,

$$\int_{-\infty}^{\infty} x_k' e^{-b_k x_k'^2} dx_k' \int_{-\infty}^{\infty} x_l' e^{-b_l x_l'^2} dx_l' = 0.$$

Hence

$$p_{ij} = R |c_{ij}| \int_{-\infty}^{\infty} \ldots \int_{-\infty}^{\infty} \sum_{k=1}^{k=m} c_{ik} c_{jk} x_k'^2 e^{-\Sigma_r b_r x_r'^2} dx_1' \ldots dx_m'.$$

We know, further, that

$$\int_{-\infty}^{\infty} e^{-b_k x_k'^2} \, dx_k' = \frac{\sqrt{\pi}}{\sqrt{b_k}},$$

$$\int_{-\infty}^{\infty} x_k'^2 e^{-b_k x_k'^2} \, dx_k' = \frac{\sqrt{\pi}}{2 \, (b_k)^{\frac{3}{2}}}.$$

Hence $\qquad p_{ij} = |c_{ij}| \dfrac{R}{2} \dfrac{\pi^{\frac{m}{2}}}{(b_1 b_2 \dots b_m)^{\frac{1}{2}}} \sum_{k=1}^{k=m} \dfrac{c_{ik} c_{jk}}{b_k}.$

Hence, by (15)

$$p_{ij} = R \frac{|c_{ij}|}{2 \, |a_{ij}|} \frac{\pi^{\frac{m}{2}}}{(b_1 b_2 \dots b_m)^{\frac{1}{2}}} A_{ij}$$

$$= \frac{R \pi^{\frac{m}{2}} A_{ij}}{2 \, |a_{ij}|^{\frac{3}{2}}}.$$

Furthermore,

$$1 = R \int_{-\infty}^{\infty} \dots \int_{-\infty}^{\infty} e^{-\sum_{i,j} a_{ij} x_i x_j} \, dx_1 \dots dx_n :$$

$$= \frac{R \pi^{\frac{m}{2}} |c_{ij}|}{(b_1 \dots b_m)^{\frac{1}{2}}}$$

$$= \frac{R \pi^{\frac{m}{2}}}{\sqrt{|a_{ij}|}}.$$

Dividing out $\qquad p_{ij} = \dfrac{A_{ij}}{2 \, |a_{ij}|}.$

Here the quantities p_{ij} are known. We wish to solve for the unknown a_{ij}'s. We first write

$$P_{ij} \doteq \frac{\partial \, |p_{ij}|}{\partial p_{ij}}.$$

Since the process of interchanging each element of a non-vanishing determinant with its cofactor is an involutory one, except for multiplication by a positive or negative power of the determinant, we shall evidently have

$$a_{ij} = MP_{ij},$$

$$|a_{ij}| = M^m |p_{ij}|^{m-1},$$

$$|p_{ij}| = \frac{|A_{ij}|}{2^m |a_{ij}|^m} = \frac{1}{2^m |a_{ij}|},$$

$$\frac{1}{2^m} = M^m |p_{ij}|^m,$$

$$M = \frac{1}{2|p_{ij}|}.$$

We thus reach our final equations

$$\phi = Re^{-\Sigma a_{ij} x_i x_j},$$

$$R = \left(\frac{|a_{ij}|}{\pi^m} \right)^{\frac{1}{2}},$$

$$a_{ij} = \frac{1}{2} \frac{\partial \log |p_{ij}|}{\partial p_{ij}}, \qquad (18)$$

$$p_{ij} = \sum_{k=1}^{k=n} \frac{\delta_{ki} \delta_{kj}}{n-1}.$$

§ 2. The Error Ellipse.

Let us return to a more careful study of the case where there are but two quantities in a group.   The curves

$$a\xi^2 + 2b\xi\eta + c\eta^2 \equiv a'\xi'^2 + c'\eta'^2 = H \qquad (19)$$

are ellipses, and are called *error ellipses* or ellipses of equal probability. The meaning of the designation is easily seen. If we take a small band on either side of such an ellipse, the probability that the point representing a pair of values should lie in a small region of this band is independent of the position of the region with regard to the curve; the points should be somewhat uniformly distributed throughout the band.   To study this ellipse, we must return to our equations of transformation

$$b^2 - ac = -a'c',$$

$$a + c = a' + c',$$

the relation between the two sets of variables is

$$\xi' = \xi \cos\theta + \eta \sin\theta,$$

$$\eta' = -\xi \sin\theta + \eta \cos\theta,$$

$$\tan 2\theta = -\frac{2b}{c-a},$$

$$c' = \frac{a+c}{2} \pm b \csc 2\theta, \qquad (20)$$

$$a' = \frac{a+c}{2} \mp b \csc 2\theta,$$

the semi-axes of the ellipse are

$$(H/a')^{\frac{1}{2}} (H/c')^{\frac{1}{2}}.$$

Its area is $\qquad \dfrac{\pi H}{\sqrt{a'c'}} = \dfrac{\pi H}{\sqrt{(ac-b^2)}}.$

The probability of being between adjacent ellipses is

$$\frac{K\pi}{\sqrt{(ac-b^2)}} e^{-H} dH.$$

To find K, we have

$$\frac{K\pi}{\sqrt{(ac-b^2)}} \int_0^\infty e^{-H} dH = 1,$$

$$K = \frac{\sqrt{(ac-b^2)}}{\pi}.$$

The probability of being in a small band is

$$e^{-H} dH.$$

The probability of falling outside an ellipse H_1 is

$$\int_{H_1}^\infty e^{-H} dH = e^{-H_1}.$$

About one-half of the points should be without the ellipse

$$e^{-H_1} = \tfrac{1}{2},$$

$$H_1 = 0 \cdot 6935.$$

This is called the 'probable ellipse'. Its area is

$$\frac{0 \cdot 6935 \pi}{\sqrt{(ac-b^2)}}.$$

In judging the performance of marksmen, it has been suggested that they should be graded according to the smallness of their error ellipses, i.e. the better marksman is the

one for whom $ac - b^2$ has the larger value.   In extreme cases
this method may work badly.*

As an example of how such material may be handled, we
take a case that has perhaps more historical than mathematical
interest, the 'Big Bertha' shots that fell on Paris in 1918.
The number of shots is not very large, we take 100, which is
nearly the total, and they were not all fired from the same

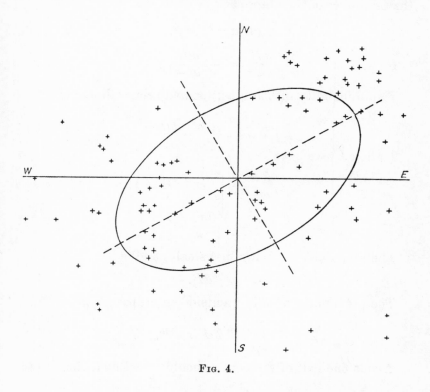

FIG. 4.

spot.   The major axis of the probable ellipse, as shown in
Fig. 4, does point in a general way in the direction whence
the firing came.   This, of course, we should expect under any
circumstances.   Errors in range are likely to show more
variation than errors in direction, and a set of shots which
took a circular distribution on a point-blank target would
take an elliptical one on a target not perpendicular to the

<hr/>

* Cf. Bertrand, loc. cit., pp. 236 ff.

central curve. The details of the calculation used in finding
the probable ellipse are

$$n = 100,$$

$$\frac{\Sigma \delta_i^2}{99} = 3{,}270, \quad \frac{\Sigma \delta_i \epsilon_i}{99} = 1{,}180, \quad \frac{\Sigma \epsilon_i^2}{99} = 2{,}030,$$

$$a = \frac{203}{1{,}049{,}140}, \quad b = \frac{-118}{1{,}049{,}140}, \quad c = \frac{327}{1{,}049{,}140},$$

$$a = 0{\cdot}000193, \quad b = -0{\cdot}000113, \quad c = 0{\cdot}000312,$$

$$\tan 2\theta = +1{\cdot}9, \quad \theta = 31°,$$

$$a' = 0{\cdot}000124, \quad c' = 0{\cdot}000380.$$

The axes of the probable ellipse are

$$\alpha = 75, \quad \beta = 43.$$

In the figure there are only 45 points within the probable
ellipse, but had it been just a little larger, fully one-half
would have been therein. The centre is close to the Louvre,
and the major axis passes close to the Gare de l'Est.

§ 3. The Correlation Coefficient.

Until recently, the only interest attached to errors in two
variables was the ballistic one, but now new applications
have arisen in connexion with statistics. A fundamental
question in many sorts of statistical work, especially in
sociological and biological sciences, is whether two characteristics which are noted in a large number of individuals are
connected in some way, or vary independently. It is evident
that the assimilation of such measurements and variations to
accidental errors of observation is very crude. The errors
here are committed by Nature as she varies one way or the
other from the average. Nevertheless, in a good many cases,
our Assumptions 1] to 6] do fit her methods of operating
with considerable closeness.

Suppose, then, that in the case of a number of individuals,
we measure the same pair of characteristics, and plot the

pairs of measurements as points in a plane. In order to bring our notation into conformity with that used by statisticians, we shall call the residuals $x_1 y_1$, $x_2 y_2$, ... $x_n y_n$. If the two characteristics were so connected that the one increased above the mean proportionately to the increase of the other, the points plotted would lie on a line of positive slope; if the increase of one were proportional to the decrease of the other, the line would have a negative slope. If the characteristics were completely independent of one another, the mean value of their product would be 0, and the axes of the ellipse would be the axes of x and y.

We write in the usual statistical notation

$$\sigma_x = \sqrt{\frac{\Sigma x_i^2}{n}}, \quad \sigma_y = \sqrt{\frac{\Sigma y_i^2}{n}}. \tag{21}$$

The number

$$r = \frac{\Sigma x_i y_i}{\sqrt{\Sigma x_i^2}\,\sqrt{\Sigma y_i^2}} = \frac{\Sigma \dfrac{x_i y_i}{n}}{\sigma_x \sigma_y} \tag{22}$$

is called the *correlation coefficient*. We suppose n so large that we may safely put

$$\frac{n-1}{n} = 1.$$

Under these circumstances, we have from (11) and (20),

$$a = \frac{\sigma_y^2}{2\,\sigma_x^2 \sigma_y^2 (1-r^2)} = \frac{1}{2\,\sigma_x^2 (1-r^2)},$$

$$b = \frac{-r}{2\,\sigma_x \sigma_y (1-r^2)},$$

$$c = \frac{1}{2\,\sigma_y^2 (1-r^2)},$$

$$\tan 2\theta = \frac{-2\,r \sigma_x \sigma_y}{\sigma_x^2 - \sigma_y^2},$$

$$\csc 2\theta = \frac{((\sigma_x^2 + \sigma_y^2)^2 - 4\,\sigma_x^2 \sigma_y^2 (1-r^2))^{\frac{1}{2}}}{2\,r \sigma_x \sigma_y},$$

$$a' = \frac{\sigma_x^2 + \sigma_y^2 \pm ((\sigma_x^2 + \sigma_y^2)^2 - 4\sigma_x^2\sigma_y^2(1-r^2))^{\frac{1}{2}}}{4\sigma_x^2\sigma_y^2(1-r^2)},$$

$$c' = \frac{\sigma_x^2 + \sigma_y^2 \mp ((\sigma_x^2 + \sigma_y^2)^2 - 4\sigma_x^2\sigma_y^2(1-r^2))^{\frac{1}{2}}}{4\sigma_x^2\sigma_y^2(1-r^2)},$$

$$\frac{1}{a'c'} = 4\sigma_x^2\sigma_y^2(1-r^2).$$

When r is close to 1 or to -1 we say that we have a strong positive or negative correlation. The difference between a' and c' will be large, and the ratio of the axes will be close to 0 or ∞. The ellipse will be excessively flat, and the two sets of residuals will tend to vary proportionately. On the other hand, when r is close to 0 we say the correlation is weak. b will be very small. Then either θ will be very small, and the probability function will be close to

$$e^{-(ax^2 + cy^2)} = e^{-ax^2} \times e^{-by^2},$$

which is characteristic of independent variation, or else σ_x is nearly equal to σ_y, a' is nearly equal to c', and we have nearly a circular distribution which would also give b close to 0.

¶ It is fair to say that the usual method of arriving at the correlation coefficient is quite different from this; for the sake of completeness we sketch the customary proceeding.*

We start, as before, with the centre of gravity of the given points as origin. There may be several x's corresponding to each y. Thus we might have on one horizontal line the points $\qquad (x_{i1}y_i)(x_{i2}y_i)\ldots(x_{im_i}y_i),$

whose centre of gravity would be the point

$$\bar{x}_i = \frac{1}{m_i}(x_{i1} + x_{i2} + \ldots x_{im_i}).$$

If now x and y varied proportionately to one another, all of the points $(\bar{x}_iy_i)$ would be collinear. When they are not,

---

* Cf. Yule, 'On the Significance of Bravais' Formula', *Proceedings of the Royal Society*, vol. lx, 1896.

let us find what line does make the best graph of $\bar{x}$ as a function of y. We shall call this a *line of regression of x on y*. We mean by the *best*, that which will minimize the sum of the squares of the weighted divergences of the values $\bar{x}$ from the corresponding values of the function. Calling the line

$$x = ky + a,$$

we must have

$$\sum_{i=1}^{i=n} m_i [\bar{x}_i - (ky_i + a)]^2 = Min.$$

Differentiating partially to a and k,

$$\sum_i m_i [\bar{x}_i - (ky_i + a)] = 0,$$

$$\sum_i m_i y_i [\bar{x}_i - (ky_i + a)] = 0,$$

$$\sum m_i \bar{x}_i = \sum m_i y_i = \sum x_{ij} = 0.$$

Here the third summation covers all the abscissae. It must not be forgotten that the origin is at the centre of gravity,

hence $$a = 0, \quad k = \frac{\sum m_i \bar{x}_i y_i}{\sum m_i y_i^2} = \frac{\sum x_k y_k}{\sum y_k^2} = r \frac{\sigma_x}{\sigma_y}.$$

The line of regression of x on y is

$$x = r \frac{\sigma_x}{\sigma_y} y.$$

In the same way the line of regression of y on x is

$$y = r \frac{\sigma_y}{\sigma_x} x.$$

The tangent of the included angle is

$$\tan \theta = \frac{r^2 - 1}{r \left(\dfrac{\sigma_x{}^2 + \sigma_y{}^2}{\sigma_x \sigma_y} \right)}.$$

When r is close to 1 or -1, the angle between the two lines of regression is close to 0 or π. Moreover, the sum of

the squares of the areas formed by the various pairs of points
with the origin is

$$\frac{1}{2} \sum_{i,j=1}^{i,j=n} [\tfrac{1}{2}(x_i y_j - x_j y_i)]^2 = \tfrac{1}{8}[\Sigma x_i^2 \Sigma y_i^2 - (\Sigma x_i y_i)^2],$$

$$= \tfrac{1}{8}\sigma_x^2 \sigma_y^2 (1 - r^2).$$

When r is close to 1 or -1, this will be close to 0, so that
all of the points will lie nearly on a line through the centre
of gravity. On the other hand, when r is close to 0, the two
lines of regression are close to the axes. For each y, the
average x is about 0, and the characteristics are practically
independent of one another.

The great trouble at present with the theory of correlation
seems to be that there is no general agreement as to how
large r^2 must be in order that we may safely conclude that
there is a real connexion between the two sets of phenomena.

¶ Besides the correlation coefficient there is another number,
called the *correlation ratio*, which the statisticians sometimes
employ. We begin with a new system of coordinates which
is independent of the unit of measure,

$$x_i' = \frac{x_i}{\sigma_x}, \quad y_i' = \frac{y_i}{\sigma_y}.$$

Then
$$\Sigma x_i'^2 = \Sigma y_i'^2 = n.$$

Let us group these according to the y's as before. We
shall have on a horizontal line

$$(x_{i1}' y_1')(x_{i2}' y_i') \dots (x_{im_i}' y_i'), \quad \Sigma_i m_i = n.$$

The dispersion of the abscissas is

$$\sqrt{\Sigma_j (x_{ij} - \bar{x}_i')^2}.$$

The total dispersion is

$$\sqrt{\Sigma_{ij}(x_{ij}' - \bar{x}_i')^2} = \sqrt{(n - \Sigma_i m_i \bar{x}_i'^2)},$$

$$\sqrt{\frac{\Sigma_i m_i \bar{x}_i'^2}{n}} = \sqrt{\left(1 - \frac{\Sigma_{ij}(x_{ij}' - \bar{x}_i')^2}{n}\right)} = h_{x' y'}.$$

This is called the *correlation ratio* of x' on y'.   It is equal to unity when, and only when, y is a single valued function of x.   If the points $\bar{x}_i'\, y_i$ all lie on a straight line we have

$$\bar{x}' = ly',$$

$$l = \frac{\bar{x}_i'}{y_i} = \sqrt{\left(\frac{\Sigma\,(m_i \bar{x}_i'^2)}{\Sigma\,(m_i y_i'^2)}\right)} = h_{x'y'}.$$

The corresponding points $\bar{x}y$ must lie in the line

$$\bar{x} = h_{x'y'}\frac{\sigma_x}{\sigma_y}y$$

which must be the regression of x on y, hence

$$h x_{x'y'} = r.$$

CHAPTER IX

INDIRECT OBSERVATIONS

§ 1. Least Square Method for Combining Indirect Observations.

IT frequently happens in physical measurements that we are not able to make a direct examination of the quantities which interest us, but must deduce their values from the observations of certain functions of them. We are faced in such cases with the problem of combining the observations in such a fashion as will best help us to estimate the values of the quantities in which we are interested.

We first ask a question in pure mathematics. Suppose that we observe the values of n differentiable functions of m variables, what are the values of the variables ? There are three obvious cases :

A) $n < m$. The problem is indeterminate if the functions be independent; we can find no unique solution when the number of equations is less than the number of unknowns.

B) $n = m$. The problem is determinate (usually) and depends upon our analytical skill in solving the equations.

C) $n > m$. If the observed values contained no error whatever, some of the equations would result from the others, and we should fall back on a previous case. But, owing to accidental errors of observation, the system is incompatible and the question is, ' What do we propose to do about it ? ' An easy plan would be to discard some of the equations and solve the others, but we have no sure guide as to which equations might better be discarded, and we should certainly lose some accuracy, just as it is less accurate to take a single measurement of a quantity than to take the average of several discordant measurements.

In order to solve our problem, we must decide on the meaning of the phrase ' best values for the unknowns '. This we shall do as we proceed with our analysis. Suppose that we have observed the values of n functions, not necessarily distinct, of m variables. These observational equations shall be

$$f_1(u_1, u_2, \ldots u_m) = x_1,$$
$$f_2(u_1, u_2, \ldots u_m) = x_2, \qquad (1)$$
$$\cdot \quad \cdot \quad \cdot \quad \cdot \quad \cdot$$
$$f_n(u_1, u_2, \ldots u_m) = x_n.$$

The x's are observed values. Let us assume that we know the weights of our observations, although we do not assume that we know the probable errors. We assume also that the number of equations is greater than the number of the unknowns, and that the equations are inconsistent, so that we cannot discard some and solve the rest.

Postulate 1] *The best values for the unknowns are those which will give a maximum value to the probability of obtaining just this series of measurements.*

Assumption 1] *The error of each observation follows the Gaussian law with a proper precision.*

Assumption 2] *We can make first approximations to the unknowns so accurate that in correcting the values of the f_i, corrections above the first order may be neglected.*

Let X_i be the true value for the function f_i, the true error shall be $x_i - X_i = \xi_i$ and the precision k_i. We may follow the reasoning of the previous chapter, which shows that all values of $u_1, u_2, \ldots u_m$ are equally likely. Our problem then is to maximize

$$e^{-(k_1^2 \xi_1^2 + k_2^2 \xi_2^2 + \ldots + k_n^2 \xi_n^2)},$$

and this amounts, in turn, to minimizing

$$k_1^2 \xi_1^2 + k_2^2 \xi_2^2 + \ldots + k_n^2 \xi_n^2. \qquad (2)$$

If we had taken as one of our assumptions that requiring this expression to be a minimum, we might have abandoned the assumption that the measures followed the law of Gauss. It will be well, in our present work, to use a large assortment of symbols. Let us assume that the true values of the unknowns are $U_1, U_2, \ldots U_m$. These we do not know, and never shall know. Let us assume that our good first approximations are $\omega_1, \omega_2, \ldots \omega_m$, and that their true errors are $\epsilon_1, \epsilon_2, \ldots \epsilon_m$. Then we have the true equations

$$f_i(\omega_1 + \epsilon_1, \omega_2 + \epsilon_2, \ldots \omega_m + \epsilon_m) = X_i,$$

and by Assumption 2] these may be written

$$f_i(\omega_1, \omega_2, \ldots \omega_m) + \sum_j \frac{\partial f_i}{\partial \omega_j} \epsilon_j = X_i = x_i - \xi_i,$$

hence the expression to minimize is

$$\sum_i k_i^2 \left[f_i(\omega_1 - \omega_m) - x_i + \sum_j \frac{\partial f_i}{\partial \omega_j} \epsilon_j \right]^2.$$

We shall equate to 0 each of the partial derivatives of this with regard to $\epsilon_1, \epsilon_2, \ldots \epsilon_m$. We do not know the values of the precisions, but we assumed that we knew the weights which are proportional to their squares. Hence we have m equations

$$\sum_{i,j} p_i \frac{\partial f_i}{\partial \omega_j} \frac{\partial f_i}{\partial \omega_k} \epsilon_j = \sum_i p_i \frac{\partial f_i}{\partial \omega_k} (x_i - f_i). \tag{3}$$

It is well to write these at length, using a symbolism which is classical in this sort of work. We write, by definition,

$$\sum_i r_i s_i = [rs], \quad \sum_i r_i s_i t_i = [rst].$$

Then we have m equations

$$\left[p \frac{\partial f}{\partial \omega_1} \frac{\partial f}{\partial \omega_1} \right] \epsilon_1 + \left[p \frac{\partial f}{\partial \omega_1} \frac{\partial f}{\partial \omega_2} \right] \epsilon_2 + \ldots + \left[p \frac{\partial f}{\partial \omega_1} \frac{\partial f}{\partial \omega_m} \right] \epsilon_m$$
$$= \left[p \frac{\partial f}{\partial \omega_1} (x - f) \right],$$

$$\left[p \frac{\partial f}{\partial \omega_2} \frac{\partial f}{\partial \omega_1} \right] \epsilon_1 + \left[p \frac{\partial f}{\partial \omega_2} \frac{\partial f}{\partial \omega_2} \right] \epsilon_2 + \ldots + \left[p \frac{\partial f}{\partial \omega_2} \frac{\partial f}{\partial \omega_m} \right] \epsilon_m$$
$$= \left[p \frac{\partial f}{\partial \omega_2} (x - f) \right], \tag{4}$$

$$\cdots$$

$$\left[p \frac{\partial f}{\partial \omega_m} \frac{\partial f}{\partial \omega_1} \right] \epsilon_1 + \left[p \frac{\partial f}{\partial \omega_m} \frac{\partial f}{\partial \omega_2} \right] \epsilon_2 + \ldots + \left[p \frac{\partial f}{\partial \omega_m} \frac{\partial f}{\partial \omega_m} \right] \epsilon_m$$
$$= \left[p \frac{\partial f}{\partial \omega_m} (x - f) \right].$$

These equations are called the *normal equations*. The principal difficulty is to remember how to write them down. An easy way is as follows. We begin with n incompatible equations, called *residual equations*,

$$\frac{\partial f_1}{\partial \omega_1}\epsilon_1 + \frac{\partial f_1}{\partial \omega_2}\epsilon_2 + \ldots + \frac{\partial f_1}{\partial \omega_m}\epsilon_m = x_1 - f_1(\omega_1 \ldots \omega_m),$$

$$\frac{\partial f_2}{\partial \omega_1}\epsilon_1 + \frac{\partial f_2}{\partial \omega_2}\epsilon_2 + \ldots + \frac{\partial f_2}{\partial \omega_m}\epsilon_m = x_2 - f_2(\omega_1 \ldots \omega_m), \qquad (5)$$

$$\frac{\partial f_n}{\partial \omega_1}\epsilon_1 + \frac{\partial f_n}{\partial \omega_2}\epsilon_2 + \ldots + \frac{\partial f_n}{\partial \omega_m}\epsilon_m = x_n - f_n(\omega_1 \ldots \omega_m).$$

These equations would become compatible if we replaced the quantities $x_1, x_2, \ldots x_n$ by their true values $X_1, X_2, \ldots X_n$. Multiply the first equation through by p_1 times the first coefficient, the second by p_2 times the first coefficient, and so on. The sum will be the first normal equation. For the kth normal equation we use the kth coefficient each time.

The case which arises most often in practice is that where the given functions are linear. Here we do not bother at all about the first approximations $\omega_1, \omega_2, \ldots \omega_m$, but take as corrections the unknowns themselves. It makes for clearness, also, to use a variety of letters, rather than to use double subscripts. We write the residual equations

$$a_1 u_1 + b_1 u_2 + \ldots + m_1 u_m = x_1,$$
$$a_2 u_1 + b_2 u_2 + \ldots + m_2 u_m = x_2,$$
$$\cdot \quad \cdot \quad \cdot \qquad\qquad\qquad (6)$$
$$a_n u_1 + b_n u_2 + \ldots + m_n u_m = x_n.$$

The normal equations then are

$$[paa]\,u_1 + [pab]\,u_2 + \ldots + [pam]\,u_m = [pax],$$
$$[pba]\,u_1 + [pbb]\,u_2 + \ldots + [pbm]\,u_m = [pbx],$$
$$\cdot \quad \cdot \quad \cdot$$
$$[pma]\,u_1 + [pmb]\,u_2 + \ldots + [pmm]\,u_m = [pmx].$$

$$|\,[paa]\,[pbb]\ldots[pmm]\,| = \Delta. \qquad (8)$$

$$u_1 = \frac{\begin{vmatrix} [pax] & [pab] & \ldots & [pam] \\ [pbx] & [pbb] & \ldots & [pbm] \\ \cdot & \cdot & \cdot & \cdot \\ [pmx] & [pmb] & \ldots & [pmm] \end{vmatrix}}{\Delta}. \qquad (9)$$

At this point we must consider a troublesome little theoretical difficulty which most writers on the present subject calmly ignore, namely, the possibility that the denominator might be 0. Fortunately this cannot happen. Let us replace the normal equations by the true equations

$$\sqrt{p_1}\,a_1 U_1 + \sqrt{p_1}\,b_1 U_2 + \dots + \sqrt{p_1}\,m_1 U_m = \sqrt{p_1}\,X_1,$$
$$\sqrt{p_2}\,a_2 U_1 + \sqrt{p_2}\,b_2 U_2 + \dots + \sqrt{p_2}\,m_2 U_m = \sqrt{p_2}\,X_2,$$
$$\cdots$$
$$\sqrt{p_n}\,a_n U_1 + \sqrt{p_n}\,b_n U_2 + \dots + \sqrt{p_n}\,m_n U_m = \sqrt{p_n}\,X_n.$$

These equations being true are certainly consistent, and the determinant of a set of m of them cannot vanish in every case unless there be not enough independent equations to determine the U's. But Δ is the sum of the squares of these m row determinants, hence it cannot vanish.

As an example of how to work these processes in practice, we take a problem in levelling :

A above $O = 573 \cdot 08$ ft. B above $A = 2 \cdot 60$ ft. D above $B = 170 \cdot 28$ ft. B above $O = 575 \cdot 27$ ft. C above $B = 167 \cdot 33$ ft. D above $C = 3 \cdot 80$ ft. D above $E = 425 \cdot 0$ ft. E above $O = 319 \cdot 91$ ft. E above $O = 319 \cdot 75$ ft.

We assume that all observations are equally trustworthy, and take the weights equal to 1. We have

Residual equations.   Normal equations.

$$u_1 = 573 \cdot 08$$
$$-u_1 + u_2 = 2 \cdot 60$$
$$-u_2 + u_4 = 170 \cdot 28$$
$$u_2 = 575 \cdot 27$$
$$-u_2 + u_3 = 167 \cdot 33$$
$$-u_3 + u_4 = 3 \cdot 80$$
$$u_4 - u_5 = 425 \cdot 0$$
$$u_5 = 319 \cdot 91$$
$$u_5 = 319 \cdot 75$$

$$2u_1 - u_2 = 570 \cdot 48$$
$$-u_1 + 4u_2 - u_3 - u_4 = 240 \cdot 26$$
$$-u_2 + 2u_3 - u_4 = 163 \cdot 53$$
$$-u_2 - u_3 + 3u_4 - u_5 = 599 \cdot 08$$
$$-u_4 + 3u_5 = 214 \cdot 66$$

Eliminate u_5 from the last two,
$$-3u_2 - 3u_3 + 8u_4 = 2011 \cdot 90.$$
Eliminate u_1 from the first two,
$$7u_2 - 2u_3 - 2u_4 = 1051.$$

Double the third,
$$-2u_2 + 4u_3 - 2u_4 = 327 \cdot 06.$$

Eliminate u_4 twice,
$$25u_2 - 11u_3 = 6215 \cdot 90,$$
$$9u_2 - 6u_3 = 723 \cdot 94.$$

Dividing by 3, $3u_2 - 2u_3 = 241 \cdot 31.$

Multiply by 6 and subtract from the equation two places above, $7u_3 + u_3 = 4768 \cdot 04.$

Double and add to the preceding,
$$17u_2 = 9777 \cdot 39,$$
$$u_2 = 575 \cdot 14.$$

Hence, finally,
$$u_1 = 572 \cdot 81, \quad u_2 = 575 \cdot 14, \quad u_3 = 742 \cdot 05, \quad u_4 = 745 \cdot 43,$$
$$u_5 = 320 \cdot 03.$$

In this particular case the coefficients in the normal equations are unusually simple, and for that reason these equations are easily solved. Unfortunately, things do not always turn out so pleasantly. We must exhibit the standard method to be followed in the usual difficult cases.

Two remarks are necessary at the outset. The first is that it is necessary to provide some check on our work as we proceed. The second that the determinant of the coefficients in the normal equations is symmetric. In consequence, if we write all that lies above the principal diagonal, we know the rest. The method we shall pursue has two characteristics. There is a check which is carried along automatically, and each time we get a new set of equations with one less variable, the determinant of the coefficients is symmetric.

We first re-write the residual equations, putting the con-

Problem.

The following observations for level were made :

A above $O = 115 \cdot 52$. B above $A = 60 \cdot 12$. B above $O = 177 \cdot 04$. C above $A = 234 \cdot 12$. C above $B = 171 \cdot 0$. E above $C = 632 \cdot 25$. E above $D = 211 \cdot 01$. D above $B = 596 \cdot 12$. D above $C = 427 \cdot 18$.

Find the various differences in level.

stant on the left and calling it r_i. Then we suppress the equality sign and put in a column of numbers $s_1, s_2, \dots s_n$, each of which is the sum of the coefficients and constants in its row; this column we call check.

$$a_1 u_1 + b_2 u_2 + m_1 u_m \ r_1 \ s_1,$$
$$a_2 u_1 + b_2 u_2 + m_2 u_m \ r_2 \ s_2,$$
$$\cdot \quad \cdot \quad \cdot \quad \cdot \quad \cdot \quad \cdot$$
$$a_n u_1 + b_n u_2 + m_n u_m \ r_n \ s_n.$$

From these we get the normal equations which we write in a similar manner, omitting whatever is below the principal diagonal,

$$[paa] u_1 + [pab] u_2 + [pac] u_3 + [pam] u_m \ [par] \ [pas] \qquad \text{I}$$
$$[pbb] u_2 + [pbc] u_3 + [pbm] u_m \ [pbr] \ [pbs] \qquad \text{II}$$
$$[pcc] u_3 + [pcm] u_m \ [pcr] \ [pcs] \qquad \text{III}$$
$$\cdot \quad \cdot \quad \cdot$$
$$[pmm] u_m [pmr] [pms]. \qquad \text{M}$$

The last column is the check, and the sum of coefficients and constants on its row. To check a row not written in full, start at the top row and add downwards in any column to the diagonal, then to the right. The sum should be the check after the last term added. We next divide the first equation by $[paa]$,

$$u_1 + \frac{[pab]}{[paa]} u_2 + \frac{[pac]}{[paa]} u_3 + \dots \frac{[pam]}{[paa]} u_m \frac{[par]}{[paa]} \frac{[pas]}{[paa]}. \qquad \text{I}'$$

We now manipulate equations I and I′ as follows. We multiply I′ by the coefficient of u_2 in I and subtract from II, we multiply I′ by the coefficient of u_3 in I and subtract from III, and so on. We get finally a new set of equations with the following properties:

A) u_1 has been eliminated, so that there are $m-1$ equations in as many unknowns.

B) The determinant of the coefficients is symmetric.

C) The term in the last column checks the others.

These equations are identical in form with those numbered I, II, ... M. We start again and eliminate another variable in the same way.

As an example, let us try the equations we had before:

$$2u_1 - u_2 \qquad\qquad -570{\cdot}48 - 569{\cdot}48 \qquad \text{I}$$

$$4u_2 - u_3 - u_4 \qquad -240{\cdot}26 - 239{\cdot}26 \qquad \text{II}$$

$$2u_3 - u_4 \qquad -163{\cdot}53 - 163{\cdot}53 \qquad \text{III}$$

$$3u_4 - u_5 - 599{\cdot}08 - 599{\cdot}08 \qquad \text{IV}$$

$$3u_5 - 214{\cdot}66 - 212{\cdot}66 \qquad \text{V}$$

$$u_1 - \tfrac{1}{2}u_2 \qquad\qquad -285{\cdot}24 - 285{\cdot}74 \qquad \text{I}'$$

$$\cdot \quad \cdot \quad \cdot \quad \cdot \quad \cdot \quad \cdot \quad \cdot \quad \cdot \quad \cdot$$

$$\tfrac{7}{2}u_2 - u_3 - u_4 \qquad -525{\cdot}50 - 524{\cdot}0 \qquad \text{I}$$

$$2u_3 - u_4 \qquad -163{\cdot}53 - 163{\cdot}53 \qquad \text{II}$$

$$3u_4 - u_5 - 599{\cdot}08 - 599{\cdot}08 \qquad \text{III}$$

$$3u_5 - 214{\cdot}66 - 212{\cdot}66 \qquad \text{IV}$$

$$u_2 - \tfrac{2}{7}u_3 - \tfrac{2}{7}u_4 - 150{\cdot}14 - 149{\cdot}71 \qquad \text{I}'$$

$$\cdot \quad \cdot \quad \cdot \quad \cdot \quad \cdot \quad \cdot \quad \cdot \quad \cdot \quad \cdot$$

$$\tfrac{12}{7}u_3 - \tfrac{9}{7}u_4 \qquad -313{\cdot}67 - 313{\cdot}24 \qquad \text{I}$$

$$\tfrac{19}{7}u_4 - u_5 - 749{\cdot}22 - 748{\cdot}79 \qquad \text{II}$$

$$3u_5 - 214{\cdot}66 - 212{\cdot}66 \qquad \text{III}$$

$$u_3 - \tfrac{3}{4}u_4 \qquad -182{\cdot}97 - 182{\cdot}72 \qquad \text{I}'$$

$$\cdot \quad \cdot \quad \cdot \quad \cdot \quad \cdot \quad \cdot \quad \cdot \quad \cdot \quad \cdot$$

$$\tfrac{7}{4}u_4 - u_5 - 984{\cdot}47 - 983{\cdot}72 \qquad \text{I}$$

$$3u_5 - 214{\cdot}66 - 212{\cdot}66 \qquad \text{II}$$

$$u_4 - \tfrac{4}{7}u_5 - 562{\cdot}55 - 562{\cdot}13 \qquad \text{I}'$$

$$\cdot \quad \cdot \quad \cdot \quad \cdot \quad \cdot \quad \cdot \quad \cdot \quad \cdot \quad \cdot$$

$$\tfrac{17}{7}u_5 = 777{\cdot}21.$$

We thus get

$$u_1 = 572{\cdot}81; \quad u_2 = 575{\cdot}14; \quad u_3 = 742{\cdot}06; \quad u_4 = 745{\cdot}43;$$
$$u_5 = 320{\cdot}03.$$

We must further caution the reader not to sit in the seat of the scornful, saying that this method turns out ever so much more cumbersome than the other. So it does in the present case, and so it often will when the coefficients in the normal equations are particularly simple. It is wiser in such cases to solve by the first method that comes to hand. But when the coefficients are complicated, the computer who waits for inspiration to find the best way to handle his equations, will probably be ill inspired. Should the reader be anxious to practice this standard proceeding on more complicated equations, he will have no difficulty in finding equations that will give him all the practice he desires.

¶ We now turn to a question of great theoretical importance, the weight to be attached to the solutions of the normal equations. This calculation is so difficult that almost all text-books omit it. The following development is the easiest that we have seen. Let us begin by replacing our incorrect residual equations by the true equations

$$a_1 U_1 + b_1 U_2 + \dots + m_1 U_m = X_1,$$
$$a_2 U_1 + b_2 U_2 + \dots + m_2 U_m = X_2,$$
$$\cdot \quad \cdot \quad \cdot \quad \cdot \quad \cdot \quad \cdot \quad \cdot \tag{10}$$
$$a_n U_1 + b_n U_2 + \dots + m_n U_m = X_n.$$

We have also a set of true equations, analogous to the normal equations

$$[paa] U_1 + [pab] U_2 + \dots + [pam] U_m = [paX],$$
$$[pba] U_1 + [pbb] U_2 + \dots + [pbm] U_m = [pbX], \tag{11}$$
$$\cdot \quad \cdot \quad \cdot \quad \cdot \quad \cdot \quad \cdot \quad \cdot \quad \cdot$$
$$[pma] U_1 + [pmb] U_2 + \dots + [pmm] U_m = [pmX].$$

Corresponding to the true errors ξ_i of the observed quantities, we shall have true errors of the quantities to be computed, namely,
$$\eta_i = u_i - U_i. \tag{12}$$

It must be noted that there are n ξ's but only m η's. From (11) and (9)

$$[paa] \eta_1 + [pab] \eta_2 + \dots + [pam] \eta_m = [pa\xi],$$
$$[pba] \eta_1 + [pbb] \eta_2 + \dots + [pbm] \eta_m = [pb\xi],$$
$$\cdot \quad \cdot \quad \cdot \quad \cdot \quad \cdot \quad \cdot \quad \cdot \quad \cdot \tag{13}$$
$$[pma] \eta_1 + [pmb] \eta_2 + \dots + [pmm] \eta_m = [pm\xi];$$

the solutions are

$$\eta_1 = \frac{[pa\xi]\dfrac{\partial \Delta}{\partial [paa]} + [pb\xi]\dfrac{\partial \Delta}{\partial [pba]} + \dots + [pm\xi]\dfrac{\partial \Delta}{\partial [pma]}}{\Delta}. \tag{14}$$

$$\eta_2 = \frac{[pa\xi]\frac{\partial \Delta}{\partial [pab]} + [pb\xi]\frac{\partial \Delta}{\partial [pbb]} + \dots + [pm\xi]\frac{\partial \Delta}{\partial |pmb]}}{\Delta}. \quad (15)$$

We have further, by the elementary theory of determinants,

$$1 = \frac{[paa]\frac{\partial \Delta}{\partial [paa]} + [pba]\frac{\partial \Delta}{\partial [pba]} + \dots + [pma]\frac{\partial \Delta}{\partial [pma]}}{\Delta}. \quad (16)$$

$$0 = \frac{[pak]\frac{\partial \Delta}{\partial [paa]} + [pbk]\frac{\partial \Delta}{\partial [pba]} + \dots + [pmk]\frac{\partial \Delta}{\partial |pma]}}{\Delta} \, a \neq k. \quad (17)$$

$$1 = \frac{[pab]\frac{\partial \Delta}{\partial [pab]} + [pbb]\frac{\partial \Delta}{\partial [pbb]} + \dots + [pmb]\frac{\partial \Delta}{\partial [pmb]}}{\Delta}. \quad (18)$$

$$0 = \frac{[pak]\frac{\partial \Delta}{\partial [pab]} + [pbk]\frac{\partial \Delta}{\partial [pbb]} + \dots + [pmk]\frac{\partial \Delta}{\partial |pbm]}}{\Delta} \, b \neq k. \quad (19)$$

We have assumed throughout that we knew the weights of our observations, but not the corresponding precisions, whose squares are proportional to them,

$$p_i = \rho \, 2 \, k_i^2. \quad (20)$$

Here ρ is a multiplier to be determined later. The quantities η_i are linear homogeneous combinations of the true errors ξ_i, hence, by VII 12] they follow the Gaussian exponential law. We must find their precisions, K_i. This we get by that same theorem, namely,

$$\frac{1}{2 K_1^2} = \frac{\sum_j p_j^2 \left[a_j \frac{\partial \Delta}{\partial [paa]} + b_j \frac{\partial \Delta}{\partial [pba]} + \dots + m_j \frac{\partial \Delta}{\partial [pma]} \right]^2 \frac{1}{2 k_j^2}}{\Delta^2},$$

$$= \rho \frac{[paa]\left(\frac{\partial \Delta}{\partial [paa]}\right)^2 + [pbb]\left(\frac{\partial \Delta}{\partial [pba]}\right)^2 + 2 [pab]\frac{\partial \Delta}{\partial |paa]}\frac{\partial \Delta}{\partial [pba]} + \dots}{\Delta^2}$$

If we multiply equation (16) by $\dfrac{\partial \Delta}{\partial [paa]}$, and each equation (17) by $\dfrac{\partial \Delta}{\partial [pak]}$ and add, we find

$$\frac{1}{2\,K_i{}^2} = \frac{\rho\,\Delta\,\dfrac{\partial \Delta}{\partial [paa]}}{\Delta^2} = \rho\,\frac{\partial \log \Delta}{\partial [paa]}. \qquad (21)$$

Another method of finding this would have been to find the mean value of $\eta_1{}^2$. If we seek the mean value of $\eta_1 \eta_2$ we shall find, using equations (16)–(19),

Mean value $\qquad \eta_1 \eta_2 = \rho\,\dfrac{\partial \log \Delta}{\partial [pab]}. \qquad (22)$

Lastly, we find similarly
Mean value

$$\eta_1 \xi_1 = \rho \left[a_1 \frac{\partial \log \Delta}{\partial [paa]} + b_1 \frac{\partial \log \Delta}{\partial [pba]} + \dots + m_1 \frac{\partial \log \Delta}{\partial [pma]} \right]. \qquad (23)$$

Why trouble about these last mean values? They are needful to determine ρ. In the residual equations (6) let us put the solutions of the normal equation and add corrections δ_i on the right so that

$$a_i u_1 + b_i u_2 + \dots + m_i u_m = X_i + \delta_i.$$

We have also

$$a_i\,U_1 + b_i\,U_2 + \dots + m_i\,U_m = X_i.$$

Subtracting $\quad a_i \eta_1 + b_i \eta_2 + \dots + m_i \eta_m - \xi_i = \delta_i.$

Let us square each of these equations, multiply by the corresponding p_i, and take the mean value of the sums, in view of (16)–(23).

The expression $[p\delta\delta]$, which is an observed quantity, is equal to its own mean value. The equivalent expression on the left contains only terms of the types (21), (22), and (23):

$$[p\delta\delta] \equiv \sum_{i=1}^{i=n} p_i \delta_i{}^2 = (n-m)\,\rho. \qquad (24)$$

Summing up, we get the final expression

$$\frac{1}{2\,K_1^{\,2}} = \frac{\partial \log \Delta}{\partial\,[paa]}\frac{[p\delta\delta]}{(n-m)}\,;\quad \frac{1}{2\,K_2^{\,2}} = \frac{\partial \log \Delta}{\partial\,[pbb]}\frac{[p\delta\delta]}{(n-m)}\,. \qquad (25)$$

Probable error of $\quad u_1 = 0{\cdot}6745 \left(\dfrac{\partial \log \Delta}{\partial\,[paa]}\dfrac{[p\delta\delta]}{(n-m)}\right)^{\frac{1}{2}}. \qquad (26)$

It is clear that a similar type of calculation could be applied in the more general case (5).

§ 2. Conditioned Observations.

It sometimes happens that the quantities which we seek are not independent, but are connected by certain identical relations. The problem is to find the best values for them subject to these restrictions. To begin with the most general case, suppose that our quantities $u_1,\ u_2,\ \dots\ u_m$ are connected by the relation

$$\phi_1(u_1, u_2, \dots u_m)$$
$$= \phi_2(u_1, u_2, \dots u_m) = \dots \phi_l(u_1, u_2, \dots u_m) = 0. \qquad (27)$$

We assume that Assumption 2] may be extended to these functions also, so that we may write these equations

$$\phi_1(\omega_1 \dots \omega_m) + \sum_i \frac{\partial \phi_1}{\partial \omega_i}\epsilon_i = \dots \phi_l(\omega_1 \dots \omega_m) + \sum_i \frac{\partial \phi_l}{\partial \omega_i}\epsilon_i = 0. \qquad (28)$$

We have now a problem in relative minima, namely, to minimize

$$\sum_{i=1}^{i=n} p_i \left[f_i(\omega_1 \dots \omega_m) - x_i + \sum_j \frac{\partial f_i}{\partial a_j}\epsilon_j \right]^2$$
$$- \sum_{k=1}^{k=l} r_k \left[\phi_k(\omega_1 \dots \omega_m) + \sum_j \frac{\partial \phi_k}{\partial \omega_j}\epsilon_j \right]. \qquad (29)$$

The m partial derivatives of this, and the l equations (28) will be sufficient to determine the corrections ϵ_j and the multipliers r_k.

A simple case arising frequently in practice is that where we observe directly the quantities which we desire to calculate, and where there is but one identical relation.   We have here a simpler form for (29), namely

$$\sum_{i=1}^{i=m} p_i \epsilon_i^2 - r \left[\phi\,(\omega_1 \ldots \omega_m) + \sum_j \frac{\partial \phi}{\partial \omega_j}\, \epsilon_j \right]. \tag{30}$$

$$2\,p_j \epsilon_j = r \frac{\partial \phi}{\partial \omega_j},$$

$$\phi + \sum_j \frac{r}{2} \frac{1}{p_j} \left(\frac{\partial \phi}{\partial \omega_j}\right)^2 = 0,$$

$$\epsilon_i = \frac{-\dfrac{\phi}{p_i} \dfrac{\partial \phi}{\partial \omega_i}}{\sum_j \dfrac{1}{p_j} \left(\dfrac{\partial \phi}{\partial \omega_j}\right)^2} \tag{31}$$

Example 1] *The observed values of the angles of a triangle are θ_1, θ_2, θ_3; what are the best values?*

$$\phi = \theta_1 + \theta_2 + \theta_3 - \pi,$$
$$u_i = \theta_i - \tfrac{1}{3}(\theta_1 + \theta_2 + \theta_3 - \pi).$$

Example 2] *The observed sides of a right triangle are a, b, c; what are the best values?*

$$\phi = a^2 + b^2 - c^2,$$

$$u_1 = a \left[1 - \frac{a^2 + b^2 - c^2}{2\,(a^2 + b^2 + c^2)} \right], \quad u_2 = b \left[1 - \frac{a^2 + b^2 - c^2}{2\,(a^2 + b^2 + c^2)} \right],$$

$$u_3 = c \left[1 + \frac{a^2 + b^2 - c^2}{2\,(a^2 + b^2 + c^2)} \right].$$

§ 3.   Curve Fitting.

An interesting application of the method of least squares is to the problem of finding a curve of given type which will best represent a given function.   The problem, stated in this bald fashion, is evidently indeterminate, until we define the term *best represent* by means of some postulates.   Still,

---

Problem.

The sides of a triangle of homogeneous material are measured, and the area is determined by weight.   Find the best values for the sides.

there are several standard artifices which can be fairly well justified.

Suppose, first, that we wish to find a power series development for a given function $\phi(x)$. The reader might be inclined to answer immediately that this is a very old problem indeed; we have merely to take Maclaurin's series. The Maclaurin series is, indeed, absolutely correct if *all the terms be included*. This can never be done in practice. When we take merely a finite number of terms, the Maclaurin series has merely the property that it is the best possible representation of the function very near the origin, i.e. that it takes the same value there as does the function, and that if $n+1$ terms be taken the first n derivatives take the same value at the origin, whether we differentiate the function or the series. This does not by any means show that we could not perhaps find another polynomial of the same degree which gave a better average representation of the function throughout a certain interval. Let us write the general polynomial of degree n

$$a_0 + a_1 x + a_2 x^2 + \ldots + a_n x^n.$$

How shall we determine the coefficients so that this shall best represent a given function throughout an interval? The most obvious way would be to divide the interval into n equal parts and determine the a's so that at each of the $n+1$ bounding points the function and the polynomial had the same values. This would be the method of interpolation.

A little reflection will now lead us to the idea that it is unwise to limit ourselves to $n+1$ points. Why not take a good many more points, so that the number of equations will be larger than that of unknowns, and solve by the methods developed in the present chapter? Let us take the points $x_0, x_1, \ldots x_n$ equally spaced by the interval Δx.

The residual equations are

$$a_0 + a_1 x_0 + a_2 x_0^2 + \ldots + a_n x_0^n = \phi(x_0),$$
$$a_0 + a_1 x_1 + a_2 x_1^2 + \ldots + a_n x_1^n = \phi(x_1),$$
$$\cdot \quad \cdot \quad \cdot$$
$$a_0 + a_1 x_n + a_2 x_n^2 + \ldots + a_n x_n^n = \phi(x_n).$$

The normal equations are

$$a_0 \sum_i 1 + \quad a_1 \sum_i x_i \quad + \ldots + \ a_n \sum_i x_i{}^n \ = \sum_i \phi(x_i),$$

$$a_0 \sum_i x_i + \quad a_1 \sum_i x_i{}^2 \quad + \ldots + a_n \sum_i x_i{}^{n+1} = \sum_i x_i \phi(x_i),$$

$$\bullet \quad \bullet \quad \bullet \tag{32}$$

$$a_0 \sum_i x_i{}^n + a_1 \sum_i x_i{}^{n+1} + \ldots + \ a_n \sum_i x_i{}^{2n} = \sum_i x_i{}^n \phi(x_i).$$

The next step is obvious. Why not keep x_0 and x_n fixed, multiply each of these equations by Δx and take the limit as $\Delta x \rightarrow 0$?

$$a_0 \int_{x_0}^{x_n} dx + \quad a_1 \int_{x_0}^{x_n} x\, dx \quad + \ldots + \ a_n \int_{x_0}^{x_n} x^n dx \ = \int_{x_0}^{x_n} \phi(x)\, dx,$$

$$a_0 \int_{x_0}^{x_n} x\, dx + \quad a_1 \int_{x_0}^{x_n} x^2 dx \quad + \ldots + a_n \int_{x_0}^{x_n} x^{n+1} dx = \int_{x_0}^{x_n} x\, \phi(x)\, dx,$$

$$\bullet \quad \bullet \quad \bullet \tag{33}$$

$$a_0 \int_{x_0}^{x_n} x^n dx + a_1 \int_{x_0}^{x_n} x^{n+1} dx + \ldots + \ a_n \int_{x_0}^{x_n} x^{2n} dx = \int_{x_0}^{x_n} x^n \phi(x)\, dx.$$

Note that these equations determine $a_0, a_1, \ldots a_n$ so that

$$\int_{x_0}^{x_n} [a_0 + a_1 x + \ldots + a_n x^n - \phi(x)]^2\, dx \text{ is a minimum.}$$

Example] *Find the value for* $\sin x$ *in the interval* $-\dfrac{\pi}{2}$ *to* $\dfrac{\pi}{2}$

in the form of a polynomial

$$a_0 + a_1 x + a_2 x^2 + a_3 x^3 + a_4 x^4.$$

To begin with, it is well to have this polynomial vanish with x. Moreover, we should like it, like $\sin x$, to be an odd function. Hence we write

$$a_1 x + a_3 x^3 = \sin x.$$

$$\int_0^{\frac{\pi}{2}} a_1 x^2 dx + \int_0^{\frac{\pi}{2}} a_3 x^4 dx = \int_0^{\frac{\pi}{2}} x \sin x\, dx,$$

$$\int_0^{\frac{\pi}{2}} a_1 x^4 dx + \int_0^{\frac{\pi}{2}} a_3 x^6 dx = \int_0^{\frac{\pi}{2}} x^3 \sin x\, dx,$$

$$\left(\frac{\pi}{2}\right)^3 \frac{a_1}{3} + \left(\frac{\pi}{2}\right)^5 \frac{a_3}{5} = 1,$$

$$\left(\frac{\pi}{2}\right)^5 \frac{a_1}{5} + \left(\frac{\pi}{2}\right)^7 \frac{a_3}{7} = 3\left[\left(\frac{\pi}{2}\right)^2 - 2\right],$$

$$a_1 + \left(\frac{\pi}{2}\right)^2 \frac{3}{5} a_3 = 3\left(\frac{2}{\pi}\right)^3,$$

$$\left(\frac{\pi}{2}\right)^7 \frac{4}{7 \cdot 5^2} a_3 = \frac{3\pi^2}{5} - 6,$$

$$a_3 = -0 \cdot 1450,$$

$$a_1 = 0 \cdot 9888.$$

In the usual Maclaurin series

$$a_3 = -0 \cdot 1667 \quad a_1 = 1.$$

For $x = \frac{\pi}{2}$, the present series gives

$$\sin \frac{\pi}{2} = 0 \cdot 991.$$

Two terms of Maclaurin's series will give

$$\sin \frac{\pi}{2} = 0 \cdot 924.$$

There frequently arise cases where we do not wish to express a given function in power series, but in some other shape. Suppose, for instance, that we wanted a trigonometric series for the interval from $-\pi$ to $+\pi$ of the form

$$a_0 + a_1 \cos x + a_2 \cos 2x + a_3 \cos 3x + \dots$$
$$+ b_1 \sin x + b_2 \sin 2x + b_3 \sin 3x + \dots.$$

We replace our equations (33) by

$$\int_{-\pi}^{\pi} \left[\sum_k a_k \cos kx + b_k \sin kx\right] dx = \int_{-\pi}^{\pi} \phi(x)\, dx.$$

$$\int_{-\pi}^{\pi} \cos lx \left[\sum_k a_k \cos kx + b_k \sin kx\right] dx = \int_{-\pi}^{\pi} \cos lx\, \phi(x)\, dx,$$

$$\int_{-\pi}^{\pi} \sin mx \left[\sum_k a_k \cos kx + b_k \sin kx\right] dx = \int_{-\pi}^{\pi} \sin mx\, \phi(x)\, dx.$$

Now $\displaystyle\int_{-\pi}^{\pi} \sin mx \sin kx\, dx = 0.$ $m \neq k,$

$$\int_{-\pi}^{\pi} \sin kx \cos lx\, dx = 0,$$

$$\int_{-\pi}^{\pi} \cos kx \cos lx\, dx = 0.$$ $l \neq k,$

$$\int_{-\pi}^{\pi} \sin^2 kx\, dx = \pi.$$ $k \neq 0,$

$$\int_{-\pi}^{\pi} \cos^2 kx\, dx = \pi.$$ $k \neq 0,$

$$a_0 = \frac{1}{2\pi} \int_{-\pi}^{\pi} \phi(x)\, dx,$$

$$a_k = \frac{1}{\pi} \int_{-\pi}^{\pi} \cos kx\, \phi(x)\, dx,$$

$$b_k = \frac{1}{\pi} \int_{-\pi}^{\pi} \sin kx\, \phi(x)\, dx.$$

All this, however, is nothing in the world but the usual determination for the coefficients in a Fourier series, so that we reach the interesting result that whereas a finite number of terms of a Maclaurin series does not give the best polynomial development of a given function over any interval, any number of terms of the Fourier series will give, for the interval $-\pi$ to π, the best development involving just those terms.

¶ Let us take a still more general case, and try to represent ϕ by a function of known type and undetermined coefficients

$$f(x, a_0, a_1, \ldots a_n).$$

Following our precedent in the case of a polynomial where we had an infinite number of points, we should like to minimize

$$\int_{x_0}^{x_N} (f - \phi)^2\, dx.$$

Problem.

Calculate $\cos x$ in the same way.

To do this, we equate to 0 the partial derivatives of this integral with regard to the a's, and throw in the supplementary condition that the area under the two curves should be the same. We get

$$\int_{x_1}^{x_N} f(x)\, dx = \int_{x_1}^{x_N} \phi(x)\, dx,$$

$$\int_{x_1}^{x_N} \frac{\partial f}{\partial a_i} f(x)\, dx = \int_{x_1}^{x_N} \frac{\partial f}{\partial a_i} \phi(x)\, dx. \tag{34}$$

The trouble here is the very prosaic one that, except when f is a polynomial, the eliminations are altogether unmanageable. We must seek another method.* If we look closely at the equations (33) and inquire into their geometrical meaning, we find it to be this. The first $n+1$ moments of the areas under the curve ϕ and under the polynomial, about the y axis, are equal to one another. This suggests the idea that, in the general case, we should find the coefficients by generalizing the process of equating these moments. We thus replace the equations (34) by

$$\int_{x_0}^{x_N} f(x)\, dx = \int_{x_0}^{x_N} \phi(x)\, dx,$$

$$\int_{x_0}^{x_N} x^k f(x)\, dx = \int_{x_0}^{x_N} x^k \phi(x)\, dx. \tag{35}$$

These equations will usually be easier to handle in practice. It is to be noted also that we pass from (34) to (35) by expanding f in Maclaurin's series.

¶ The problem in practice frequently assumes a different form, in that the function ϕ is not given, merely the $n+1$ pairs of points $(x_0\, y_0), (x_1\, y_1) \ldots (x_n\, y_n)$. Let us imagine that these are joined by a broken line which must replace the curve ϕ. We are faced with the laborious mathematical problem of calculating the moments about the y axis of a series of trapezoids standing on the x axis. For simplicity

---

* Cf. Karl Pearson, ' On the Systematic Fitting of Curves ', *Biometrika*, vol. i, 1901-2, and vol. ii, 1902-3.

we shall assume that the intervals on the x axis are all equal, so that
$$x_{k+1} - x_k = b,$$
$$x_k = x_0 + kb.$$

For the upper (or lower) side of the $(k+1)$th trapezoid
$$y = y_k + \frac{(y_{k+1} - y_k)}{b}(x - x_k).$$

The mth moment of this trapezoid is

$$\int_{x_k}^{x_k+b} \left[y_k + \frac{(y_{k+1}-y_k)}{b}(x-x_k) \right] x^m \, dx$$

$$= \frac{1}{b} \left[y_k x^{m+1} \left(\frac{x_k+b}{m+1} - \frac{x}{m+2} \right) + y_{k+1} x^{m+1} \left(\frac{x}{m+2} - \frac{x_k}{m+1} \right) \right]_{x_k}^{x_k+b}$$

$$= \frac{1}{b(m+1)(m+2)} \{ y_k \left[(x_k+b)^{m+2} - x_k{}^{m+2} - b(m+2)x_k{}^{m+1} \right]$$
$$+ y_{k+1} \left[x_k{}^{m+2} - (x_k+b)^{m+2} + b(m+2)(x_k+b)^{m+1} \right] \}.$$

We get the total coefficient of y_k by adding the first part of this to the last of the preceding term, namely

$$\frac{1}{b(m+1)(m+2)} \left[(x_k+b)^{m+2} + (x_k-b)^{m+2} - 2x_k{}^{m+2} \right]$$

$$= 2b \left[\frac{x_k{}^m}{2!} + \frac{m(m-1)}{4!} x_k{}^{m-2} b^2 \right.$$
$$\left. + \frac{m(m-1)(m-2)(m-3)}{6!} x_k{}^{m-4} b^4 \ldots \right].$$

There remain the end y's, each of which appears in only one term. The total coefficient of y_0 is

$$\frac{1}{b(m+1)(m+2)} \left[(x_0+b)^{m+2} - x_0{}^{m+2} - b(m+2)x_0{}^{m+1} \right]$$

$$= 2b \left[\frac{x_0{}^m}{2!} + \frac{m(m-1)}{4!} x_0{}^{m-2} b^2 \right.$$
$$\left. + \frac{m(m-1)(m-2)(m-3)}{6!} x_0{}^{m-4} b^4 + \ldots \right]$$

$$- \frac{b}{(m+1)(m+2)} \left[(x_0-b)^{m+2} - x_0{}^{m+2} + (m+2)x_0{}^{m+1} b \right].$$

The total coefficient of y_n is

$$\frac{1}{b(m+1)(m+2)}\left[(x_n-b)^{m+2}-x_n^{m+2}+b(m+2)x_n^{m+1}\right]$$

$$= 2b\left[\frac{x_n^m}{2!} + \frac{m(m-1)}{4!}x_n^{m-2}b^2\right.$$

$$\left. + \frac{m(m-1)(m-2)(m-3)}{6!}x_n^{m-4}b^4 + \cdots\right]$$

$$- \frac{b}{(m+1)(m+2)}\left[(x_n+b)^{m+2}-x_n^{m+2}-(m+2)x_n^{m+1}b\right].$$

Lastly, if we put

$$s_r = \frac{1}{r!}\sum_{k=0}^{k=n}x_k^r y_k.$$

the total mth moment is

$$m!\quad 2b\left[\frac{1}{2!}s_m + \frac{1}{4!}s_{m-2}b^2 + \frac{1}{6!}s_{m-4}b^4 + \cdots\right]$$

$$- \frac{b}{(m+1)(m+2)}\left\{y_0\left[(x_0-b)^{m+2}-x_0^{m+2}+(m+2)x_0^{m+1}b\right]\right.$$

$$\left. + y_n\left[(x_n+b)^{m+2}-x_n^{m+2}-(m+2)x_n^{m+1}b\right]\right\}. \qquad (36)$$

This unlovely formula probably represents the simplest form attainable. It is visibly simpler in the case where

$$y_0 = y_n = 0.$$

The whole subject of curve fitting leads us naturally to a topic which has attained a large development, through the efforts of the large number of writers · on mathematical statistics. In England Karl Pearson has founded a whole school, and on the Continent the Scandinavians have shown themselves particularly skilful in developing the theory. A thorough discussion of all of these new methods will be found in Arne Fisher's *Mathematical Theory of Probabilities* *

* 2nd edition, New York, 1922, Parts II and III.

CHAPTER X

THE STATISTICAL THEORY OF GASES

§ 1. General Properties of Perfect Gases

IN Chapter V, which dealt with geometrical probability, we excused ourselves for lingering over such an elegant trifle on the ground of the connexion with the kinetic theory of gas, and the methods of statistical mechanics. It is now time to give a very summary introduction to these extended topics.* We shall content ourselves with giving the method for deriving Maxwell's expression for normal distribution, and critical comments thereon; it is not our business to deduce physical properties.

A gas, for our present purposes, is conceived as a very large agglomeration of very small molecules in rapid motion. We consider the case of a gas confined in some vessel, and, *as a first approximation*, make the following assumptions:

I) The vessel is of finite volume, with perfectly elastic walls which are surfaces given by differentiable equations.

II) All gas molecules are smooth, incompressible, perfectly elastic spheres of uniform diameter σ and mass, acting under the influence of no forces.

It is evident that, under Newton's second law, each molecule will be in a state of rectilinear motion at uniform velocity, or at rest, except when its course is altered by a collision with a boundary wall or with another molecule. We are not concerned with the actual shell of the vessel, but

---

* In the present chapter I have leaned very heavily on Castelnuovo, loc. cit., ch. xiii.   For a more detailed study see Jeans, *Dynamical Theory of Gases*, 3rd edition, Cambridge, 1921, chs. ii–iv.

with a surface parallel thereto, a radius distance inside, for this is the effective limit for the centre of a molecule; when we speak of the boundary, we mean this latter surface. The laws of collision will then be the following:

A) When two spheres collide, the motion of their centre of gravity is unaltered, and the vector velocity of one centre with regard to the other is replaced by its reflection in the common tangent plane at the point of impact.

B) If the centre of a sphere meet a boundary, the vector velocity after impact is the reflection of the vector velocity before impact, in the tangent plane to the boundary at that point.

It is possible that some molecules will strike exactly into cracks between two parts of the surface, which amounts to a molecule centre striking a double curve of the boundary, but this case will occur an infinitesimal number of times, and may be overlooked.

Since the rotations of the spheres are of no importance, the essential point to be borne in mind is that the total vis viva of the system will be constant. The phenomena which we call 'temperature' and 'pressure' depend upon molecular velocities; it is with them that we shall be specially occupied.

Let the total number of molecules be n. The coordinates of the centre of the ith molecule shall be $x_i y_i z_i$, the components of its velocity $u_i v_i w_i$. Since the motion is un-accelerated, a knowledge at any instant of the $6n$ quantities $x_1 y_1 z_1 \ldots x_n y_n z_n u_1 v_1 w_1 \ldots u_n v_n w_n$ will give a complete account of the state of the gas. Moreover, this knowledge will, theoretically, serve to predict the exact state at any future instant; in other words, the whole history is determined by the initial conditions of situation and velocity.

§ 2.　Representation in Hyperspace.

There is a great saving in words, in dealing with the gas problem, if we use the language, or jargon, of the geometry of many dimensions. The reader must not allow himself to be unduly alarmed by this proceeding. If an object be determined by N independent variables, we say that each of its determinations corresponds to *a point in a space of N dimensions*. When the variables are connected by one or more equations, we say that we have a *variety* in the original space, the number of dimensions of the variety being that of the space, less the number of independent equations. A variety of $N-1$ dimensions is called a *hypersurface*, if the equation be linear we call it a *hyperplane*. When we speak of the *distance* of two points, we mean the expression obtained by analogy from the expression for the distance of two points in three dimensional space in terms of their rectangular cartesian coordinates. The general laws for combining distances are the same no matter how many the dimensions.

We start with a space of $6n$ dimensions where a point has the coordinates $x_1 y_1 z_1 \ldots x_n y_n z_n u_1 v_1 w_1 \ldots u_n v_n w_n$. Such a point will represent the state of a gas of n molecules. As the gas changes with time, so does the point move in the given space. What is the nature of its path? Since each molecule is moving at a uniform velocity along a straight path we have

$$
\begin{aligned}
x_i &= \bar{x}_i + t\bar{u}_i & u_i &= \bar{u}_i, \\
y_i &= \bar{y}_i + t\bar{v}_i & v_i &= \bar{v}_i, \\
z_i &= \bar{z}_i + t\bar{w}_i & w_i &= \bar{w}_i.
\end{aligned} \tag{1}
$$

The representing point is moving along, at uniform velocity, on a path parallel to the flat variety of $3n$ dimensions obtained by giving the last three coordinates fixed values. There will be a sharp break in this path corresponding to each collision in the gas. To understand these, we must first note that in the space of $6n$ dimensions there are certain limiting hypersurfaces which the representing point cannot pass. The centre of no molecule can pass the boundary, and the distance between two centres can never be less than σ, hence

$$
f(x_i y_i z_i) \geqq 0 \quad \phi(x_i y_i z_i) \geqq 0 \ldots i = 1, 2, \ldots n,
$$
$$
(x_j - x_k)^2 + (y_j - y_k)^2 + (z_j - z_k)^2 - \sigma^2 \geqq 0 \ \ j, k = 1, \ldots n. \tag{2}
$$

Moreover, the vis viva of the system has the constant value E, hence

$$\sum_{i=1}^{i=n} (u_i^2 + v_i^2 + w_i^2) - E = 0. \tag{3}$$

The representing point in $6n$ dimensions must thus remain on the hypersurface (3) moving along a straight line. At the moment of a collision in the gas it takes a sharp jump along one of the hypersurfaces (2).

We get a clearer idea by using a slightly simpler representation, namely, taking the space of $3n$ dimensions, where a point has the coordinates $x_1 y_1 z_1 \ldots x_n y_n z_n$. The $3n$ quantities $u_1 v_1 w_1 \ldots u\ v_n w_n$ are the components of the velocity of this point, the path will be rectilinear, and the velocity uniform until the moment when there is a collision in the gas. If a molecule collide with the boundary $f = 0$ we have the following relation between the components of velocity before and after:

$$u_i' = - \frac{2\left[u_i \frac{\partial f}{\partial x_i} + v_i \frac{\partial f}{\partial y_i} + w_i \frac{\partial f}{\partial z_i} \right] \frac{\partial f}{\partial x_i}}{\left[\left(\frac{\partial f}{\partial x_i} \right)^2 + \left(\frac{\partial f}{\partial y_i} \right)^2 + \left(\frac{\partial f}{\partial z_i} \right)^2 \right]} + u_i. \tag{4}$$

There will be similar equations for v_i' and w_i'. On the other hand, if the molecules $x_j y_j z_j$ and $x_k y_k z_k$ collide, we have

$$x_k = x_j + l\sigma \qquad y_k = y_j + m\sigma \qquad z_k = z_j + n\sigma,$$
$$b^2 + m^2 + n^2 = 1,$$
$$u_j' + u_k' = u_j + u_k ; \ v_j' + v_k' = v_j + v_k; \ w_j' + w_k' = w_j + w_k,$$
$$u_j' - u_k' = -2l\left[l(u_j - u_k) + m(v_j - v_k) + n(w_j - w_k) \right] + u_j - u_k,$$
$$u_j' = -l\left[l(u_j - u_k) + m(v_j - v_k) + n(w_j - w_k) \right] + u_j,$$
$$u_k' = l\left[l(u_j - u_k) + m(v_j - v_k) + n(w_j - w_k) \right] + u_k. \tag{5}$$

These equations have a simple meaning. Let us suppose that the laws of elastic bodies are the same in the space of $3n$ dimensions as they are in our space, i.e. when an elastic point encounters a hypersurface, it bounds off with a vector velocity which is the reflection in the tangent hyperplane of the previous vector velocity. The interpretation of equations (4) and (5) is then as follows : *

Theorem 1] *If n gas molecules be represented by a single point in a space of n dimensions, the alterations of the gas are perfectly represented by the motion of this point as it traces a straight line with the uniform velocity given by* (1) *or rebounds elastically from one of the hypersurfaces given by* (2), *the square of its velocity being constantly given by* (3).

There is another conclusion of a more complicated nature which can be drawn from equations (4) and (5). We have

$$\left[\frac{\partial\,(u_i{}'v_i{}'w_i{}')}{\partial\,(u_i v_i w_i)}\right]^2 = \left[\frac{\partial\,(u_j{}'v_j{}'w_j{}'u_k{}'v_k{}'w_k{}')}{\partial\,(u_j v_j w_j u_k v_k w_k)}\right]^2 = 1,$$

so that

$$\frac{\partial\,(x_1{}'y_1{}'z_1{}' \ldots x_n{}'y_n{}'z_n{}'u_1{}'v_1{}'w_1{}' \ldots u_n{}'v_n{}'w_n{}')}{\partial\,(x_1 y_1 z_1 \ldots x^n y_n z_n u_1 v_1 w_1 \ldots u_n v_n w_n)} = \pm 1.$$

If, then, we express our volume element in $6n$ dimensions as we do in 3 dimensions, we see that the transformations (4) and (5) are of a sort to preserve volumes. Suppose that the probability that a point in this space should lie close to an assigned position be proportional to a quantity differing by an infinitesimal of higher order from

$$dx_1 dy_1 dz_1 \ldots dx_n dy_n dz_n \ldots du_1 dv_1 dw_1 \ldots du_n dv_n dw_n,$$

the element of volume, then after any time there is an equal probability that it will lie equally near to the transformed position. This leads to:

Assumption 1] *The probability that a gas should have properties analytically expressible in terms of the $6n$ coordinates is proportional to the volume of that portion of the space of $6n$ dimensions in which the representing point must then lie.*

Our work in geometrical probability shows how arbitrary this assumption is, for it amounts to assuming that

$$x_1 y_1 z_1 \ldots u_n v_n w_n$$

* Cf. Borel, 'Sur les principes de la théorie cinétique du gaz', *Annales de. l'École Normale,* Series 2, vol. xxvi, 1904, p. 24.

are the natural independent variables, and that the element of volume is given by the differential expression above. From this assumption, and from the proof that the large Jacobian written above is equal to 1, we deduce:

Theorem 2] *If a set of gas molecules be such that at a time t_1 there is a certain probability that it will possess a property of the type mentioned in Assumption 1] then there is an equal probability that at the time t_2 it will possess the transformed property.*

It is scarcely necessary to warn the reader that the word 'probability' as used in this chapter must be understood in the statistical sense that we defined in Ch. I and have consistently used throughout the present work.

§ 3.   First Deduction of Maxwell's Law.

Our Theorem 2] tells us that the probability that a gas should have certain property is proportional to the volume of a certain region in the space of $6n$ dimensions. If, however, this property have to do merely with the vector velocities of the particles, as the only limitation on these is the equation (3), we may confine ourselves to a representation in a space of $3n$ dimensions only, where the coordinates are

$$u_1 v_1 w_1 \ldots u_n v \ w_n.$$

Now, by the form of Assumption 1) the probability that a certain gas should have a certain property is proportional to the volume of a certain region in this space of $3n$ dimensions, not proportional to the hyper-area cut by the region from the hyper-sphere (3).   The element of volume is

$$du_1 dv_1 dw_1 \ldots du_n dv_n dw_n = (du_1 dv_1 dw_1) \ldots (du_n dv_n dw_n),$$

and is the product of n different volume elements in the three-dimensional space u, v, w.   Hence the probability sought is proportional to the product of n different volumes in three-dimensional space.   These n points we shall call 'velocity points'.

Suppose next that the three-dimensional velocity space u, v, w is divided into a very large number v of cells of equal volume V. When we say a large number, we mean that, as a first approximation, the coordinates of all points in one cell may be taken as identical. We shall assume, however, that n is so large that it is well above ν. The probability that the first a_1 points shall be in the first cell, the second a_2 in the second, the last a_ν in the last is proportional to

$$V^{a_1} \times V^{a_2} \times \ldots \times V^{a_\nu},$$

and since we have

$$a_1 + a_2 + \ldots + a_\nu = n \tag{6}$$

this is V^n.

On the other hand, the probability that *some* a_1 lie in the first cell, *some* a_2 in the second, *some* a_ν in the last is proportional to this number multiplied by the number of ways in which we can divide n objects into distinguishable groups of $a_1, a_2, \ldots a_\nu$ respectively. This is given by Ch. II (3), so that our probability is proportional to

$$P = \frac{n!\, V^n}{a_1!\, a_2!\, \ldots a_\nu!}. \tag{7}$$

Our fundamental question is to find a set of values

$$u_1 v_1 w_1 \ldots u_n v_n w_n$$

subject to (3), which will make this a maximum.

Since P is a maximum with its logarithm, we must maximize

$$\log(n!) - \log(a_1!) - \log(a_2!) - \ldots - \log(a_\nu!).$$

By Stirling's formula

$$\log(r!) = (r + \tfrac{1}{2}) \log r - r + \tfrac{1}{2} \log 2\pi.$$

Hence, we must minimize

$$\sum_{i=1}^{i=\nu} (a_i + \tfrac{1}{2}) \log a_i.$$

Assuming all of the a_i's are large, it will suffice to minimize

$$\sum_{i=1}^{i=\nu} a_i \log a_i,$$

$$\sum_{i=1}^{i=\nu} a_i = n, \quad \sum_{i=1}^{i=\nu} a_i (u_i^2 + v_i^2 + w_i^2) = E.$$

Strictly speaking, the quantities a_i are integers, but we may obtain a sufficiently accurate answer by treating them as if they were capable of continuous variation, and looking for a relative minimum. We have thus

$$\frac{\partial}{\partial a_l}\Big[\sum_{i=1}^{i=\nu} a_i\{\log a_i - r(u_i^2 + v_i^2 + w_i^2) - s\} + rE + sn\Big] = 0,$$

$$\log a_l = r(u_i^2 + v_i^2 + w_i^2) - 1 + s.$$

In view of (3) we must expect a_l to decrease as $u^2 + v^2 + w^2$ increases, so that we write

$$a_l = k_l e^{-h_l^2 (u_l^2 + v_l^2 + w_l^2)}.$$

In words, this tells us that the most likely distribution of velocities is that where the number close to the values u, v, w is proportional to

$$nke^{-h^2 (u^2 + v^2 + w^2)}\, du\, dv\, dw.$$

To find the values of the constants, we have, first,

$$n = nk \int_{-\infty}^{\infty} e^{-h^2 u^2}\, du \int_{-\infty}^{\infty} e^{-h^2 v^2}\, dv \int_{-\infty}^{\infty} e^{-h^2 w^2}\, dw,$$

$$k = \Big(\frac{h}{\sqrt{\pi}}\Big)^3.$$

This process is very much the sort of 'near mathematics' to which we have frequently resorted, for we have integrated between infinite limits, whereas in view of (3) every velocity component must be less than $\sqrt{E}$. However, since the value of $e^{-h^2 u^2}$ is very small for every large u, the error is not serious. To find h, we must remember that the number of molecules in a cell is about n times the probability that a molecule should be in that cell, hence

$$E = n\Big(\frac{h}{\sqrt{\pi}}\Big)^3 \int_{-\infty}^{\infty}\int_{-\infty}^{\infty}\int_{-\infty}^{\infty} (u^2 + v^2 + w^2)\, e^{-h^2 (u^2 + v^2 + w^2)}\, du\, dv\, dw$$

$$= 3n\Big(\frac{h}{\sqrt{\pi}}\Big)^3 \int_{-\infty}^{\infty} u^2 e^{-h^2 u^2}\, du \int_{-\infty}^{\infty} e^{-h^2 v^2}\, dv \int_{-\infty}^{\infty} e^{-h^2 w^2}\, dw$$

$$= \frac{3n}{2h^2},$$

$$h = \sqrt{\frac{3n}{2E}}.$$

Theorem 3] *The most probable distribution of velocities among the molecules of a gas is that where the number of those having velocities within the limits $u \pm \frac{1}{2}du$, $v \pm \frac{1}{2}dv$, $w \pm \frac{1}{2}dw$ is nearly equal to*

$$n \left(\frac{h}{\sqrt{\pi}}\right)^3 e^{-h^2(u^2+v^2+w^2)} \, du \, dv \, dw,$$

$$h = \sqrt{\frac{3\,n}{2\,E}}.$$

Here n is the number of molecules, E the given vis viva, the mass of each being taken as 2.

This is Maxwell's law for the distribution of velocities; a gas in this condition is said to be in a *normal state*. The equation is so well known historically that we reproduce his original proof.*

'Let N be the whole number of particles. Let u, v, w be the components of the velocity in the three rectangular directions, and let the number of particles for which u lies between u and $u + du$ be $Nf(u)\,du$, where f is a function to be determined.

The number of particles for which v lies between v and $v + dv$ will be $Nf(v)\,dv$, and the number for which w lies between w and $w + dw$ will be $Nf(w)\,dw$, where f always stands for the same function.

Now the existence of the velocity u does not, in any way, affect the existence of the velocities v or w, since they are at right angles to each other and independent, so that the number of particles whose velocities lie between u and $u + du$ and between v and $v + dv$, and also between w and $w + dw$, is

$$Nf(u)f(v)f(w)\,du\,dv\,dw.$$

If we imagine N particles to start from the origin at the same instant, then this will be the number in the unit of volume $du\,dv\,dw$ after the unit of time, and the number per unit volume will be $Nf(u)f(v)f(w)$.

But the directions of the coordinates are perfectly arbitrary,

* Maxwell, *Collected Works*, vol. i, pp. 380 ff.   Also Jeans, loc. cit., p. 55.

and therefore this number must depend upon the distance from the origin alone; that is

$$f(u)f(v)f(w) = \phi(u^2 + v^2 + w^2).$$

Solving this functional equation, we find

$$f(u) = Ce^{-Au^2} \qquad \phi(u^2 + v^2 + w^2) = C^3 e^{-A(u^2 + v^2 + w^2)}.$$

This simple proof is, unfortunately, very unsound, as it is not at all clear that the components of the velocities may be treated as independent variables, and in fact, if one component were equal to the square root of the vis viva, all others would have to be equal to 0.*

¶ § 4. Amplification of the Preceding Proof.

There are certain points in the deduction of the Normal Law of Maxwell which deserve more careful mathematical investigation: it is now time to return to them. Logically, we should have cleaned up everything as we went along, but this would have burdened the argument to an unbearable extent.

The first point to notice is the fundamental role played by Stirling's formula. Now that formula, as stated in Ch. III, tells us that

$$1 < \frac{r!}{r^r e^{-r}(2\pi r)^{\frac{1}{2}}} < 1 + \frac{1}{10r};$$

hence the error made in evaluating

$$\log a_1! + \log a_2! + \ldots + \log a_v!$$

is of the same order of magnitude as

$$\frac{1}{10}\left(\frac{1}{a_1} + \frac{1}{a_2} + \ldots + \frac{1}{a_v}\right)$$

or as $\qquad\qquad v/a_k.$

Both of these quantities are large; it is not clear what the nature of their ratio will be.

* Cf. Bertrand, loc. cit., p. 30.

To begin with, it should be noticed that there is no harm done if, in deducing our general law, we reject a small number of molecules. In fact we may reject a number increasing with n, provided that it does not increase as fast as n. v depends upon the number of cells; it will remain constant if the total volume in the u, v, w space remain fixed. But we have no right to assume that this total volume does not increase with n, for it is limited only by (3) and the vis viva clearly increases with the number of molecules. We shall not go far wrong in assuming that E increases proportionately with n. In order to keep the volume below a certain upper limit, we may have to reject a certain number of molecules of the highest velocity. But if we put $E = \rho n$, we see that the number of molecules, the squares of whose velocities are greater than ρ, cannot increase proportionately with n; hence the number rejected will increase less rapidly than n, and do no harm. We may choose v once for all, and then assume that all of the a's are so large that v/a_k is small.

The following difficulty is more serious. If we take different velocity points in the same cell of u, v, w space, their coordinates are not identical. We have the more exact equation

$$\sum_{k=1}^{k=v} \sum_{j=1}^{j=a_k} [(u_k + \delta_j u_k)^2 + (v_k + \delta_j v_k)^2 + (w_k + \delta_j w_k)^2] - E = 0.$$

We may imagine that every increment $\delta_j u_k$, $\delta_j v_k$, $\delta_j w_k$ lies within the small limits $\pm \dfrac{\theta}{2}$, where θ is very small, thanks to the size of v.

The point in the space of $3n$ dimensions with coordinates

$$(u_1 + \delta_1 u_1)\,(v_1 + \delta_1 v_1)\,(u_1 + \delta_1 w_1) \ldots$$
$$(u_v + \delta_v u_v)\,(v_v + \delta_v v_v)\,(w_v + \delta_v w_v) + \ldots,$$

which represents a distribution of velocities in v cells, will lie in a $3n$ dimensional hypercube of edge θ. The quantity which we call E is the square of the distance of this point from the origin and the total variation of this cannot exceed the length of a diagonal of the small hypercube $\theta \sqrt{3n}$.

The difference of the distances of two points from a third point is less than their distance from one another; hence

$$\sqrt{\overline{\sum_{k=1}^{k=\nu} a_k \left(u_k{}^2 + v_k{}^2 + w_k{}^2\right)}} - \sqrt{E} \leqq \theta \sqrt{3\,n},$$

$$\sum_{k=1}^{k=\nu} a_k \left(u_k{}^2 + v_k{}^2 + w_k{}^2\right) - \left(\sqrt{E} + y\,\theta \sqrt{3\,n}\right)^2 = 0,$$

$$-1 \leqq y \leqq 1.$$

We find, as before,

$$a_l = k e^{-h^2 \left(u_l{}^2 + v_l{}^2 + w_l{}^2\right)},$$

$$k = \left(\frac{h}{\sqrt{\pi}}\right)^3,$$

$$\left(\sqrt{E} + y\,\theta \sqrt{3\,n}\right)^2 = \frac{3\,n}{2\,h^2},$$

$$\frac{1}{2\,h^2} = \frac{E}{3\,n} \left[1 + 2\,y\,\theta \sqrt{\frac{3\,n}{E}} + \frac{3\,n}{E}\,y^2\,\theta^2\right].$$

Since θ is very small, $\sqrt{\dfrac{3\,n}{2\,E}}$ is a good value for h.

¶ § 5. Probability of a Nearly Normal State.

We have seen that the most probable distribution of velocities is that given by Maxwell's law for the normal state, given in Theorem 3]. This knowledge does not, however, carry us very far, as we have not much idea how likely it is that the distribution of velocities in a given gas will be according to this law, or nearly so. This difficult problem must now claim our attention.

Let us begin by shifting slightly the number of molecules in each cell so that the number in the ith cell is now

$$a_i{}' = a_i + \alpha_i,$$

$$\sum_{l=1}^{l=v} \alpha_l = 0, \quad \sum_{l=1}^{l=v} \alpha_l \left(u_l{}^2 + v_l{}^2 + w_l{}^2\right) = 0. \qquad (8)$$

We replace (7) by

$$P' = \frac{n! \, V^n}{a_1'! \, a_2'! \dots a_v'!}.$$ (9)

$$\log P' = (n + \tfrac{1}{2}) \log n + n \log V - \left(\frac{v-1}{2}\right) \log 2\pi$$

$$- \sum_{l=1}^{l=v} (a_l + \alpha_l + \tfrac{1}{2}) \log (a_l + \alpha_l)$$

$$= \log P - \sum_{l=1}^{l=v} \left[\alpha_l \log a_l + (a_l + \alpha_l + \tfrac{1}{2}) \log \left(1 + \frac{\alpha_l}{a_l}\right) \right]$$

$$= \log P - \sum_{l=1}^{l=v} \left[\alpha_l \log a_l + \alpha_l + \frac{\alpha_l^2}{2a_l} \right],$$

nearly.

Since

$$a_l = ke^{-h^2(u_l^2 + v_l^2 + w_l^2)}$$

by (8),

$$\sum_{l=1}^{l=v} \alpha_l (\log a_l + 1) = \sum_{l=1}^{l=v} \alpha_l [\log k + 1 - h^2 (u_l^2 + v_l^2 + w_l^2)] = 0,$$

$$\log P' = \log P - \sum_{l=1}^{l=v} \frac{\alpha_l^2}{2 a_l},$$

$$P' = P e^{-\Sigma \frac{\alpha_l^2}{2a}}.$$

We wish to find the sum of the values P' for all integral sets of values $\alpha_1 \dots \alpha_v$ compatible with (8) and with a condition of size, let us say

$$\sum_{l=1}^{l=v} \frac{\alpha_l^2}{2 a_l} \leq \frac{z_0}{2}.$$ (10)

We seek the value of

$$\pi = P \Sigma e^{-\frac{1}{2} \Sigma \frac{\alpha_l^2}{a_l}},$$

for all integral values of $\alpha_1 \dots \alpha_v$ compatible with (8) and (10).

It is clear that we must, first of all, replace our summation by some sort of definite integral. Let the number of groups of a's be N, the corresponding values of P' being $P_1', P_2', \ldots P_N'$.

$$\pi = \sum_{i=1}^{i=N} P_i'.$$

Consider the space of ν dimensions where a point has coordinates $a_1, a_2, \ldots a_\nu$. Equations (8) give us two hyperplanes in this, and (10) a hyperellipsoid. The section is a hyperellipsoid in a space of $\nu - 2$ dimensions whose volume we call W. Let each point within this hyperellipsoid with integral coordinates be enclosed in a separate region of volume dv; then

$$P_i' = \frac{N}{W} \int P_i' \, dv,$$

where the integral is extended throughout the whole of the region including the point. As N is very large indeed, and the region small, this is close to the value obtained by replacing P_i' by the continuous variable P'. Then

$$P_i' = \frac{N}{W} \int P' \, dv,$$

approximately, and so

$$\pi = \frac{N}{W} \int P' \, dv,$$

where this integral is taken over the whole of the hyperellipsoid. We may re-write this

$$\pi = \frac{NP}{W} \int \ldots \int e^{-\frac{1}{2} \Sigma \frac{d_l^2}{a_l}} \, da_1 \, da_2 \ldots da_\nu.$$

We next put

$$\frac{1}{2} \sum_{l=1}^{l=\nu} \frac{d_l^2}{a_l} = z.$$

By altering z we have a set of concentric ellipsoids. If the volume of one of these be written $f(z)$, then

$$\pi = \frac{NP}{W} \int_0^{\frac{z_0}{2}} e^{-z} f'(z) \, dz, \quad W = \int_0^{\frac{z_0}{2}} f'(z) \, dz = f\left(\frac{z_0}{2}\right),$$

$$\pi = \frac{NP}{f\left(\frac{z_0}{2}\right)} \int_0^{\frac{z_0}{2}} e^{-z} f'(z) \, dz.$$

A change in z is in the nature of a central similitude in the space of ν dimensions, which carries each of the hyperplanes (8) into itself, and permutes the hyperellipsoids in this space. Hence it permutes also the hyperellipsoids in the space of $\nu - 2$ dimensions, and we shall have a relation

$$f(z) = Kz^{\frac{\nu=2}{2}},$$

as we prove by beginning with the case where all of the a's are equal, and then imposing a homogeneous strain.

$$f\left(\frac{z_0}{2}\right) = K\left(\frac{z_0}{2}\right)^{\frac{\nu\,\cdot 2}{2}},$$

$$\pi = \frac{(\nu-2)\,NP}{2\left(\dfrac{z_0}{2}\right)^{\frac{\nu-2}{2}}} \int_0^{\frac{z_0}{2}} e^{-z} z^{\frac{\nu}{2}-2}\, dz.$$

Now if z_0 be allowed to increase indefinitely we shall eventually include all sets of integral values of $\alpha_1, \alpha_2, \ldots \alpha_\nu$ compatible with (8) and our probability π becomes a certainty. Moreover, the integrand becomes tiny when z is very large, so we assume that we get certainty by integrating out to infinity. Lastly, $\dfrac{N}{\left(\dfrac{z_0}{2}\right)^{\frac{\nu-2}{2}}}$ is proportional to the number of integral points divided by the volume of the hyperellipsoid and varies little from a fixed constant μ. Hence

$$\pi = \frac{\nu-2}{2}\,\mu P \int_0^{\frac{z_0}{2}} e^{-z} z^{\frac{\nu}{2}-2}\, dz,$$

$$1 = \frac{\nu-2}{2}\,\mu P \int_0^{\infty} e^{-z} z^{\frac{\nu}{2}-2}\, dz = \frac{\nu-2}{2}\,\mu P \Gamma\left(\frac{\nu}{2}-1\right),$$

$$\pi = \frac{1}{\Gamma\left(\dfrac{\nu}{2}-1\right)} \int_0^{\frac{z_0}{2}} e^{-z} z^{\frac{\nu}{2}-2}\, dz. \tag{11}$$

The only quantity here which depends on n is z_0, for we have already seen that v may be chosen once for all. If n increase indefinitely, we may expect a_l to increase about in proportion. If we allow a_l to increase in about the same ratio, then z_0 will increase about proportionately with n and π will approach 1 as a limit.

We can express this more accurately. The quantities a_l are those which give the most likely distribution, the a_l's are discrepancies, and the ratios $\dfrac{a_l}{a_l} = \beta_l$ are the relative discrepancies. We have the inequality

$$\sum_{l=1}^{l=v} \frac{a_l}{z_0}\beta_l^2 \leqq 1. \tag{12}$$

If we start with the β_l's, then from (12) we may assume the a_l's to increase proportionately with z_0.

Theorem 4] *The probability that the distribution of velocities shall differ from the normal one in such a way that each relative discrepancy is less than some assigned quantity, will approach 1 as a limit if the number of molecules increase indefinitely and the vis viva increase proportionately with them.*

Theorem 5] *If the number of molecules be very large, and if a gas be taken at random, it is practically certain that the distribution of velocities will differ but little from the normal one.*

Theorem 6] *If a large number of gas specimens be examined, each containing the same number of molecules of the same size and mass, with the same vis viva and equal containers, in the vast majority of cases the distribution of velocities will differ but little from the normal one.*

We have stated this theorem in three different ways, in order to contrast them with another statement which seems less legitimate:

'This completes our information about the motion of the gas. At any instant it is infinitely probable that it is in the normal state. In the course of the motion departures from the normal state will occur, but it is infinitely probable that these will occupy but an infinitesimal fraction of the time occupied by the motion.'*

This conclusion seems unwarranted. Returning to the representation by means of points in higher space each representing point will trace a trajectory made up of rectilinear segments, followed by jumps along the hypersurfaces (2). If a large number of representing points be started on their journeys at the same moment, a large majority of them will always be found in regions corresponding to normal distributions of velocity. But it does not seem at all clear that the paths are such that a minority of points may not stay most of the time in regions corresponding to abnormal distributions of velocity.† Perhaps the best statement we can make is the following : ‡

Theorem 7] *If a gas specimen be chosen at random from a very large number, all with equal containers and equal vires vivae, it is immensely probable that it will have a nearly normal distribution of velocities most of the time.*

§ 6. Distribution in Space.

The work which we have done so far has been exclusively on the distribution of velocities; the question arises naturally whether we may not carry on a similar discussion of the distribution of the molecules in space.

We begin by replacing our coordinates u, v, w by x, y, z. These must all be finite since the gas is supposed to be in a finite container. This container we may imagine divided into a number of equal cells as before. At this point the analogy breaks down. In the case of velocities, starting with the assumption that the probability that a gas was in a certain state was proportional to the volume of a certain region in the space of $6n$ dimensions, we noted that the limiting conditions (2) do not involve the velocity coordinates.

* Jeans, loc. cit., p. 55.
† This possibility is hinted at ibid., following paragraph.
‡ The discussion of these points in Castelnuovo, loc. cit., pp. 290 ff., is admirable.

Hence the probability was proportional to the volume of a region in a $3n$ dimensional space and that was proportional to the product of the volumes of n regions in the three-dimensional space u, v, w. But a similar line of reasoning is not applicable to the x, y, z coordinates, for they appear in (2). The matter is even more evident on purely physical grounds. The velocity coordinates of non-colliding molecules are totally independent, and are in no danger of 'crowding' one another, but the fact that a certain molecule lies in a certain small region reduces the probability that a second molecule should be therein. This shows the illegitimacy of the 'assumption of molecular chaos' which is used to deduce Maxwell's Law from dynamical considerations. This assumption may be stated as follows: *

'It is usual to assume that the molecules having velocity components within any specified limits are, at every instant throughout the motion of the gas, distributed at random, independent of the positions or velocities of the other molecules, provided, only, that two molecules do not occupy the same space.'

The matter assumes quite a different aspect when we assume that the diameters of the molecules are negligible. Here we retain only those inequalities (2) which have to do with the container, and these involve the positions of the molecules separately. Equation (3) drops away. We may repeat our previous reasoning: where the quantity called r_l is equal to 0, the a_i's will all be equal.

Theorem 8] *When the radii of the molecules are negligible, the most likely distribution is a uniform one throughout the container.*

The reasoning previously employed to find P_i' is still valid:

¶ Theorem 9] *When the radii of the molecules are negligible, there is a very great probability that at any instant the distribution will be nearly uniform throughout the container.*

¶ Theorem 10] *When the radii of the molecules are negligible, the assumption of molecular chaos is legitimate.*

* Jeans, loc. cit., p. 17.

CHAPTER XI

THE PRINCIPLES OF LIFE INSURANCE *

§ 1. Calculation of Life Probabilities.

THE fundamental question on which the whole theory of
life insurance is based is the probability that a certain individual shall survive a certain time. From one point of
view the statement of this question is nonsense on its face:
our times are in the hands of God; the probability does not
exist. But let us remember that from the very start we have
clung closely to a statistical definition of probability; that
definition will stand us in good stead now. The problem
means essentially this. An individual is classed as a member
of a recognized category of a sort that has been long under
observation. What proportion of that category may we, as
a result of statistical inquiry, expect to survive the time in
question?

The category in which a healthy individual is usually classed,
for purposes of life insurance, is that of his age. The fundamental problem can be put in the following more exact form:

'What is the probability that a healthy individual of age x
will survive one year?' The probability that he will survive
two years is the product of the probability that he will
survive one year, multiplied by the probability that a person
one year older will also survive one year, and so on for
a number of years. The question of how to compute these
probabilities statistically is ever so much harder than one
would suppose at first. One would be inclined to say: 'Why,

---

* The masterwork on the subject of the present chapter is the *Institute of
Actuaries Text-book*, Part II, by George King, 2nd edition, London, 1902. See
also Czuber, loc. cit., vol. ii.

all you have to do is to take a census of a large number of persons of age x at a certain date, check them up a year later to see how many are alive, and form the quotient.' Unfortunately, this is quite impracticable. To begin with, the category is too elastic. If at a certain date two persons give their ages as x, one may be 364 days older than the other, a serious divergence in the later ages. In fact it might be wiser to assign the age $x-1$ to the one, or $x+1$ to the other. Moreover, unless all of the individuals were soldiers or convicts or of some other non-representative sort, it is impossible to keep track of them all. Some will escape observation during the course of the year, and it will be impossible to say at the end of that time whether they are alive or dead.

Difficulties of a somewhat different sort arise when we try to compute the probability of surviving from birth and death statistics. If a man be born in the year 1900 and die in the year 1925, he may die at the age of 24 or 25. If in the year 1925 a man give his age as 25 years, he may have been born in the year 1899 or the year 1900. If a man born in 1900 die at the age of 25 years, he may die in 1925 or 1926.

Further complications arise for an insurance company which tries to calculate life probabilities from its own experience. Suppose that, at the beginning of a certain year, the number of persons insured of a given age is known. A year later the books of the company are re-examined and the number of persons, ostensibly a year older, is observed. The ratio will by no means give the probability for surviving one year; the two sets of figures bear on different, if overlapping, categories. Among those who appear in the second count are some who did not appear the year before, because they took out their first policies during that year. On the other hand, of those whose names appear the first year, some will disappear, and the company will not know whether they survive or not. It is still worse if the company make use of the lists of deaths, for those who die during the year at the same age will have been born in two different years, and will appear under different years in the birth registers, and some will have taken out their first insurance in the course of the year.

It is evident that, in view of all these difficulties, no perfect calculation is possible; the best we can do is to adopt certain arbitrary, if plausible, conventions. To begin with, different insurance companies combine their experience. Some of the best life tables are those of twenty British companies, and the large American companies combine their experience also. Secondly, statistics are made up as of January 1, but each individual is given a fictitious birthday, the 1st of July nearest to the date of his actual birth. This corresponds to the tolerably reasonable assumption that those who announce a certain age on January 1 have their birthdays scattered pretty evenly over a twelvemonth. In the same way, it is assumed that all who take out or surrender their policies during a year, do so on July 1. Let L_x be the number of persons aged x whose names appear on the company's books on the 1st of January,* the number giving their age as $x+1$ a year later shall be L_{x+1}. Let p_x be the chance that a person aged x will survive one year. Let i_x be the number of new policy-holders aged x who enter during the year, e_x the number who left. The probability of surviving half a year will be about $1 - \frac{1}{2}(1 - p_x) = \frac{1}{2}(1 + p_x)$.

Now L_{x+1} is made up of the survivors of L_x plus the surviving immigrants, and less the surviving emigrants, i. e.

$$L_{x+1} = L_x p_x - \frac{e_x}{2}(1 + p_x) + \frac{i_x}{2}(1 + p_x),$$

$$p_x = \frac{L_{x+1} + \frac{1}{2}(e_x - i_x)}{L_x - \frac{1}{2}(e_x - i_x)}. \tag{1}$$

It must not be imagined that after the various p_x's have been calculated in this way the results are in final shape. It is clear that no one will be perfectly accurate, not even the best value obtainable. In fact if we plot each p_x as an ordinate corresponding to the abscissa x, we have points of

---

* The notation used throughout this chapter is the universal one adopted at the second International Actuarial Congress, London, 1898.

a broken line that waves up and down. The next step is
to 'graduate' these results, and consists essentially in altering
the ordinates slightly so that the resulting points lie on
a smooth curve, which sinks continuously after the years of
early childhood. This graduation may be accomplished in
a large number of ways. We may replace the middle one
of each triad of successive points by the centre of gravity of
the triangle with these points as vertices. This 'will bring
down the mighty from their seat, and exalt the lowly and
meek'. If need be, the process may be repeated several
times. Another plan is to take a number of points greater
than three and find, by least squares, the parabola of vertical
axis which lies nearest to them. A very simple way is to
plot the points and then run a smooth curve as near them as
possible with the aid of a spline or some other instrument.
Practical actuaries seem to find this method as good as
any other.*

An ideal way to calculate the probability of survival would
be to find an explicit function for p_x. Various attempts have
been made to find some such function, the most successful
being that of the English actuary Makeham, whose method
we shall now explain.†

Let l_x be the number of persons, all born at practically the
same time, who reach the age x. The probability of surviving
one year is

$$p_x = \frac{l_{x+1}}{l_x}. \tag{2}$$

Let $-\Delta l_x$ be the number of persons of the category x
who die in a short space of time Δx thereafter. Then the
instantaneous death-rate, called the 'instantaneous force of
mortality', is

$$\mu_x = \lim_{\Delta_x \to 0} \frac{-\Delta l_x}{l_x \Delta x} = -\frac{d \log l_x}{dx}. \tag{3}$$

According to Makeham's assumption, death will arise from
one of two general causes. The first is accident, and may be

---

* Cf. Czuber, loc. cit., vol. ii, pp. 167-200.

†. Makeham, *Journal of the* (British) *Institute of Actuaries*, London, Jan. 1860.
Unfortunately, I have not been able to verify this reference.

looked at as a constant throughout, for younger men are more active than old ones, and have greater recuperative power, but also take more risks. The second is decrease in power to resist disease. If we overlook the accidental deaths for a moment, we might fairly assume that the rate at which people were dying at any instant was inversely proportional to a function $f(x)$ which represents the force of resistance to disease. Hence

$$\mu_x = A + \frac{B}{f(x)}.$$

With regard to $f(x)$, Makeham assumes that in any short interval a man loses a constant proportion of such force of resistance as he still has.

We now have the data necessary to calculate the number of living l_x; we change constants at pleasure throughout our integration

$$\frac{df(x)}{f(x)} = -p\,dx,$$

$$f(x) = re^{-px},$$

$$\mu_x = A + Bc^x,$$

$$\log l_x = -Ax - Dc^x - F,$$

$$l_x = ks^x g^{(c^x)}. \tag{4}$$

$$p_x = sg^{(c^x)\,(c-1)}. \tag{5}$$

A simpler formula was devised some time earlier by Gompertz.* He overlooked the element of chance, and therefore made $A = 0$ and $s = 1$, thus getting

$$l_x = kg^{(c^x)}, \qquad p_x = g^{(c^x)\,(c-1)}. \tag{6}$$

We may find the values of the constants in Makeham's formula from four observations as follows:

$$\log l_x = \log k + x \log s + c^x \log g,$$

$$\log l_{x+t} = \log k + (x+t) \log s + c^t c^x \log g,$$

$$\log l_{x+2t} = \log k + (x+2t) \log s + c^{2t} c^x \log g,$$

$$\log l_{x+3t} = \log k + (x+3t) \log s + c^{3t} c^x \log g.$$

* Gompertz, 'On the Nature of the Function expressive of the Law of Human Mortality', *Philosophical Transactions, Royal Society*, 1825.

The first differences are

$$\Delta \log l_x = t \log s + (c^t - 1) c^x \log g,$$
$$\Delta \log l_{x+t} = t \log s + c^t (c^t - 1) c^x \log g,$$
$$\Delta \log l_{x+2t} = t \log s + c^{2t} (c^t - 1) c^x \log g.$$

The second differences are

$$\Delta_2 \log l_x = (c^t - 1)^2 c^x \log g,$$
$$\Delta_2 \log l_{x+t} = c^t (c^t - 1)^2 c^x \log g.$$
$$\log (\Delta_2 \log l_{x+t}) - \log (\Delta_2 \log l_x) = t \log c.$$

The other constants are then easily found.

Another, and better, plan is to use all available data and determine the constants by least squares. We write

$$\log p_x = \log s + c^x (c - 1) \log g.$$

The constants, of which $\log s$ and $(c - 1) \log g$ appear linearly, may be found by the methods explained in Ch. IX.*

How much confidence should we place in Makeham's formula? It is evident that the assumptions on which it is based are nothing more than reasonably plausible. The test is whether it really checks up in practice. This is the case to a really surprising extent. A life table calculated by Makeham's formula is better than any but the very best table calculated by other means. This is strikingly brought out by the following figures,† where, unfortunately, we have available not Makeham's formula but the less accurate one of Gompertz. The values tabulated are for l_x:

x	Gompertz Formula.	20 British Co.'s.	Duvillard.	Deparcieux.	Northampton.
30	890	890	890	890	890
40	839	813	750	797	737
50	745	718	603	704	579
60	584	584	434	561	413
70	355	382	238	375	250
80	125	142	71	143	95

If we assume that the best tables are those of 20 British Companies, we see that this table shows that the Gompertz figures are as accurate as Deparcieux, and distinctly better

* Czuber, loc. cit., vol. ii, pp. 181 ff.
† Bertrand, loc. cit., p. 318.

than Duvillard or Northampton. As a matter of fact, Makeham tables are used in practice. As for the Gompertz formula, that is useful for calculating the probabilities for contingencies depending on two lives. We see from (6) that the probability that a person aged (x) and another aged x' should both survive is p_y, where

$$c^x + c^{x'} = c^y.$$

This formula would not hold for two persons intimately connected, like husband and wife, for the death of one would be likely to hasten the death of the other.

§ 2. Endowments and Annuities.

Before taking up the subject-matter of the present section, we must say a word or two about the mathematics of finance. In calculating all sorts of insurance values, it must be understood that the word 'interest' always means 'compound interest'. If, thus, i be the rate (usually in the neighbourhood of $3\frac{1}{2}$ per cent.), the amount of \$1 at the end of n years is

$$(1 + i)^n.$$

To find the present worth of \$1 payable at the end of that time, we write $(1 + i)^{-1} = v$; the present worth, or discounted value, is v^n.

With regard to calculating compound interest, we note that if the interest be compounded m times per year, the amount at the end of n years will be

$$\left(1 + \frac{i}{m}\right)^{mn}.$$

Allowing m to increase indefinitely, the amount at interest continuously compounded is e^{in}; if we put $e^{i'} = (1 + i)$ we see that compound interest or present worth can be reckoned by assuming the new rate i' with continuous compounding. This new rate is called the 'force of interest'.

A sum of money to be paid at the end of a certain time, provided that a stated individual is still alive, is called an 'endowment'. What is the present value of \$1 payable at the end of n years, in case a person now aged x is then alive?

$$_nE_x = v^n\frac{l_{x+n}}{l_x} = \frac{v^{x+n}l_{x+n}}{v^x l_x}.$$

Every practising actuary is provided with a series of tables called 'commutation tables' which contain the fundamental data needed for his purposes.* The first column in such tables contains the age x, the second

$$D_x = v^x l_x, \tag{7}$$

so that the fundamental endowment formula is

$$_nE_x = D_{x+n}/D_x. \tag{8}$$

A sum of money which shall be paid at the end of each year that an individual survives is called an 'Annuity'; the value of an annuity of \$1 based on the life of an individual aged x is

$$a_x = \frac{D_{x+1} + D_{x+2} + \cdots}{D_x}.$$

Sometimes it is required that the first payment shall be made immediately. In that case the sum is called an 'Annuity due'; the Germans have more sonorous titles, calling them annuities 'postnumerando' and 'praenumerando' respectively. In the third column of the commutation tables are the quantities

$$N_x = \sum_{i=1}^{i=\omega-x} D_{x+i}, \tag{9}$$

where ω is the age, usually about 100, where an individual may reasonably be supposed to be certainly dead. We have, then, for an annuity

$$a_x = N_x/D_x, \tag{10}$$

and for an annuity due †

$$1 + a_x = N_{x-1}/D_x. \tag{11}$$

¶ It is interesting to compare the value of a_x with that

---

* Cf. King, loc. cit., pp. 512–45.

† This is the standard notation. Some authors, as Czuber, loc. cit., write $N_x = \sum_{i=0}^{i=\omega-x} D_{x+i}$ and a_x where we write $1 + a_x$. Thus they write (10), meaning (11).

of a certain payment to be made yearly during the season e_x, the expected life of the individual, i.e. the mean life of one of his age,

$$e_x = \frac{l_{x+1} + l_{x+2} + \ldots + l_\omega}{l_x}. \tag{12}$$

The value of the certain payment is

$$v + v^2 + v^3 + \ldots + v^{e_x} = v\left[\frac{v^{e_x} - 1}{v - 1}\right]$$

$$= \frac{1}{i}\left[1 - (1 + i)^{-e_x}\right].$$

We wish to compare this with

$$a_x = \frac{v l_{x+1} + v^2 l_{x+2} + \ldots + v^{\omega - x} l_\omega}{l_x}$$

$$< v\frac{l_{x+1}}{l_x} + v^2\frac{l_{x+2}}{l_x} + \ldots + v^{e_x}\frac{l_{x+e_x}}{l_x} + v^{e_x+1}\left[\frac{l_{x+e_x+1} + \ldots + l_\omega}{l_x}\right].$$

To prove that this is less than the other, we must show

$$v^{e_x+1}\left[\frac{l_{x+e_x+1} + \ldots + l_\omega}{l_x}\right] < v\left(1 - \frac{l_{x+1}}{l_x}\right) + v^2\left(1 - \frac{l_{x+2}}{l_x}\right) + \ldots$$

$$+ v^{e_x}\left(1 - \frac{l_{x+e_x}}{l_x}\right).$$

The right-hand side is greater than

$$v^{e_x+1}\left[\left(1 - \frac{l_{x+1}}{l_x}\right) + \left(1 - \frac{l_{x+2}}{l_x}\right) + \ldots + \left(1 - \frac{l_{x+e_x}}{l_x}\right)\right]$$

$$= v^{e_x+1}\left[e_x - \frac{l_{x+1} + l_{x+2} + \ldots + l_{x+e_x}}{l_x}\right]$$

$$= v^{e_x+1}\left[\frac{l_{x+e_x+1} + \ldots + l_\omega}{l_x}\right].$$

Problem.

Find the value of $_{|n}a_x$ an annuity limited to n payments, of $_{m|}a_x$ an annuity whose first payment will be at the end of m years, and of $_{m|n}a_x$ which is both limited and postponed.

The inequality is thus established, and the certain payment has the greater value.

It is sometimes important to know the value of an annuity which increases each year. Let the first payment be $1, the second $2, the third $3, and so on. We have here, really, an annuity for $1, another for the same sum deferred one year, a third deferred two years, and so on. The value is thus

$$\frac{1}{D_x}\left[\begin{array}{l}D_{x+1}+D_{x+2}+\ldots+D_{x+3}+\ldots \\ \qquad\quad D_{x+2}+D_{x+3}+\ldots \\ \qquad\qquad\qquad +D_{x+3}+\ldots\end{array}\right]$$

$$= \frac{1}{D_x}[N_x + N_{x+1} + N_{x+2} + \ldots].$$

The fourth column in the commutation table is

$$S_x = \sum_{t=0}^{t=\omega-x} N_{x+t}. \tag{13}$$

The value of our complicated annuity is then

$$S_x/D_x. \tag{14}$$

§ 3. Single Payment Insurance.

There are two sorts of benefits which a Life Insurance Company is called upon to pay: annuities if people survive, insurance if they die. We have calculated the values of the principle types of the former benefit; we must now calculate the latter. In passing, we note that whereas when a man wishes to take out an insurance policy he must pass a careful physical examination, and give evidence that he does not follow an unusually dangerous calling, when it comes to annuities, the worse a man's health and the more dangerous his calling, the better the Company will be pleased.

What is the present value of $1 to be paid at the end of the year in which a person aged x dies? We call this A_x and note that we have various mutually exclusive possibilities that he may die in any one of the succeeding years.

$$A_x = v\left[1 - \frac{l_{x+1}}{l_x}\right] + v^2\left[\frac{l_{x+1}}{l_x}\left(1 - \frac{l_{x+2}}{l_{x+1}}\right)\right]$$

$$+ v^3\frac{l_{x+3}}{l^x}\left[\left(1 + \frac{l_{x+3}}{l_{x+2}}\right)\right] + \cdots$$

$$= v(1 + a_x) - a_x$$

$$= \frac{vN_{x-1} - N_x}{D_x}.$$

This formula might have been predicted by the following reasoning. The Company agrees that if the man be alive at the beginning of any year it will pay \$1 either to him or to his 'heirs or assigns' at the end of the year. The man agrees that if he be alive at the end of the year, he will pay that dollar back. The man agrees to pay the Company an annuity of \$1, the Company agrees to pay an annuity due for the same amount, but as each payment is postponed a year, the whole must be discounted once. The difference between these two benefits gives the formula above. It must be added, however, that this is not the best type of formula for computation. We shall add to our commutation table columns based on those who die, not on those who survive. The number who die at the age x is

$$d_x = l_x - l_{x+1}. \tag{15}$$

$$A_x = \frac{vd_x}{l_x} + \frac{v^2 d_{x+1}}{l_x} + \cdots$$

$$= \frac{v^{x+1}d_x + v^{x+2}d_{x+1} + \cdots}{v^x l_x}.$$

Let $\qquad v^{y+1}d_y = C_y, \tag{16}$

$$M_x = \sum_{t=0}^{t=\omega-x} C_{x+t}, \tag{17}$$

$$A_x = M_x/D_x. \tag{18}$$

Let us, lastly, suppose that the amount of the insurance will be \$1 if the man die in the first year, \$2 if in the second, and so on. We have

$$\frac{1}{D_x}[M_x + M_{x+1} + \cdots].$$

We make a last column in our commutation tables,

$$R_x = \sum_{t=0}^{t=\omega-x} M_{x+t}; \tag{19}$$

the value of this increasing insurance is then

$$R_x/D_x. \tag{20}$$

A much more frequent form of contract is the so-called 'endowment' policy, where the Company agrees to insure a life for n years, and to pay the amount at the end of that time in case the person is still alive. This is clearly the sum of an insurance limited to a certain number of years, and an endowment postponed the same number of years, namely

$$A_{x\overline{n}|} = (M_x - M_{x+n} + D_{x+n})/D_x. \tag{21}$$

This may be transformed in a number of ways which we shall not stop to explain.

We have, so far, assumed that the insurance would be paid at the end of the year of death; that is not an arrangement which usually commends itself in practice, most beneficiaries not caring to wait so long.

Suppose that an annuity of \$1 is to be paid in m equal instalments. Its value is increased, partly because the beneficiary receives his money earlier each year, partly because he receives some payments in the year of death. The present value of the last payment to be made each year is a_x/m.

An annuity due of $1/m$ payable at the beginning of each year would have the value

$$\frac{1}{m}(1 + a_x).$$

Let us assume that the intervening benefits decrease proportionately; the total value of the annuity is now

$$\frac{1}{m}a_x + \frac{1}{m}\left(a_x + \frac{1}{m}\right) + \frac{1}{m}\left(a_x + \frac{2}{m}\right) + \dots$$

$$a_x^{(m)} = a_x + \frac{m-1}{2m}. \tag{22}$$

Problem.

Calculate the value of $_{m|}A_x$ an insurance where the liability begins only after m years, of $_{|n}A_x$ where it ceases after n years, and of $_{m|n}A_x$ where it is limited both ways.

For a continuous annuity we should have

$$\bar{a}_x = a_x + \tfrac{1}{2}. \tag{23}$$

In the same way, an insurance policy receives an enhanced value if the payment be made at the end of a stated fraction of the year, say $1/m$th, in which death occurs, for the Company loses interest on its money from the end of that term to the end of the year. Assuming, for simplicity, that the probability of death is the same throughout all intervals of the year, a rather inaccurate assumption, and that the interest lost is only simple interest, the loss to the Company is

$$A_x \frac{1}{m} \left[\frac{m-1}{m} i + \frac{m-2}{m} i + \ldots + \frac{1}{m} i \right] = A_x \frac{m-1}{2m} i ;$$

hence the value under the present contract is

$$A_x^{(m)} = A_x \left(1 + \frac{m-1}{2m} i \right). \tag{24}$$

For immediate payment at death, we have

$$\bar{A}_x = A_x (1 + i/2). \tag{25}$$

§ 4. Premiums.

In all the calculations made so far we have merely considered the present value of the benefit to be obtained. In the majority of cases, however, the beneficiary is by no means in a position to pay down at once the full value of his benefit, but arranges for payments at stated intervals. Suppose, for instance, instead of making a single payment for a simple life policy, the beneficiary wishes to make equal annual payments, beginning immediately, as long as he lives. What he undertakes to do is, thus, to pay to the Company an annuity due for the amount of the premium P_x, and this must have the same present value as the insurance, hence

$$P_x (1 + a_x) = A_x,$$

$$P_x = \frac{M_x}{N_{x-1}}. \tag{26}$$

The premium for a policy payable immediately at death is

$$\bar{P}_x = \frac{M_x}{N_{x-1}}\left(1 + \frac{i}{2}\right).$$

When the beneficiary wishes to limit himself to at most n payments, we have

$$_{|n}P_x\left(1 + _{|n},\, a_x\right) = A_x,$$

$$_{|n}P_x = \frac{M_x}{N_{x-1} - N_{x+n-1}}. \tag{27}$$

The annual premium for an n-year endowment policy will be

$$P_{x\overline{n}|} = \frac{M_x - M_{x+n} + D_{x+n}}{N_{x-1} - N_{x+n-1}}. \tag{28}$$

A not uncommon practice in the case of both insurance and endowments is to arrange that the premium or premiums shall all be returned with the benefit. It is not quite clear why any one should desire this type of policy, except that it has the appearance of giving the beneficiary something for nothing, which is always popular. Let us begin with the simplest case, and find the single premium for an endowment, which shall give the beneficiary, if alive, the sum of \$1 plus the premium. We have

$$\pi_x = \frac{(1 + \pi_x)\, D_{x+n}}{D_x},$$

$$\pi_x = \frac{D_{x+n}}{D_x - D_{x+n}}. \tag{29}$$

What will be the single premium for a simple life policy, premium to be returned with the insurance?

$$\pi_x = \frac{(1 + \pi_x)\, M_x}{D_x},$$

$$\pi_x = \frac{M_x}{D_x - M_x}. \tag{30}$$

If immediate payment be required, we must multiply M_x

Problem.

    Calculate the increased cost of $P_{x\overline{n}|}$ for immediate payment at death.

by $1 + \dfrac{i}{2}$. Single premium for n-year endowment policy, premium to be returned

$$\pi_x = (1 + \pi_x)\frac{M_x - M_{x+n} + D_{x+n}}{D_x},$$

$$\pi_x = \frac{M_x - M_{x+n} + D_{x+n}}{(D_x - D_{x+n}) - (M_x - M_{x+n})}. \tag{31}$$

Annual premium on simple life policy, all premiums to be returned. Here the payment side is an annuity due of the amount of the premium. The benefit side is two policies, one for $1, the other of increasing amount, starting with the premium, and increasing by that amount every year. We get from (11), (18), and (20)

$$\pi_x \frac{N_{x-1}}{D_x} = \frac{M_x}{D_x} + \pi_x \frac{R_x}{D_x},$$

$$\pi_x = \frac{M_x}{N_{x-1} - R_x}. \tag{32}$$

Let us look a little more closely into the wisdom of stipulating that the premiums shall be returned. Let us take this last case of simple life policy, premium to be returned. The beneficiary's expectation is here

$$1 + \pi_x \frac{l_{x+1}}{l_x} + \pi_x \frac{l_{x+2}}{l_x} + \ldots = 1 + \pi_x e_x,$$

the ratio of benefit expected to premium is, by (32),

$$\frac{N_{x-1} - R_x}{M_x} + e_x.$$

The ratio of benefit expected to premium, when premiums are not returned, is N_{x-1}/M_x.

Problems.

1. Find single premium for n-year endowment policy, with return of premiums, if payment be made immediately after death.

2. Find premium for n-year endowment policy, all premiums to be returned.

To compare these, we must compare R_x/M_x with e_x. Turning to a $3\frac{1}{2}$ per cent. commutation table, we find the figures :

x	R_x/M_x	e_x
25	30	29
40	22	20
60	13	9

As the ratio of expected benefit to premium is greater in the simple case than where premiums are returned, the former would seem to be the better for the beneficiary.

At this point it is necessary to emphasize in the strongest terms the fact that the premiums which we have calculated, differ very widely from those charged in practice by commercial insurance companies. These net premiums fail to provide any reserve to meet the following contingencies :

(1) Cost of operation, and interest on capital invested.

(2) Fluctuations in the death-rate.

(3) Fluctuation from the theoretical number of deaths, according to Bernoulli's theorem.

(4) Decrease in rate of interest obtainable on invested funds.

In order to meet these various contingencies, the premiums are usually 'loaded' to a greater or less extent. The different companies do not announce to the world the different bases which they take for calculating this loading, and this reticence is very natural, but the result is a rather remarkable diversity in practice. As an example, we quote a few figures, the supposed age of the insured being 35 years :

	Net Premium.	P.D.Q. Company.	X.Y.Z. Company.
20 payment life	0.0311	0.03328	0.03834
20 year endowment	0.0422	0.0467	0.05147

The net figures are calculated from a $3\frac{1}{2}$ per cent. commutation table, the others from a card published by the P. D. Q. Company showing how much less its rates were than those of some score of competitors. The X. Y. Z. was chosen for comparison because of its high premiums and great size. The great difference in the premiums is doubtless explained in large measure by differences in systems of loading. Thus, some companies follow the plan of loading the first premiums very heavily, then dividing large slices of profit among the policy-holders. Insurance companies doing this have a habit of employing such adjectives as 'mutual' or 'co-operative' to describe themselves. We quote from the card where these figures are found :

'The P. D. Q. Company is distinguished for low rates of premium on all forms of insurance, also for low expense rate and its mortality, since organization is lower than that of any other American Company for a like period. All of its policies are on the "participating plan", that is, the difference between the premium and the cost of insurance is determined by experience, and returned to the policy-holder.'

The only insurance system with which the writer is familiar, where only net premiums seem to be charged, is the United States War Risk Insurance.

§ 5. Surrender Values.

At the moment when an individual takes out an insurance policy, his mathematical expectation is 0, that is to say, the sum which he expects to pay in net premiums has the same present value as the benefit looked for. As time goes on this equation ceases to hold. The expected benefit is greater than the expected outlay, and it would be increasingly advantageous to the Company for him to cancel the contract. The difference between what the Company expects to receive from the premiums stipulated for in the past, and what it would expect from an individual of the same age, insuring himself for the first time, is called the 'Surrender value', and is about the sum which, in practice, a Company is willing to pay to a policy-holder, after the first few years, in return for giving up his insurance. It can be calculated in various ways.

Suppose that an individual aged $x + n$ took out a simple life policy at the age x. The surrender value will be the difference between the value of a new policy for a man of his

present age and the value of an annuity due of the amount
of his present premium, namely,

$$_nV_x = A_{x+n} - (1 + a_{x+n})\,P_x$$

$$= \frac{M_{x+n}}{D_{x+n}} - \frac{N_{x+n-1}}{D_{x+n}}\,\frac{M_x}{N_{x-1}}$$

$$= \frac{M_{x+n}N_{x-1} - M_xN_{x+n-1}}{D_{x+n}N_{x-1}}. \tag{33}$$

This method of calculating is called the 'prospective method'.
It is interesting to compare it with the 'retrospective method',
which may be explained as follows.

At the time when the contract was first made, the pros-
pective value of the first n payments was $(1 +\,_{|\,n-1}a_x)\,P_x$.
These payments had two functions: to provide for a temporary
insurance for n years, and to provide the surrender value at
the end of that time. The difference between the limited
annuity due and the temporary insurance is the surrender
value, multiplied by the probability that the individual will
survive n years, and discounted for n years, i.e. an n years
endowment to the amount of the surrender value. We
thus have

$$_nV_x\frac{D_{x+n}}{D_x} = \frac{N_{x-1} - N_{x+n-1}}{D_x}\,\frac{M_x}{N_{x-1}} - \frac{(M_x - M_{x+n})}{D_x}$$

$$= \frac{M_{x+n}N_{x-1} - M_xN_{x+n-1}}{D_xN_{x-1}}$$

$$_nV_x = \frac{M_{x+n}N_{x-1} - M_xN_{x+n-1}}{D_{x+n}N_{x-1}}. \tag{34}$$

As a matter of fact, policy-holders do not usually surrender
their policies, and, in consequence, a large insurance company
is obliged to have continually on hand a very large reserve.
This great sum of money gives to the Company much importance in the world of finance. Moreover, there is rather a nice
ethical question as to who is, in reality, the owner of this
reserve, and this question is by no means of merely academic
interest, for it was once raised in a big lawsuit involving one of

the largest of the American companies. The policy-holders maintained that the reserve was really the totality of surrender values, and so belonged to them, or at least they should have a voice in determining how it should be managed. The directors of the Company contended that as long as the institution was in a sound financial condition, and of this there was never the slightest question, and as long as they met all of their obligations with reasonable promptness, it was nobody's business but their own, what they did with the reserve. This line of reasoning would seem flawless, were it not for the allurement of mutuality or co-operation which many companies hold out to prospective policy-holders. Just how much right has a policy-holder in a mutual company to a voice in its management? Questions of this sort are interesting and important, but can hardly be said to fall naturally under the head of mathematical probability.

TABLE A

The Common Logarithms of e^x and e^{-x}.

x	$\log_{10} e^x$	$\log_{10} e^{-x}$	x	$\log_{10} e^x$	$\log_{10} e^{-x}$
0.00001	0.0000043429	$\overline{1}$.9999956571	0.08000	0.0347435586	$\overline{1}$.9652564414
0.00002	0.0000086859	$\overline{1}$.9999913141	0.09000	0.0390865034	$\overline{1}$.9609134966
0.00003	0.0000130288	$\overline{1}$.9999869712	0.10000	0.0434294482	$\overline{1}$.9565705518
0.00004	0.0000173718	$\overline{1}$.9999826282	0.20000	0.0868588964	$\overline{1}$.9131411036
0.00005	0.0000217747	$\overline{1}$.9999782853	0.30000	0.1302883446	$\overline{1}$.8697116554
0.00006	0.0000260577	$\overline{1}$.9999739423	0.40000	0.1737177928	$\overline{1}$.8262822072
0.00007	0.0000304006	$\overline{1}$.9999695994	0.50000	0.2171472410	$\overline{1}$.7828527590
0.00008	0.0000347436	$\overline{1}$.9999652564	0.60000	0.2605766891	$\overline{1}$.7394233109
0.00009	0.0000390865	$\overline{1}$.9999609135	0.70000	0.3040061373	$\overline{1}$.6959938627
0.00010	0.0000434294	$\overline{1}$.9999565706	0.80000	0.3474355855	$\overline{1}$.6525644145
0.00020	0.0000868589	$\overline{1}$.9999131411	0.90000	0.3908650337	$\overline{1}$.6091349663
0.00030	0.0001302883	$\overline{1}$.9998697117	1.00000	0.4342944819	$\overline{1}$.5657055181
0.00040	0.0001737178	$\overline{1}$.9998262822	2.00000	0.8685889638	$\overline{1}$.1314110362
0.00050	0.0002171472	$\overline{1}$.9997828528	3.00000	1.3028834457	$\overline{2}$.6971165543
0.00060	0.0002605767	$\overline{1}$.9997394233	4.00000	1.7371779276	$\overline{2}$.2628220724
0.00070	0.0003040061	$\overline{1}$.9996959939	5.00000	2.1714724095	$\overline{3}$.8285275905
0.00080	0.0003474356	$\overline{1}$.9996525644	6.00000	2.6057668914	$\overline{3}$.3942331086
0.00090	0.0003908650	$\overline{1}$.9996091350	7.00000	3.0400613733	$\overline{4}$.9599386267
0.00100	0.0004342945	$\overline{1}$.9995657055	8.00000	3.4743558552	$\overline{4}$.5256441448
0.00200	0.0008685890	$\overline{1}$.9991314110	9.00000	3.9086503371	$\overline{4}$.0913496629
0.00300	0.0013028834	$\overline{1}$.9986971166	10.00000	4.3429448190	$\overline{5}$.6570551810
0.00400	0.0017371779	$\overline{1}$.9982628221	20.00000	8.6858896381	$\overline{9}$.3141103619
0.00500	0.0021714724	$\overline{1}$.9978285276	30.00000	13.0288344571	$\overline{14}$.9711655429
0.00600	0.0026057669	$\overline{1}$.9973942331	40.00000	17.3717792761	$\overline{18}$.6282207239
0.00700	0.0030400614	$\overline{1}$.9969599386	50.00000	21.7147240952	$\overline{22}$.2852759048
0.00800	0.0034743559	$\overline{1}$.9965256441	60.00000	26.0576689142	$\overline{27}$.9423310858
0.00900	0.0039086503	$\overline{1}$.9960913497	70.00000	30.4006137332	$\overline{31}$.5993862668
0.01000	0.0043429448	$\overline{1}$.9956570552	80.00000	34.7435585523	$\overline{35}$.2564414477
0.02000	0.0086858896	$\overline{1}$.9913141104	90.00000	39.0865033713	$\overline{40}$.9134966287
0.03000	0.0130288345	$\overline{1}$.9869711655	100.00000	43.4294481903	$\overline{44}$.5705518097
0.04000	0.0173717793	$\overline{1}$.9826282207	200.00000	86.8588963807	$\overline{87}$.1411036193
0.05000	0.0217147241	$\overline{1}$.9782852759	300.00000	130.2883445710	$\overline{131}$.7116554290
0.06000	0.0260576689	$\overline{1}$.9739423311	400.00000	173.7177927613	$\overline{174}$.2822072387
0.07000	0.0304006137	$\overline{1}$.9695993863	500.00000	217.1472409516	$\overline{218}$.8527590484

Note : $\log e^{x+y} = \log e^x + \log e^y$. Thus, $\log e^{113.1478} = 49.139465180$.

TABLE B

The Probability Integral.

$$\left(\frac{2}{\sqrt{\pi}}\int_0^x e^{-x^2}\,dx.\right)$$

x	0	1	2	3	4	5	6	7	8	9
0.00	0.00000	00113	00226	00339	00451	00564	00677	00790	00903	01016
0.01	0.01128	01241	01354	01467	01580	01792	01805	01918	02031	02144
0.02	0.02256	02369	02482	02595	02708	02820	02933	03046	03159	03271
0.03	0.03384	03497	03610	03722	03835	03948	04060	04173	04286	04398
0.04	0.04511	04624	04736	04849	04962	05074	05187	05299	05412	05525
0.05	0.05637	05750	05862	05975	06087	06200	06312	06425	06537	06650
0.06	0.06762	06875	06987	07099	07212	07324	07437	07549	07661	07773
0.07	0.07886	07998	08110	08223	08335	08447	08559	08671	08784	08896
0.08	0.09008	09120	09232	09344	09456	09568	09680	09792	09904	10016
0.09	0.10128	10240	10352	10464	10576	10687	10799	10911	11023	11135
0.10	0.11246	11358	11470	11581	11693	11805	11916	12028	12139	12251
0.11	0.12362	12474	12585	12697	12808	12919	13031	13142	13253	13365
0.12	0.13476	13587	13698	13809	13921	14032	14143	14254	14365	14476
0.13	0.14587	14698	14809	14919	15030	15141	15252	15363	15473	15584
0.14	0.15695	15805	15916	16027	16137	16248	16358	16468	16579	16689
0.15	0.16800	16910	17020	17130	17241	17351	17461	17571	17681	17791
0.16	0.17901	18011	18121	18231	18341	18451	18560	18670	18780	18890
0.17	0.18999	19109	19218	19328	19437	19547	19656	19766	19875	19984
0.18	0.20094	20203	20312	20421	20530	20639	20748	20857	20966	21075
0.19	0.21184	21293	21402	21510	21619	21728	21836	21945	22053	22162
0.20	0.22270	22379	22487	22595	22704	22812	22920	23028	23136	23244
0.21	0.23352	23460	23568	23676	23784	23891	23999	24107	24214	24322
0.22	0.24430	24537	24643	24752	24859	24967	25074	25181	25288	25395
0.23	0.25502	25609	25716	25823	25930	26037	26144	26250	26357	26463
0.24	0.26570	26677	26783	26889	26996	27102	27208	27314	27421	27527
0.25	0.27633	27739	27845	27950	28056	28162	28268	28373	28479	28584
0.26	0.28690	28795	28901	29006	29111	29217	29322	29427	29532	29637
0.27	0.29742	29847	29952	30056	30161	30266	30370	30475	30579	30684
0.28	0.30788	30892	30997	31101	31205	31309	31413	31517	31621	31725
0.29	0.31828	31922	32036	32139	32243	32346	32450	32553	32656	32760
0.30	0.32863	32966	33069	33172	33275	33378	33480	33583	33686	33788
0.31	0.33891	33993	34096	34198	34300	34403	34505	34607	34709	34811
0.32	0.34913	35014	35116	35218	35319	35421	35523	35624	35725	35827
0.33	0.35928	36029	36130	36231	36332	36433	36534	36635	36735	36836
0.34	0.36936	37037	37137	37238	37338	37438	37538	37638	37738	37838
0.35	0.37938	38038	38138	38237	38337	38436	38536	38635	38735	38834
0.36	0.38933	39032	39131	39230	39329	39428	39526	39625	39724	39822
0.37	0.39921	40019	40117	40215	40314	40412	40510	40608	40705	40803
0.38	0.40901	40999	41096	41194	41291	41388	41486	41583	41680	41777
0.39	0.41874	41971	42068	42164	42261	42358	42454	42550	42647	42743
0.40	0.42839	42935	43031	43127	43223	43319	43415	43510	43606	43701
0.41	0.43797	43892	43988	44083	44178	44273	44368	44463	44557	44652
0.42	0.44747	44841	44936	45030	45124	45219	45313	45407	45501	45595
0.43	0.45689	45872	45876	45970	46063	46157	46250	46343	46436	46529
0.44	0.46623	46715	46808	46901	46994	47086	47179	47271	47364	47456
0.45	0.47548	47640	47732	47824	47916	48008	48100	48191	48283	48374
0.46	0.48466	48557	48648	48739	48830	48921	49012	49103	49193	49284
0.47	0.49375	49465	49555	49646	49736	49826	49916	50006	50096	50185
0.48	0.50275	50365	50454	50543	50633	50722	50811	50900	50989	51078
0.49	0.51167	51256	51344	51433	51521	51609	51698	51786	51874	51962

TABLES

The Probability Integral.

$$\left(\frac{2}{\sqrt{\pi}} \int_0^x e^{-x^2} dx. \right)$$

x	0	1	2	3	4	5	6	7	8	9
0.50	0.52050	52138	52226	52313	52401	52488	52576	52663	52750	52837
0.51	0.52924	53011	53098	53185	53272	53358	53445	53531	53617	53704
0.52	0.53790	53876	53962	54048	54134	54219	54305	54390	54476	54561
0.53	0.54646	54732	54817	54902	54987	55071	55156	55241	55325	55410
0.54	0.55494	55578	55662	55746	55830	55914	55998	56082	56165	56249
0.55	0.56332	56416	56499	56582	56665	56748	56831	56914	56996	57079
0.56	0.57162	57244	57326	57409	57491	57573	57655	57737	57818	57900
0.57	0.57982	58063	58144	58226	58307	58388	58469	58550	58631	58712
0.58	0.58792	58873	58953	59034	59114	59194	59274	59354	59434	59514
0.59	0.59594	59673	59753	59832	59912	59991	60070	60149	60228	60307
0.60	0.60386	60464	60543	60621	60700	60778	60856	60934	61012	61090
0.61	0.61168	61246	61323	61401	61478	61556	61633	61710	61787	61864
0.62	0.61941	62018	62095	62171	62248	62324	62400	62477	62553	62629
0.63	0.62705	62780	62856	62932	63007	63083	63158	63233	63309	63384
0.64	0.63459	63533	63608	63683	63757	63832	63906	63981	64055	64129
0.65	0.64203	64277	64351	64424	64498	64572	64645	64718	64791	64865
0.66	0.64938	65011	65083	65156	65229	65301	65374	65446	65519	65591
0.67	0.65663	65735	65807	65878	65950	66022	66093	66165	66236	66307
0.68	0.66378	66449	66520	66591	66662	66732	66803	66873	66944	67014
0.69	0.67084	67154	67224	67294	67364	67433	67503	67572	67642	67711
0.70	0.67780	67849	67918	67987	68056	68125	68193	68262	68330	68398
0.71	0.68467	68535	68603	68671	68738	68806	68874	68941	69009	69076
0 72	0.69146	69210	69278	69344	69411	69478	69545	69611	69678	69744
0.73	0.69810	69877	69943	70009	70075	70140	70206	70272	70337	70403
0.74	0.70468	70533	70598	70663	70728	70793	70858	70922	70987	71051
0.75	0.71116	71180	71244	71308	71372	71436	71500	71563	71627	71690
0.76	0.71754	71817	71880	71943	72006	72069	72132	72195	72257	72320
0.77	0.72382	72444	72507	72569	72631	72693	72755	72816	72878	72940
0.78	0.73001	73062	73124	73185	73246	73307	73368	73429	73489	73550
0.79	0.73610	73671	73731	73791	73851	73911	73971	74031	74091	74151
0.80	0.74210	74270	74329	74388	74447	74506	74565	74624	74683	74742
0.81	0.74800	74859	74917	74976	75034	75092	75150	75208	75266	75323
0.82	0.75381	75439	75496	75553	75668	75668	75725	75782	75839	75896
0.83	0.75952	76009	76066	76122	76178	76234	76291	76347	76403	76459
0.84	0.76514	76570	76626	76681	76736	76792	76847	76902	76957	77012
0.85	0.77067	77122	77176	77231	77285	77340	77394	77448	77502	77556
0.86	0.77610	77664	77718	77771	77825	77878	77932	77985	78038	78091
0.87	0.78144	78197	78250	78302	78355	78408	78460	78512	78565	78617
0.88	0.78669	78721	78773	78824	78876	78928	78979	79031	79082	79133
0.89	0.79184	79235	79286	79337	79388	79439	79489	79540	79590	79641
0 90	0.79691	79741	79791	79841	79891	79941	79990	80040	80090	80139
0.91	0.80188	80238	80287	80336	80385	80434	80482	80531	80580	80628
0.92	0.80677	80725	80773	80822	80870	80918	80966	81013	81061	81109
0.93	0.81156	81204	81251	81299	81346	81393	81440	81487	81534	81580
0.94	0.81627	81674	81720	81767	81813	81859	81905	81951	81997	82043
0.95	0.82089	82135	82180	82226	82271	82317	82362	82407	82452	82497
0.96	0.82542	82587	82632	82677	82721	82766	82810	82855	82899	82943
0.97	0.82987	83031	83075	83119	83162	83206	83250	83293	83337	83380
0.98	0.83423	83466	83509	83552	83595	83638	83681	83723	83766	83808
0.99	0.83851	83893	83935	83977	84020	84061	84103	84145	84187	84229

The Probability Integral.

$$\left(\frac{2}{\sqrt{\pi}} \int_0^x e^{-x^2} dx. \right)$$

x	0	1	2	3	4	5	6	7	8	9
1.00	0.84270	84312	84353	84394	84435	84477	84518	84559	84600	84640
1.01	0.84681	84722	84762	84803	84843	84883	84924	84964	85004	85044
1.02	0.85084	85124	85163	85203	85243	85282	85322	85361	85400	85439
1.03	0.85478	85517	85556	85595	85634	85673	85711	85750	85788	85827
1.04	0.85865	85903	85941	85979	86017	86055	86093	86131	86169	86206
1.05	0.86244	86281	86318	86356	86393	86430	86467	86504	86541	86578
1.06	0.86614	86651	86688	86724	86760	86797	86833	86869	86905	86941
1.07	0.86977	87013	87049	87085	87120	87156	87191	87227	87262	87297
1.08	0.87333	87368	87403	87438	87473	87507	87542	87577	87611	87646
1.09	0.87680	87715	87749	87783	87817	87851	87885	87919	87953	87987
1.10	0.88021	88054	88088	88121	88155	88188	88221	88254	88287	88320
1.11	0.88353	88386	88419	88452	88484	88517	88549	88582	88614	88647
1.12	0.88679	88711	88743	88775	88807	88839	88871	88902	88934	88966
1.13	0.88997	89029	89060	89091	89122	89154	89185	89216	89247	89277
1.14	0.89308	89339	89370	89400	89431	89461	89492	89522	89552	89582
1.15	0.89612	89642	89672	89702	89732	89762	89792	89821	89851	89880
1.16	0.89910	89939	89968	89997	90027	90056	90085	90114	90142	90171
1.17	0.90200	90229	90257	90286	90314	90343	90371	90399	90428	90456
1.18	0.90484	90512	90540	90568	90595	90623	90651	90678	90706	90733
1.19	0.90761	90788	90815	90843	90870	90897	90924	90951	90978	91005
1.20	0.91031	91058	91085	91111	91138	91164	91191	91217	91243	91269
1.21	0.91296	91322	91348	91374	91399	91425	91451	91477	91502	91528
1.22	0.91553	91579	91604	91630	91655	91680	91705	91730	91755	91780
1.23	0.91805	91830	91855	91879	91904	91929	91953	91978	92002	92026
1.24	0.92051	92075	92099	92123	92147	92171	92195	92219	92243	92266
1.25	0.92290	92314	92337	92361	92384	92408	92431	92454	92477	92500
1.26	0.92524	92547	92570	92593	92615	92638	92661	92684	92706	92729
1.27	0.92751	92774	92796	92819	92841	92863	92885	92907	92929	92951
1.28	0.92973	92995	93017	93039	93061	93082	93104	93126	93147	93168
1.29	0.93190	93211	93232	93254	93275	93296	93317	93338	93369	93380
1.30	0.93401	93422	93442	93463	93484	93504	93525	93545	93566	93586
1.31	0.93606	93627	93647	93667	93687	93707	93727	93747	93767	93787
1.32	0.93807	93826	93846	93866	93885	93905	93924	93944	93963	93982
1.33	0.94002	94021	94040	94059	94078	94097	94116	94135	94154	94173
1.34	0.94191	94210	94229	94247	94266	94284	94303	94321	94340	94358
1.35	0.94376	94394	94413	94431	94449	94467	94485	94503	94521	94538
1.36	0.94556	94574	94592	94609	94627	94644	94662	94679	94697	94714
1.37	0.94731	94748	94766	94783	94800	94817	94834	94851	94868	94885
1.38	0.94902	94918	94935	94952	94968	94985	95002	95018	95035	95051
1.39	0.95067	95084	95100	95116	95132	95148	95165	95181	95197	95213
1.40	0.95229	95244	95260	95276	95292	95307	95323	95339	95354	95370
1.41	0.95385	95401	95416	95431	95447	95462	95477	95492	95507	95523
1.42	0.95538	95553	95566	95582	95597	95612	95627	95642	95656	95671
1.43	0.95686	95700	95715	95729	95744	95758	95773	95787	95801	95815
1.44	0.95830	95844	95858	95872	95886	95900	95914	95928	95942	95956
1.45	0.95970	95983	95997	96011	96024	96038	96051	96065	96078	96092
1.46	0.96105	96119	96132	96145	96159	96172	96185	96198	96211	96224
1.47	0.96237	96250	96263	96276	96289	96302	96315	96327	96340	96353
1.48	0.96365	96378	96391	96403	96416	96428	96440	96453	96465	96478
1.49	0.96490	96502	96514	96526	96539	96551	96563	96575	96587	96599

TABLES

The Probability Integral.

$$\left(\frac{2}{\sqrt{\pi}}\int_0^x e^{-x^2}dx.\right)$$

x	0	2	4	6	8	x	0	2	4	6	8
1.50	0.96611	96634	96658	96681	96705	2.00	0.99532	99536	99540	99544	99548
1.51	0.96728	96751	96774	96796	96819	2.01	0.99552	99556	99560	99564	99568
1.52	0.96841	96864	96886	96908	96930	2.02	0 99572	99576	99580	99583	99587
1.53	0.96952	96973	96995	97016	97037	2.03	0.99591	99594	99598	99601	99605
1.54	0.97059	97080	97100	97121	97142	2.04	0.99609	99612	99616	99619	99622
1.55	0.97162	97183	97203	97223	97243	2.05	0.99626	99629	99633	99636	99639
1.56	0.97263	97283	97302	97322	97341	2.06	0.99642	99646	99649	99652	99655
1.57	0.97360	97379	97398	97417	97436	2.07	0.99658	99661	99664	99667	99670
1.58	0.97455	97473	97492	97510	97528	2.08	0.99673	99676	99679	99682	99685
1.59	0.97546	97564	97582	97600	97617	2.09	0.99688	99691	99694	99697	99699
1.60	0.97635	97652	97670	97687	97704	2.10	0.99702	99705	99707	99710	99713
1.61	0.97721	97738	97754	97771	97787	2.11	0.99715	99718	99721	99723	99726
1.62	0.97804	97820	97836	97852	97868	2.12	0.99728	99731	99733	99736	99738
1.63	0.97884	97900	97916	97931	97947	2.13	0.99741	99743	99745	99748	99750
1.64	0.97962	97977	97993	98008	98023	2.14	0.99753	99755	99757	99759	99762
1.65	0.98038	98052	98067	98082	98096	2.15	0.99764	99766	99768	99770	99773
1.66	0.98110	98125	98139	98153	98167	2.16	0.99775	99777	99779	99781	99783
1.67	0.98181	98195	98209	98222	98236	2.17	0.99785	99787	99789	99791	99793
1.68	0.98249	98263	98276	98289	98302	2.18	0.99795	99797	99799	99801	99803
1.69	0.98315	98328	98341	98354	98366	2.19	0.99805	99806	99808	99810	99812
1.70	0.98379	98392	98404	98416	98429	2.20	0.99814	99815	99817	99819	99821
1.71	0.98441	98453	98465	98477	98489	2.21	0.99822	99824	99826	99827	99829
1.72	0.98500	98512	98524	98535	98546	2.22	0.99831	99832	99834	99836	99837
1.73	0.98558	98569	98580	98591	98602	2.23	0.99839	99840	99842	99843	99845
1.74	0.98613	98624	98635	98646	98657	2.24	0.99846	99848	99849	99851	99852
1.75	0.98667	98678	98688	98699	98709	2.25	0.99854	99855	99857	99858	99859
1.76	0.98719	98729	98739	98749	98759	2.26	0.99861	99862	99863	99865	99866
1.77	0.98769	98779	98789	98798	98808	2.27	0.99867	99869	99870	99871	99873
1.78	0.98817	98827	98836	98846	98855	2.28	0.99874	99875	99876	99877	99879
1.79	0.98864	98873	98882	98891	98900	2.29	0.99880	99881	99882	99883	99885
1.80	0.98909	98918	98927	98935	98944	2.30	0.99886	99887	99888	99889	99890
1.81	0.98952	98961	98969	98978	98986	2.31	0.99891	99892	99893	99894	99896
1.82	0.98994	99003	99011	99019	99027	2.32	0.99897	99898	99899	99900	99901
1.83	0.99035	99043	99050	99058	99066	2.33	0.99902	99903	99904	99905	99906
1.84	0.99074	99081	99089	99096	99104	2.34	0.99906	99907	99908	99909	99910
1.85	0.99111	99118	99126	99133	99140	2.35	0.99911	99912	99913	99914	99915
1.86	0.99147	99154	99161	99168	99175	2.36	0.99915	99916	99917	99918	99919
1.87	0.99182	99189	99196	99202	99209	2.37	0.99920	99920	99921	99922	99923
1.88	0.99216	99222	99229	99235	99242	2.38	0.99924	99924	99925	99926	99927
1.89	0.99248	99254	99261	99267	99273	2.39	0.99928	99928	99929	99930	99930
1.90	0.99279	99285	99291	99297	99303	2.40	0.99931	99932	99933	99933	99934
1.91	0.99309	99315	99321	99326	99332	2.41	0.99935	99935	99936	99937	99937
1.92	0.99338	99343	99349	99355	99360	2.42	0.99938	99939	99939	99940	99940
1.93	0.99366	99371	99376	99382	99387	2.43	0.99941	99942	99942	99943	99943
1.94	0.99392	99397	99403	99408	99413	2.44	0.99944	99945	99945	99946	99946
1.95	0.99418	99423	99428	99433	99438	2.45	0.99947	99947	99948	99949	99949
1.96	0.99443	99447	99452	99457	99462	2.46	0.99950	99950	99951	99951	99952
1.97	0.99466	99471	99476	99480	99485	2.47	0.99952	99953	99953	99954	99954
1.98	0.99489	99494	99498	99502	99507	2.48	0.99955	99955	99956	99956	99957
1.99	0.99511	99515	99520	99524	99528	2.49	0.99957	99958	99958	99958	99959
2.00	0.99532	99536	99540	99544	99548	2.50	0.99959	99960	99960	99961	99961

The Probability Integral.

$$\left(\frac{2}{\sqrt{\pi}} \int_0^x e^{-x^2} dx. \right)$$

x	0	1	2	3	4	5	6	7	8	9
2.5	0.99959	99961	99963	99965	99967	99969	99971	99972	99974	99975
2.6	0.99976	99978	99979	99980	99981	99982	99983	99984	99985	99986
2.7	0.99987	99987	99988	99989	99989	99990	99991	99991	99992	99992
2.8	0.99992	99993	99993	99994	99994	99994	99995	99995	99995	99996
2.9	0.99996	99996	99996	99997	99997	99997	99997	99997	99997	99998
3.0	0.99998	99998	99998	99998	99998	99998	99998	99998	99999	99999

The value, I, of the Probability Integral may always be found from the convergent series

$$I = \frac{2}{\sqrt{\pi}} \left(x - \frac{x^3}{3 \cdot 1 !} + \frac{x^5}{5 \cdot 2 !} - \frac{x^7}{7 \cdot 3 !} + \cdots \right),$$

but for large values of x, the semiconvergent series

$$I = 1 - \frac{e^{-x}}{x \sqrt{\pi}} \left(1 - \frac{1}{2 x^2} + \frac{1 \cdot 3}{(2 x^2)^2} - \frac{1 \cdot 3 \cdot 5}{(2 x^2)^3} + \cdots \right)$$

is convenient.

INDEX OF AUTHORS

SUBJECT-INDEX

Catalogue of Dover
SCIENCE BOOKS

BOOKS THAT EXPLAIN SCIENCE

THE NATURE OF LIGHT AND COLOUR IN THE OPEN AIR, M. Minnaert. Why is falling snow sometimes black? What causes mirages, the fata morgana, multiple suns and moons in the sky; how are shadows formed? Prof. Minnaert of U. of Utrecht answers these and similar questions in optics, light, colour, for non-specialists. Particularly valuable to nature, science students, painters, photographers. "Can best be described in one word—fascinating!" Physics Today. Translated by H. M. Kremer-Priest, K. Jay. 202 illustrations, including 42 photos. xvi + 362pp. 5⅜ x 8.   T196 Paperbound **$1.95**

THE RESTLESS UNIVERSE, Max Born. New enlarged version of this remarkably readable account by a Nobel laureate. Moving from sub-atomic particles to universe, the author explains in very simple terms the latest theories of wave mechanics. Partial contents: air and its relatives, electrons and ions, waves and particles, electronic structure of the atom, nuclear physics. Nearly 1000 illustrations, including 7 animated sequences. 325pp. 6 x 9.   T412 Paperbound **$2.00**

MATTER AND LIGHT, THE NEW PHYSICS, L. de Broglie. Non-technical papers by a Nobel laureate explain electromagnetic theory, relativity, matter, light, radiation, wave mechanics, quantum physics, philosophy of science. Einstein, Planck, Bohr, others explained so easily that no mathematical training is needed for all but 2 of the 21 chapters. "Easy simplicity and lucidity . . . should make this source-book of modern physcis available to a wide public," Saturday Review. Unabridged. 300pp. 5⅜ x 8.   T35 Paperbound **$1.60**

THE COMMON SENSE OF THE EXACT SCIENCES, W. K. Clifford. Introduction by James Newman, edited by Karl Pearson. For 70 years this has been a guide to classical scientific, mathematical thought. Explains with unusual clarity basic concepts such as extension of meaning of symbols, characteristics of surface boundaries, properties of plane figures, vectors, Cartesian method of determining position, etc. Long preface by Bertrand Russell. Bibliography of Clifford. Corrected. 130 diagrams redrawn. 249pp. 5⅜ x 8.
                                                              T61 Paperbound **$1.60**

THE EVOLUTION OF SCIENTIFIC THOUGHT FROM NEWTON TO EINSTEIN, A. d'Abro. Einstein's special, general theories of relativity, with historical implications, analyzed in non-technical terms. Excellent accounts of contributions of Newton, Riemann, Weyl, Planck, Eddington, Maxwell, Lorentz, etc., are treated in terms of space, time, equations of electromagnetics, finiteness of universe, methodology of science. "Has become a standard work," Nature. 21 diagrams. 482pp. 5⅜ x 8.   T2 Paperbound **$2.00**

BRIDGES AND THEIR BUILDERS, D. Steinman, S. R. Watson. Engineers, historians, everyone ever fascinated by great spans will find this an endless source of information and interest. Dr. Steinman, recent recipient of Louis Levy Medal, is one of the great bridge architects, engineers of all time. His analysis of great bridges of history is both authoritative and easily followed. Greek, Roman, medieval, oriental bridges; modern works such as Brooklyn Bridge, Golden Gate Bridge, etc. described in terms of history, constructional principles, artistry, function. Most comprehensive, accurate semi-popular history of bridges in print in English. New, greatly revised, enlarged edition. 23 photographs, 26 line drawings. xvii + 401pp. 5⅜ x 8.   T431 Paperbound **$1.95**

CONCERNING THE NATURE OF THINGS, Sir William Bragg. Christmas lectures at Royal Society by Nobel laureate, dealing with atoms, gases, liquids, and various types of crystals. No scientific background is needed to understand this remarkably clear introduction to basic processes and aspects of modern science. "More interesting than any bestseller," London Morning Post. 32pp. of photos. 57 figures. xii + 232pp. 5⅜ x 8.   T31 Paperbound **$1.35**

THE RISE OF THE NEW PHYSICS, A. d'Abro. Half million word exposition, formerly titled "The Decline of Mechanism," for readers not versed in higher mathematics. Only thorough explanation in everyday language of core of modern mathematical physical theory, treating both classical, modern views. Scientifically impeccable coverage of thought from Newtonian system through theories of Dirac, Heisenberg, Fermi's statistics. Combines history, exposition; broad but unified, detailed view, with constant comparison of classical, modern views. "A must for anyone doing serious study in the physical sciences," J. of the Franklin Inst. "Extraordinary faculty . . . to explain ideas and theories . . . in language of everyday life," Isis. Part I of set: philosophy of science, from practice of Newton, Maxwell, Poincaré, Einstein, etc. Modes of thought, experiment, causality, etc. Part II: 100 pp. on grammar, vocabulary of mathematics, discussions of functions, groups, series, Fourier series, etc. Remainder treats concrete, detailed coverage of both classical, quantum physics: analytic mechanics, Hamilton's principle, electromagnetic waves, thermodynamics, Brownian movement, special relativity, Bohr's atom, de Broglie's wave mechanics, Heisenberg's uncertainty, scores of other important topics. Covers discoveries, theories of d'Alembert, Born, Cantor, Debye, Euler, Foucault, Galois, Gauss, Hadamard, Kelvin, Kepler Laplace, Maxwell, Pauli, Rayleigh Volterra, Weyl, more than 180 others. 97 illustrations. ix + 982pp. 5⅜ x 8.
T3 Vol. 1 Paperbound **$2.00**
T4 Vol. II Paperbound **$2.00**

SPINNING TOPS AND GYROSCOPIC MOTION, John Perry. Well-known classic of science still unsurpassed for lucid, accurate, delightful exposition. How quasi-rigidity is induced in flexible, fluid bodies by rapid motions; why gyrostat falls, top rises; nature, effect of internal fluidity on rotating bodies; etc. Appendixes describe practical use of gyroscopes in ships, compasses, monorail transportation. 62 figures. 128pp. 5⅜ x 8.
T416 Paperbound **$1.00**

FOUNDATIONS OF PHYSICS, R. B. Lindsay, H. Margenau. Excellent bridge between semi-popular and technical writings. Discussion of methods of physical description, construction of theory; valuable to physicist with elementary calculus. Gives meaning to data, tools of modern physics. Contents: symbolism, mathematical equations; space and time; foundations of mechanics; probability; physics, continua; electron theory; relativity; quantum mechanics; causality; etc. "Thorough and yet not overdetailed. Unreservedly recommended," Nature. Unabridged corrected edition. 35 illustrations. xi + 537pp. 5⅜ x 8.   S377 Paperbound **$2.45**

FADS AND FALLACIES IN THE NAME OF SCIENCE, Martin Gardner. Formerly entitled "In the Name of Science," the standard account of various cults, quack systems, delusions which have masqueraded as science: hollow earth fanatics, orgone sex energy, dianetics, Atlantis, Forteanism, flying saucers, medical fallacies like zone therapy, etc. New chapter on Bridey Murphy, psionics, other recent manifestations. A fair reasoned appraisal of eccentric theory which provides excellent innoculation. "Should be read by everyone, scientist or non-scientist alike," R. T. Birge, Prof. Emeritus of Physics, Univ. of Calif.; Former Pres., Amer. Physical Soc. x + 365pp. 5⅜ x 8.   T394 Paperbound **$1.50**

ON MATHEMATICS AND MATHEMATICIANS, R. E. Moritz. A 10 year labor of love by discerning, discriminating Prof. Moritz, this collection conveys the full sense of mathematics and personalities of great mathematicians. Anecdotes, aphorisms, reminiscences, philosophies, definitions, speculations, biographical insights, etc. by great mathematicians, writers: Descartes, Mill, Locke, Kant, Coleridge, Whitehead, etc. Glimpses into lives of great mathematicians, from Archimedes to Euler, Gauss, Weierstrass. To mathematicians, a superb browsing-book. To laymen, exciting revelation of fullness of mathematics. Extensive cross index. 410pp. 5⅜ x 8.   T489 Paperbound **$1.95**

GUIDE TO THE LITERATURE OF MATHEMATICS AND PHYSICS, N. G. Parke III. Over 5000 entries under approximately 120 major subject headings, of selected most important books, monographs, periodicals, articles in English, plus important works in German, French, Italian, Spanish, Russian (many recently available works). Covers every branch of physics, math, related engineering. Includes author, title, edition, publisher, place, date, number of volumes, number of pages. 40 page introduction on basic problems of research, study provides useful information on organization, use of libraries, psychology of learning, etc. Will save you hours of time. 2nd revised edition. Indices of authors, subjects. 464pp. 5⅜ x 8.   S447 Paperbound **$2.49**

THE STRANGE STORY OF THE QUANTUM, An Account for the General Reader of the Growth of Ideas Underlying Our Present Atomic Knowledge, B. Hoffmann. Presents lucidly, expertly, with barest amount of mathematics, problems and theories which led to modern quantum physics. Begins with late 1800's when discrepancies were noticed; with illuminating analogies, examples, goes through concepts of Planck, Einstein, Pauli, Schroedinger, Dirac, Sommerfield, Feynman, etc. New postscript through 1958. "Of the books attempting an account of the history and contents of modern atomic physics which have come to my attention, this is the best," H. Margenau, Yale U., in Amer. J. of Physics. 2nd edition. 32 tables, illustrations. 275pp. 5⅜ x 8.   T518 Paperbound **$1.45**

DOVER SCIENCE BOOKS

HISTORY OF SCIENCE
AND PHILOSOPHY OF SCIENCE

THE VALUE OF SCIENCE, Henri Poincaré. Many of most mature ideas of "last scientific universalist" for both beginning, advanced workers. Nature of scientific truth, whether order is innate in universe or imposed by man, logical thought vs. intuition (relating to Weierstrass, Lie, Riemann, etc), time and space (relativity, psychological time, simultaneity), Herz's concept of force, values within disciplines of Maxwell, Carnot, Mayer, Newton, Lorentz, etc. iii + 147pp. 5⅜ x 8. S469 Paperbound **$1.35**

PHILOSOPHY AND THE PHYSICISTS, L. S. Stebbing. Philosophical aspects of modern science examined in terms of lively critical attack on ideas of Jeans, Eddington. Tasks of science, causality, determinism, probability, relation of world physics to that of everyday experience, philosophical significance of Planck-Bohr concept of discontinuous energy levels, inferences to be drawn from Uncertainty Principle, implications of "becoming" involved in 2nd law of thermodynamics, other problems posed by discarding of Laplacean determinism. 285pp. 5⅜ x 8. T480 Paperbound **$1.65**

THE PRINCIPLES OF SCIENCE, A TREATISE ON LOGIC AND THE SCIENTIFIC METHOD, W. S. Jevons. Milestone in development of symbolic logic remains stimulating contribution to investigation of inferential validity in sciences. Treats inductive, deductive logic, theory of number, probability, limits of scientific method; significantly advances Boole's logic, contains detailed introduction to nature and methods of probability in physics, astronomy, everyday affairs, etc. In introduction, Ernest Nagel of Columbia U. says, "[Jevons] continues to be of interest as an attempt to articulate the logic of scientific inquiry." liii + 786pp. 5⅜ x 8. S446 Paperbound **$2.98**

A HISTORY OF ASTRONOMY FROM THALES TO KEPLER, J. L. E. Dreyer. Only work in English to give complete history of cosmological views from prehistoric times to Kepler. Partial contents: Near Eastern astronomical systems, Early Greeks, Homocentric spheres of Euxodus, Epicycles, Ptolemaic system, Medieval cosmology, Copernicus, Kepler, much more. "Especially useful to teachers and students of the history of science . . . unsurpassed in its field," Isis. Formerly "A History of Planetary Systems from Thales to Kepler." Revised foreword by W. H. Stahl. xvii + 430pp. 5⅜ x 8. S79 Paperbound **$1.98**

A CONCISE HISTORY OF MATHEMATICS, D. Struik. Lucid study of development of ideas, techniques, from Ancient Near East, Greece, Islamic science, Middle Ages, Renaissance, modern times. Important mathematicians described in detail. Treatment not anecdotal, but analytical development of ideas. Non-technical—no math training needed. "Rich in content, thoughtful in interpretations," U.S. Quarterly Booklist. 60 illustrations including Greek, Egyptian manuscripts, portraits of 31 mathematicians. 2nd edition. xix + 299pp. 5⅜ x 8. S255 Paperbound **$1.75**

THE PHILOSOPHICAL WRITINGS OF PEIRCE, edited by Justus Buchler. A carefully balanced expositon of Peirce's complete system, written by Peirce himself. It covers such matters as scientific method, pure chance vs. law, symbolic logic, theory of signs, pragmatism, experiment, and other topics. "Excellent selection . . . gives more than adequate evidence of the range and greatness," Personalist. Formerly entitled "The Philosophy of Peirce." xvi + 368pp. T217 Paperbound **$1.95**

SCIENCE AND METHOD, Henri Poincaré. Procedure of scientific discovery, methodology, experiment, idea-germination—processes by which discoveries come into being. Most significant and interesting aspects of development, application of ideas. Chapters cover selection of facts, chance, mathematical reasoning, mathematics and logic; Whitehead, Russell, Cantor, the new mechanics, etc. 288pp. 5⅜ x 8. S222 Paperbound **$1.35**

SCIENCE AND HYPOTHESIS, Henri Poincaré. Creative psychology in science. How such concepts as number, magnitude, space, force, classical mechanics developed, how modern scientist uses them in his thought. Hypothesis in physics, theories of modern physics. Introduction by Sir James Larmor. "Few mathematicians have had the breadth of vision of Poincaré, and none is his superior in the gift of clear exposition," E. T. Bell. 272pp. 5⅜ x 8. S221 Paperbound **$1.35**

ESSAYS IN EXPERIMENTAL LOGIC, John Dewey. Stimulating series of essays by one of most influential minds in American philosophy presents some of his most mature thoughts on wide range of subjects. Partial contents: Relationship between inquiry and experience; dependence of knowledge upon thought; character logic; judgments of practice, data, and meanings; stimuli of thought, etc. viii + 444pp. 5⅜ x 8. T73 Paperbound **$1.95**

WHAT IS SCIENCE, Norman Campbell. Excellent introduction explains scientific method, role of mathematics, types of scientific laws. Contents: 2 aspects of science, science and nature, laws of chance, discovery of laws, explanation of laws, measurement and numerical laws, applications of science. 192pp. 5⅜ x 8. S43 Paperbound **$1.25**

3

FROM EUCLID TO EDDINGTON: A STUDY OF THE CONCEPTIONS OF THE EXTERNAL WORLD, Sir Edmund Whittaker. Foremost British scientist traces development of theories of natural philosophy from western rediscovery of Euclid to Eddington, Einstein, Dirac, etc. 5 major divisions: Space, Time and Movement; Concepts of Classical Physics; Concepts of Quantum Mechanics; Eddington Universe. Contrasts inadequacy of classical physics to understand physical world with present day attempts of relativity, non-Euclidean geometry, space curvature, etc. 212pp. 5⅜ x 8.   T491 Paperbound **$1.35**

THE ANALYSIS OF MATTER, Bertrand Russell. How do our senses accord with the new physics? This volume covers such topics as logical analysis of physics, prerelativity physics, causality, scientific inference, physics and perception, special and general relativity, Weyl's theory, tensors, invariants and their physical interpretation, periodicity and qualitative series. "The most thorough treatment of the subject that has yet been published," The Nation. Introduction by L. E. Denonn. 422pp. 5⅜ x 8.   T231 Paperbound **$1.95**

LANGUAGE, TRUTH, AND LOGIC, A. Ayer. A clear introduction to the Vienna and Cambridge schools of Logical Positivism. Specific tests to evaluate validity of ideas, etc. Contents: function of philosophy, elimination of metaphysics, nature of analysis, a priori, truth and probability, etc. 10th printing. "I should like to have written it myself," Bertrand Russell. 160pp. 5⅜ x 8.   T10 Paperbound **$1.25**

THE PSYCHOLOGY OF INVENTION IN THE MATHEMATICAL FIELD, J. Hadamard. Where do ideas come from? What role does the unconscious play? Are ideas best developed by mathematical reasoning, word reasoning, visualization? What are the methods used by Einstein, Poincaré, Galton, Riemann? How can these techniques be applied by others? One of the world's leading mathematicians discusses these and other questions. xiii + 145pp. 5⅜ x 8.
T107 Paperbound **$1.25**

GUIDE TO PHILOSOPHY, C. E. M. Joad. By one of the ablest expositors of all time, this is not simply a history or a typological survey, but an examination of central problems in terms of answers afforded by the greatest thinkers: Plato, Aristotle, Scholastics, Leibniz, Kant, Whitehead, Russell, and many others. Especially valuable to persons in the physical sciences; over 100 pages devoted to Jeans, Eddington, and others, the philosophy of modern physics, scientific materialism, pragmatism, etc. Classified bibliography. 592pp. 5⅜ x 8.   T50 Paperbound **$2.00**

SUBSTANCE AND FUNCTION, and EINSTEIN'S THEORY OF RELATIVITY, Ernst Cassirer. Two books bound as one. Cassirer establishes a philosophy of the exact sciences that takes into consideration new developments in mathematics, shows historical connections. Partial contents: Aristotelian logic, Mill's analysis, Helmholtz and Kronecker, Russell and cardinal numbers, Euclidean vs. non-Euclidean geometry, Einstein's relativity. Bibliography. Index. xxi + 464pp. 5⅜ x 8.   T50 Paperbound **$2.00**

FOUNDATIONS OF GEOMETRY, Bertrand Russell. Nobel laureate analyzes basic problems in the overlap area between mathematics and philosophy: the nature of geometrical knowledge, the nature of geometry, and the applications of geometry to space. Covers history of non-Euclidean geometry, philosophic interpretations of geometry, especially Kant, projective and metrical geometry. Most interesting as the solution offered in 1897 by a great mind to a problem still current. New introduction by Prof. Morris Kline, N.Y. University. "Admirably clear, precise, and elegantly reasoned analysis," International Math. News. xii + 201pp. 5⅜ x 8.   S233 Paperbound **$1.60**

THE NATURE OF PHYSICAL THEORY, P. W. Bridgman. How modern physics looks to a highly unorthodox physicist—a Nobel laureate. Pointing out many absurdities of science, demonstrating inadequacies of various physical theories, weighs and analyzes contributions of Einstein, Bohr, Heisenberg, many others. A non-technical consideration of correlation of science and reality. xi + 138pp. 5⅜ x 8.   S33 Paperbound **$1.25**

EXPERIMENT AND THEORY IN PHYSICS, Max Born. A Nobel laureate examines the nature and value of the counterclaims of experiment and theory in physics. Synthetic versus analytical scientific advances are analyzed in works of Einstein, Bohr, Heisenberg, Planck, Eddington, Milne, others, by a fellow scientist. 44pp. 5⅜ x 8.   S308 Paperbound **60¢**

A SHORT HISTORY OF ANATOMY AND PHYSIOLOGY FROM THE GREEKS TO HARVEY, Charles Singer. Corrected edition of "The Evolution of Anatomy." Classic traces anatomy, physiology from prescientific times through Greek, Roman periods, dark ages, Renaissance, to beginning of modern concepts. Centers on individuals, movements, that definitely advanced anatomical knowledge. Plato, Diocles, Erasistratus, Galen, da Vinci, etc. Special section on Vesalius. 20 plates. 270 extremely interesting illustrations of ancient, Medieval, Renaissance, Oriental origin. xii + 209pp. 5⅜ x 8.   T389 Paperbound **$1.75**

SPACE - TIME - MATTER, Hermann Weyl. "The standard treatise on the general theory of relativity," (Nature), by world renowned scientist. Deep, clear discussion of logical coherence of general theory, introducing all needed tools: Maxwell, analytical geometry, non-Euclidean geometry, tensor calculus, etc. Basis is classical space-time, before absorption of relativity. Contents: Euclidean space, mathematical form, metrical continuum, general theory, etc. 15 diagrams. xviii + 330pp. 5⅜ x 8.   S267 Paperbound **$1.75**

4

DOVER SCIENCE BOOKS

MATTER AND MOTION, James Clerk Maxwell. Excellent exposition begins with simple particles, proceeds gradually to physical systems beyond complete analysis; motion, force, properties of centre of mass of material system; work, energy, gravitation, etc. Written with all Maxwell's original insights and clarity. Notes by E. Larmor. 17 diagrams. 178pp. 5⅜ x 8.
S188 Paperbound **$1.25**

PRINCIPLES OF MECHANICS, Heinrich Hertz. Last work by the great 19th century physicist is not only a classic, but of great interest in the logic of science. Creating a new system of mechanics based upon space, time, and mass, it returns to axiomatic analysis, understanding of the formal or structural aspects of science, taking into account logic, observation, a priori elements. Of great historical importance to Poincaré, Carnap, Einstein, Milne. A 20 page introduction by R. S. Cohen, Wesleyan University, analyzes the implications of Hertz's thought and the logic of science. 13 page introduction by Helmholtz. xlii + 274pp. 5⅜ x 8.
S316 Clothbound **$3.50**
S317 Paperbound **$1.75**

FROM MAGIC TO SCIENCE, Charles Singer. A great historian examines aspects of science from Roman Empire through Renaissance. Includes perhaps best discussion of early herbals, penetrating physiological interpretation of "The Visions of Hildegarde of Bingen." Also examines Arabian, Galenic influences; Pythagoras' sphere, Paracelsus; reawakening of science under Leonardo da Vinci, Vesalius; Lorica of Gildas the Briton; etc. Frequent quotations with translations from contemporary manuscripts. Unabridged, corrected edition. 158 unusual illustrations from Classical, Medieval sources. xxvii + 365pp. 5⅜ x 8.
T390 Paperbound **$2.00**

A HISTORY OF THE CALCULUS, AND ITS CONCEPTUAL DEVELOPMENT, Carl B. Boyer. Provides laymen, mathematicians a detailed history of the development of the calculus, from beginnings in antiquity to final elaboration as mathematical abstraction. Gives a sense of mathematics not as technique, but as habit of mind, in progression of ideas of Zeno, Plato, Pythagoras, Eudoxus, Arabic and Scholastic mathematicians, Newton, Leibniz, Taylor, Descartes, Euler, Lagrange, Cantor, Weierstrass, and others. This first comprehensive, critical history of the calculus was originally entitled "The Concepts of the Calculus." Foreword by R. Courant. 22 figures. 25 page bibliography. v + 364pp. 5⅜ x 8.
S509 Paperbound **$2.00**

A DIDEROT PICTORIAL ENCYCLOPEDIA OF TRADES AND INDUSTRY, Manufacturing and the Technical Arts in Plates Selected from "L'Encyclopédie ou Dictionnaire Raisonné des Sciences, des Arts, et des Métiers" of Denis Diderot. Edited with text by C. Gillispie. First modern selection of plates from high-point of 18th century French engraving. Storehouse of technological information to historian of arts and science. Over 2,000 illustrations on 485 full page plates, most of them original size, show trades, industries of fascinating era in such great detail that modern reconstructions might be made of them. Plates teem with men, women, children performing thousands of operations; show sequence, general operations, closeups, details of machinery. Illustrates such important, interesting trades, industries as sowing, harvesting, beekeeping, tobacco processing, fishing, arts of war, mining, smelting, casting iron, extracting mercury, making gunpowder, cannons, bells, shoeing horses, tanning, papermaking, printing, dying, over 45 more categories. Professor Gillispie of Princeton supplies full commentary on all plates, identifies operations, tools, processes, etc. Material is presented in lively, lucid fashion. Of great interest to all studying history of science, technology. Heavy library cloth. 920pp. 9 x 12.
T421 2 volume set **$18.50**

DE MAGNETE, William Gilbert. Classic work on magnetism, founded new science. Gilbert was first to use word "electricity," to recognize mass as distinct from weight, to discover effect of heat on magnetic bodies; invented an electroscope, differentiated between static electricity and magnetism, conceived of earth as magnet. This lively work, by first great experimental scientist, is not only a valuable historical landmark, but a delightfully easy to follow record of a searching, ingenious mind. Translated by P. F. Mottelay. 25 page biographical memoir. 90 figures. lix + 368pp. 5⅜ x 8.
S470 Paperbound **$2.00**

HISTORY OF MATHEMATICS, D. E. Smith. Most comprehensive, non-technical history of math in English. Discusses lives and works of over a thousand major, minor figures, with footnotes giving technical information outside book's scheme, and indicating disputed matters. Vol. I: A chronological examination, from primitive concepts through Egypt, Babylonia, Greece, the Orient, Rome, the Middle Ages, The Renaissance, and to 1900. Vol. II: The development of ideas in specific fields and problems, up through elementary calculus. "Marks an epoch . . . will modify the entire teaching of the history of science," George Sarton. 2 volumes, total of 510 illustrations, 1355pp. 5⅜ x 8. Set boxed in attractive container.
T429, 430 Paperbound, the set **$5.00**

THE PHILOSOPHY OF SPACE AND TIME, H. Reichenbach. An important landmark in development of empiricist conception of geometry, covering foundations of geometry, time theory, consequences of Einstein's relativity, including: relations between theory and observations; coordinate definitions; relations between topological and metrical properties of space; psychological problem of visual intuition of non-Euclidean structures; many more topics important to modern science and philosophy. Majority of ideas require only knowledge of intermediate math. "Still the best book in the field," Rudolf Carnap. Introduction by R. Carnap. 49 figures. xviii + 296pp. 5⅜ x 8.
S443 Paperbound **$2.00**

5

FOUNDATIONS OF SCIENCE: THE PHILOSOPHY OF THEORY AND EXPERIMENT, N. Campbell.
A critique of the most fundamental concepts of science, particularly physics. Examines why certain propositions are accepted without question, demarcates science from philosophy, etc. Part I analyzes presuppositions of scientific thought: existence of material world, nature of laws, probability, etc; part 2 covers nature of experiment and applications of mathematics: conditions for measurement, relations between numerical laws and theories, error, etc. An appendix covers problems arising from relativity, force, motion, space, time. A classic in its field. "A real grasp of what science is," Higher Educational Journal.
xiii + 565pp. 5⅝ x 8⅜. S372 Paperbound **$2.95**

THE STUDY OF THE HISTORY OF MATHEMATICS and THE STUDY OF THE HISTORY OF SCIENCE, G. Sarton. Excellent introductions, orientation, for beginning or mature worker. Describes duty of mathematical historian, incessant efforts and genius of previous generations. Explains how today's discipline differs from previous methods. 200 item bibliography with critical evaluations, best available biographies of modern mathematicians, best treatises on historical methods is especially valuable. 10 illustrations. 2 volumes bound as one.
113pp. + 75pp. 5⅜ x 8. T240 Paperbound **$1.25**

MATHEMATICAL PUZZLES

MATHEMATICAL PUZZLES OF SAM LOYD, selected and edited by **Martin Gardner.** 117 choice puzzles by greatest American puzzle creator and innovator, from his famous "Cyclopedia of Puzzles." All unique style, historical flavor of originals. Based on arithmetic, algebra, probability, game theory, route tracing, topology, sliding block, operations research, geometrical dissection. Includes famous "14-15" puzzle which was national craze, "Horse of a Different Color" which sold millions of copies. 120 line drawings, diagrams. Solutions.
xx + 167pp. 5⅜ x 8. T498 Paperbound **$1.00**

SYMBOLIC LOGIC and THE GAME OF LOGIC, Lewis Carroll. "Symbolic Logic" is not concerned with modern symbolic logic, but is instead a collection of over 380 problems posed with charm and imagination, using the syllogism, and a fascinating diagrammatic method of drawing conclusions. In "The Game of Logic" Carroll's whimsical imagination devises a logical game played with 2 diagrams and counters (included) to manipulate hundreds of tricky syllogisms. The final section, "Hit or Miss" is a lagniappe of 101 additional puzzles in the delightful Carroll manner. Until this reprint edition, both of these books were rarities costing up to $15 each. Symbolic Logic: Index. xxxi + 199pp. The Game of Logic: 96pp.
2 vols. bound as one. 5⅜ x 8. T492 Paperbound **$1.50**

PILLOW PROBLEMS and A TANGLED TALE, Lewis Carroll. One of the rarest of all Carroll's works, "Pillow Problems" contains 72 original math puzzles, all typically ingenious. Particularly fascinating are Carroll's answers which remain exactly as he thought them out, reflecting his actual mental process. The problems in "A Tangled Tale" are in story form, originally appearing as a monthly magazine serial. Carroll not only gives the solutions, but uses answers sent in by readers to discuss wrong approaches and misleading paths, and grades them for insight. Both of these books were rarities until this edition, "Pillow Problems" costing up to $25, and "A Tangled Tale" $15. Pillow Problems: Preface and Introduction by Lewis Carroll. xx + 109pp. A Tangled Tale: 6 illustrations. 152pp. Two vols.
bound as one. 5⅜ x 8. T493 Paperbound **$1.50**

NEW WORD PUZZLES, G. L. Kaufman. 100 brand new challenging puzzles on words, combinations, never before published. Most are new types invented by author, for beginners and experts both. Squares of letters follow chess moves to build words; symmetrical designs made of synonyms; rhymed crostics; double word squares; syllable puzzles where you fill in missing syllables instead of missing letter; many other types, all new. Solutions. "Excellent," Recreation. 100 puzzles. 196 figures. vi + 122pp. 5⅜ x 8.
T344 Paperbound **$1.00**

MATHEMATICAL EXCURSIONS, H. A. Merrill. Fun, recreation, insights into elementary problem solving. Math expert guides you on by-paths not generally travelled in elementary math courses—divide by inspection, Russian peasant multiplication; memory systems for pi; odd, even magic squares; dyadic systems; square roots by geometry; Tchebichev's machine; dozens more. Solutions to more difficult ones. "Brain stirring stuff . . . a classic," Genie.
50 illustrations. 145pp. 5⅜ x 8. T350 Paperbound **$1.00**

THE BOOK OF MODERN PUZZLES, G. L. Kaufman. Over 150 puzzles, absolutely all new material based on same appeal as crosswords, deduction puzzles, but with different principles, techniques. 2-minute teasers, word labyrinths, design, pattern, logic, observation puzzles, puzzles testing ability to apply general knowledge to peculiar situations, many others.
Solutions. 116 illustrations. 192pp. 5⅜ x 8. T143 Paperbound **$1.00**

MATHEMAGIC, MAGIC PUZZLES, AND GAMES WITH NUMBERS, R. V. Heath. Over 60 puzzles, stunts, on properties of numbers. Easy techniques for multiplying large numbers mentally, identifying unknown numbers, finding date of any day in any year. Includes The Lost Digit, 3 Acrobats, Psychic Bridge, magic squares, triangles, cubes, others not easily found elsewhere. Edited by J. S. Meyer. 76 illustrations. 128pp. 5⅜ ·x 8. T110 Paperbound **$1.00**

DOVER SCIENCE BOOKS

PUZZLE QUIZ AND STUNT FUN, J. Meyer. 238 high-priority puzzles, stunts, tricks—math puzzles like The Clever Carpenter, Atom Bomb, Please Help Alice; mysteries, deductions like The Bridge of Sighs, Secret Code; observation puzzlers like The American Flag, Playing Cards, Telephone Dial; over 200 others with magic squares, tongue twisters, puns, anagrams. Solutions. Revised, enlarged edition of "Fun-To-Do." Over 100 illustrations. 238 puzzles, stunts, tricks. 256pp. 5⅜ x 8. T337 Paperbound $1.00

101 PUZZLES IN THOUGHT AND LOGIC, C. R. Wylie, Jr. For readers who enjoy challenge, stimulation of logical puzzles without specialized math or scientific knowledge. Problems entirely new, range from relatively easy to brainteasers for hours of subtle entertainment. Detective puzzles, find the lying fisherman, how a blind man identifies color by logic, many more. Easy-to-understand introduction to logic of puzzle solving and general scientific method. 128pp. 5⅜ x 8. T367 Paperbound $1.00

CRYPTANALYSIS, H. F. Gaines. Standard elementary, intermediate text for serious students. Not just old material, but much not generally known, except to experts. Concealment, Transposition, Substitution ciphers; Vigenere, Kasiski, Playfair, multafid, dozens of other techniques. Formerly "Elementary Cryptanalysis." Appendix with sequence charts, letter frequencies in English, 5 other languages, English word frequencies. Bibliography. 167 codes. New to this edition: solutions to codes. vi + 230pp. 5⅜ x 8⅜.
T97 Paperbound $1.95

CRYPTOGRAPY, L. D. Smith. Excellent elementary introduction to enciphering, deciphering secret writing. Explains transposition, substitution ciphers; codes; solutions; geometrical patterns, route transcription, columnar transposition, other methods. Mixed cipher systems; single, polyalphabetical substitutions; mechanical devices; Vigenere; etc. Enciphering Japanese; explanation of Baconian biliteral cipher; frequency tables. Over 150 problems. Bibliography. Index. 164pp. 5⅜ x 8. T247 Paperbound $1.00

MATHEMATICS, MAGIC AND MYSTERY, M. Gardner. Card tricks, metal mathematics, stage mind-reading, other "magic" explained as applications of probability, sets, number theory, etc. Creative examination of laws, applications. Scores of new tricks, insights. 115 sections on cards, dice, coins; vanishing tricks, many others. No sleight of hand—math guarantees success. "Could hardly get more entertainment . . . easy to follow," Mathematics Teacher. 115 illustrations. xii + 174pp. 5⅜ x 8. T335 Paperbound $1.00

AMUSEMENTS IN MATHEMATICS, H. E. Dudeney. Foremost British originator of math puzzles, always witty, intriguing, paradoxical in this classic. One of largest collections. More than 430 puzzles, problems, paradoxes. Mazes, games, problems on number manipulations, unicursal, other route problems, puzzles on measuring, weighing, packing, age, kinship, chessboards, joiners', crossing river, plane figure dissection, many others. Solutions. More than 450 illustrations. viii + 258pp. 5⅜ x 8. T473 Paperbound $1.25

THE CANTERBURY PUZZLES H. E. Dudeney. Chaucer's pilgrims set one another problems in story form. Also Adventures of the Puzzle Club, the Strange Escape of the King's Jester, the Monks of Riddlewell, the Squire's Christmas Puzzle Party, others. All puzzles are original, based on dissecting plane figures, arithmetic, algebra, elementary calculus, other branches of mathematics, and purely logical ingenuity. "The limit of ingenuity and intricacy," The Observer. Over 110 puzzles, full solutions. 150 illustrations. viii + 225 pp. 5⅜ x 8. T474 Paperbound $1.25

MATHEMATICAL PUZZLES FOR BEGINNERS AND ENTHUSIASTS, G. Mott-Smith. 188 puzzles to test mental agility. Inference, interpretation, algebra, dissection of plane figures, geometry, properties of numbers, decimation, permutations, probability, all are in these delightful problems. Includes the Odic Force, How to Draw an Ellipse, Spider's Cousin, more than 180 others. Detailed solutions. Appendix with square roots, triangular numbers, primes, etc. 135 illustrations. 2nd revised edition. 248pp. 5⅜ x 8. T198 Paperbound $1.00

MATHEMATICAL RECREATIONS, M. Kraitchik. Some 250 puzzles, problems, demonstrations of recreation mathematics on relatively advanced level. Unusual historical problems from Greek, Medieval, Arabic, Hindu sources; modern problems on "mathematics without numbers," geometry, topology, arithmetic, etc. Pastimes derived from figurative, Mersenne, Fermat numbers: fairy chess; latruncles: reversi; etc. Full solutions. Excellent insights into special fields of math. "Strongly recommended to all who are interested in the lighter side of mathematics," Mathematical Gaz. 181 illustrations. 330pp. 5⅜ x 8. T163 Paperbound $1.75

FICTION

FLATLAND, E. A. Abbott. A perennially popular science-fiction classic about life in a 2-dimensional world, and the impingement of higher dimensions. Political, satiric, humorous, moral overtones. This land where women are straight lines and the lowest and most dangerous classes are isosceles triangles with 3° vertices conveys brilliantly a feeling for many concepts of modern science. 7th edition. New introduction by Banesh Hoffmann. 128pp. 5⅜ x 8. T1 Paperbound $1.00

SEVEN SCIENCE FICTION NOVELS OF H. G. WELLS. Complete texts, unabridged, of seven of Wells' greatest novels: The War of the Worlds, The Invisible Man, The Island of Dr. Moreau, The Food of the Gods, First Men in the Moon, In the Days of the Comet, The Time Machine. Still considered by many experts to be the best science-fiction ever written, they will offer amusements and instruction to the scientific minded reader. "The great master," Sky and Telescope. 1051pp. 5⅜ x 8. T264 Clothbound **$3.95**

28 SCIENCE FICTION STORIES OF H. G. WELLS. Unabridged! This enormous omnibus contains 2 full length novels—Men Like Gods, Star Begotten—plus 26 short stories of space, time, invention, biology, etc. The Crystal Egg, The Country of the Blind, Empire of the Ants, The Man Who Could Work Miracles, Aepyornis Island, A Story of the Days to Come, and 20 others "A master . . . not surpassed by . . . writers of today," The English Journal. 915pp. 5⅜ x 8. T265 Clothbound **$3.95**

FIVE ADVENTURE NOVELS OF H. RIDER HAGGARD. All the mystery and adventure of darkest Africa captured accurately by a man who lived among Zulus for years, who knew African ethnology, folkways as did few of his contemporaries. They have been regarded as examples of the very best high adventure by such critics as Orwell, Andrew Lang, Kipling. Contents: She, King Solomon's Mines, Allan Quatermain, Allan's Wife, Maiwa's Revenge. "Could spin a yarn so full of suspense and color that you couldn't put the story down," Sat. Review. 821pp. 5⅜ x 8. T108 Clothbound **$3.95**

CHESS AND CHECKERS

LEARN CHESS FROM THE MASTERS, Fred Reinfeld. Easiest, most instructive way to improve your game—play 10 games against such masters as Marshall, Znosko-Borovsky, Bronstein, Najdorf, etc., with each move graded by easy system. Includes ratings for alternate moves possible. Games selected for interest, clarity, easily isolated principles. Covers Ruy Lopez, Dutch Defense, Vienna Game openings; subtle, intricate middle game variations; all-important end game. Full annotations. Formerly "Chess by Yourself." 91 diagrams. viii + 144pp. 5⅜ x 8. T362 Paperbound **$1.00**

REINFELD ON THE END GAME IN CHESS, Fred Reinfeld. Analyzes 62 end games by Alekhine, Flohr, Tarrasch, Morphy, Capablanca, Rubinstein, Lasker, Reshevsky, other masters. Only 1st rate book with extensive coverage of error—tell exactly what is wrong with each move you might have made. Centers around transitions from middle play to end play. King and pawn, minor pieces, queen endings; blockage, weak, passed pawns, etc. "Excellent . . . a boon," Chess Life. Formerly "Practical End Play." 62 figures. vi + 177pp. 5⅜ x 8. T417 Paperbound **$1.25**

HYPERMODERN CHESS as developed in the games of its greatest exponent, ARON NIMZO-VICH, edited by Fred Reinfeld. An intensely original player, analyst, Nimzovich's approaches startled, often angered the chess world. This volume, designed for the average player, shows how his iconoclastic methods won him victories over Alekhine, Lasker, Marshall, Rubinstein, Spielmann, others, and infused new life into the game. Use his methods to startle opponents, invigorate play. "Annotations and introductions to each game . . . are excellent," Times (London). 180 diagrams. viii + 220pp. 5⅜ x 8. T448 Paperbound **$1.35**

THE ADVENTURE OF CHESS, Edward Lasker. Lively reader, by one of America's finest chess masters, including: history of chess, from ancient Indian 4-handed game of Chaturanga to great players of today; such delights and oddities as Maelzel's chess-playing automaton that beat Napoleon 3 times; etc. One of most valuable features is author's personal recollections of men he has played against—Nimzovich, Emanuel Lasker, Capablanca, Alekhine, etc. Discussion of chess-playing machines (newly revised). 5 page chess primer. 11 illustrations. 53 diagrams. 296pp. 5⅜ x 8. S510 Paperbound **$1.45**

THE ART OF CHESS, James Mason. Unabridged reprinting of latest revised edition of most famous general study ever written. Mason, early 20th century master, teaches beginning, intermediate player over 90 openings; middle game, end game, to see more moves ahead, to plan purposefully, attack, sacrifice, defend, exchange, govern general strategy. "Classic . . . one of the clearest and best developed studies," Publishers Weekly. Also included, a complete supplement by F. Reinfeld, "How Do You Play Chess?", invaluable to beginners for its lively question-and-answer method. 448 diagrams. 1947 Reinfeld-Bernstein text. Bibliography. xvi + 340pp. 5⅜ x 8. T463 Paperbound **$1.85**

MORPHY'S GAMES OF CHESS, edited by P. W. Sergeant. Put boldness into your game by flowing brilliant, forceful moves of the greatest chess player of all time. 300 of Morphy's best games, carefully annotated to reveal principles. 54 classics against masters like Anderssen, Harrwitz, Bird, Paulsen, and others. 52 games at odds; 54 blindfold games; plus over 100 others. Follow his interpretation of Dutch Defense, Evans Gambit, Giuoco Piano, Ruy Lopez, many more. Unabridged reissue of latest revised edition. New introduction by F. Reinfeld. Annotations, introduction by Sergeant. 235 diagrams. x + 352pp. 5⅜ x 8. T386 Paperbound **$1.75**

DOVER SCIENCE BOOKS

WIN AT CHECKERS, M. Hopper. (Formerly "Checkers.") Former World's Unrestricted Checker Champion discusses principles of game, expert's shots, traps, problems for beginner, standard openings, locating best move, end game, opening "blitzkrieg" moves to draw when behind, etc. Over 100 detailed questions, answers anticipate problems. Appendix. 75 problems with solutions, diagrams. 79 figures. xi + 107pp. 5⅜ x 8.   T363 Paperbound **$1.00**

HOW TO FORCE CHECKMATE, Fred Reinfeld. If you have trouble finishing off your opponent, here is a collection of lightning strokes and combinations from actual tournament play. Starts with 1-move checkmates, works up to 3-move mates. Develops ability to look ahead, gain new insights into combinations, complex or deceptive positions; ways to estimate weaknesses, strengths of you and your opponent. "A good deal of amusement and instruction," Times, (London). 300 diagrams. Solutions to all positions. Formerly "Challenge to Chess Players." 111pp. 5⅜ x 8.   T417 Paperbound **$1.25**

A TREASURY OF CHESS LORE, edited by Fred Reinfeld. Delightful collection of anecdotes, short stories, aphorisms by, about masters; poems, accounts of games, tournaments, photographs; hundreds of humorous, pithy, satirical, wise, historical episodes, comments, word portraits. Fascinating "must" for chess players; revealing and perhaps seductive to those who wonder what their friends see in game. 49 photographs (14 full page plates). 12 diagrams. xi + 306pp. 5⅜ x 8.   T458 Paperbound **$1.75**

WIN AT CHESS, Fred Reinfeld. 300 practical chess situations, to sharpen your eye, test skill against masters. Start with simple examples, progress at own pace to complexities. This selected series of crucial moments in chess will stimulate imagination, develop stronger, more versatile game. Simple grading system enables you to judge progress. "Extensive use of diagrams is a great attraction," Chess. 300 diagrams. Notes, solutions to every situation. Formerly "Chess Quiz." vi + 120pp. 5⅜ x 8.   T433 Paperbound **$1.00**

MATHEMATICS:
ELEMENTARY TO INTERMEDIATE

HOW TO CALCULATE QUICKLY, H. Sticker. Tried and true method to help mathematics of everyday life. Awakens "number sense"—ability to see relationships between numbers as whole quantities. A serious course of over 9000 problems and their solutions through techniques not taught in schools: left-to-right multiplications, new fast division, etc. 10 minutes a day will double or triple calculation speed. Excellent for scientist at home in higher math, but dissatisfied with speed and accuracy in lower math. 256pp. 5 x 7¼.
Paperbound **$1.00**

FAMOUS PROBLEMS OF ELEMENTARY GEOMETRY, Felix Klein. Expanded version of 1894 Easter lectures at Göttingen. 3 problems of classical geometry: squaring the circle, trisecting angle, doubling cube, considered with full modern implications: transcendental numbers, pi, etc. "A modern classic . . . no knowledge of higher mathematics is required," Scientia. Notes by R. Archibald. 16 figures. xi + 92pp. 5⅜ x 8.   T298 Paperbound **$1.00**

HIGHER MATHEMATICS FOR STUDENTS OF CHEMISTRY AND PHYSICS, J. W. Mellor. Practical, not abstract, building problems out of familiar laboratory material. Covers differential calculus, coordinate, analytical geometry, functions, integral calculus, infinite series, numerical equations, differential equations, Fourier's theorem probability, theory of errors, calculus of variations, determinants. "If the reader is not familiar with this book, it will repay him to examine it," Chem. and Engineering News. 800 problems. 189 figures. xxi + 641pp. 5⅜ x 8.   S193 Paperbound **$2.25**

TRIGONOMETRY REFRESHER FOR TECHNICAL MEN, A. A. Klaf. 913 detailed questions, answers cover most important aspects of plane, spherical trigonometry—particularly useful in clearing up difficulties in special areas. Part I: plane trig, angles, quadrants, functions, graphical representation, interpolation, equations, logs, solution of triangle, use of slide rule, etc. Next 188 pages discuss applications to navigation, surveying, elasticity, architecture, other special fields. Part 3: spherical trig, applications to terrestrial, astronomical problems. Methods of time-saving, simplification of principal angles, make book most useful. 913 questions answered. 1738 problems, answers to odd numbers. 494 figures. 24 pages of formulas, functions. x + 629pp. 5⅜ x 8.   T371 Paperbound **$2.00**

CALCULUS REFRESHER FOR TECHNICAL MEN, A. A. Klaf. 756 questions examine most important aspects of integral, differential calculus. Part I: simple differential calculus, constants, variables, functions, increments, logs, curves, etc. Part 2: fundamental ideas of integrations, inspection, substitution, areas, volumes, mean value, double, triple integration, etc. Practical aspects stressed. 50 pages illustrate applications to specific problems of civil, nautical engineering, electricity, stress, strain, elasticity, similar fields. 756 questions answered. 566 problems, mostly answered. 36pp. of useful constants, formulas. v + 431pp. 5⅜ x 8.   T370 Paperbound **$2.00**

MONOGRAPHS ON TOPICS OF MODERN MATHEMATICS, edited by J. W. A. Young. Advanced mathematics for persons who have forgotten, or not gone beyond, high school algebra. 9 monographs on foundation of geometry, modern pure geometry, non-Euclidean geometry, fundamental propositions of algebra, algebraic equations, functions, calculus, theory of numbers, etc. Each monograph gives proofs of important results, and descriptions of leading methods, to provide wide coverage. "Of high merit," Scientific American. New introduction by Prof. M. Kline, N.Y. Univ. 100 diagrams. xvi + 416pp. 6⅛ x 9¼.
S289 Paperbound **$2.00**

MATHEMATICS IN ACTION, O. G. Sutton. Excellent middle level application of mathematics to study of universe, demonstrates how math is applied to ballistics, theory of computing machines, waves, wave-like phenomena, theory of fluid flow, meteorological problems, statistics, flight, similar phenomena. No knowledge of advanced math required. Differential equations, Fourier series, group concepts, Eigenfunctions, Planck's constant, airfoil theory, and similar topics explained so clearly in everyday language that almost anyone can derive benefit from reading this even if much of high-school math is forgotten. 2nd edition. 88 figures. viii + 236pp. 5⅜ x 8.
T450 Clothbound **$3.50**

ELEMENTARY MATHEMATICS FROM AN ADVANCED STANDPOINT, Felix Klein. Classic text, an outgrowth of Klein's famous integration and survey course at Göttingen. Using one field to interpret, adjust another, it covers basic topics in each area, with extensive analysis. Especially valuable in areas of modern mathematics. "A great mathematician, inspiring teacher, . . . deep insight," Bul., Amer. Math Soc.

Vol. I. ARITHMETIC, ALGEBRA, ANALYSIS. Introduces concept of function immediately, enlivens discussion with graphical, geometric methods. Partial contents: natural numbers, special properties, complex numbers. Real equations with real unknowns, complex quantities. Logarithmic, exponential functions, infinitesimal calculus. Transcendence of e and pi, theory of assemblages. Index. 125 figures. ix + 274pp. 5⅜ x 8.
S151 Paperbound **$1.75**

Vol. II. GEOMETRY. Comprehensive view, accompanies space perception inherent in geometry with analytic formulas which facilitate precise formulation. Partial contents: Simplest geometric manifold; line segments, Grassman determinant principles, classication of configurations of space. Geometric transformations: affine, projective, higher point transformations, theory of the imaginary. Systematic discussion of geometry and its foundations. 141 illustrations. ix + 214pp. 5⅜ x 8.
S151 Paperbound **$1.75**

A TREATISE ON PLANE AND ADVANCED TRIGONOMETRY, E. W. Hobson. Extraordinarily wide coverage, going beyond usual college level, one of few works covering advanced trig in full detail. By a great expositor with unerring anticipation of potentially difficult points. Includes circular functions; expansion of functions of multiple angle; trig tables; relations between sides, angles of triangles; complex numbers; etc. Many problems fully solved. "The best work on the subject," Nature. Formerly entitled "A Treatise on Plane Trigonometry." 689 examples. 66 figures. xvi + 383pp. 5⅜ x 8.
S353 Paperbound **$1.95**

NON-EUCLIDEAN GEOMETRY, Roberto Bonola. The standard coverage of non-Euclidean geometry. Examines from both a historical and mathematical point of view geometries which have arisen from a study of Euclid's 5th postulate on parallel lines. Also included are complete texts, translated, of Bolyai's "Theory of Absolute Space," Lobachevsky's "Theory of Parallels." 180 diagrams. 431pp. 5⅜ x 8.
S27 Paperbound **$1.95**

GEOMETRY OF FOUR DIMENSIONS, H. P. Manning. Unique in English as a clear, concise introduction. Treatment is synthetic, mostly Euclidean, though in hyperplanes and hyperspheres at infinity, non-Euclidean geometry is used. Historical introduction. Foundations of 4-dimensional geometry. Perpendicularity, simple angles. Angles of planes, higher order. Symmetry, order, motion; hyperpyramids, hypercones, hyperspheres; figures with parallel elements; volume, hypervolume in space; regular polyhedroids. Glossary. 78 figures. ix + 348pp. 5⅜ x 8.
S182 Paperbound **$1.95**

MATHEMATICS: INTERMEDIATE TO ADVANCED

GEOMETRY (EUCLIDEAN AND NON-EUCLIDEAN)

THE GEOMETRY OF RENÉ DESCARTES. With this book, Descartes founded analytical geometry. Original French text, with Descartes's own diagrams, and excellent Smith-Latham translation. Contains: Problems the Construction of Which Requires only Straight Lines and Circles; On the Nature of Curved Lines; On the Construction of Solid or Supersolid Problems. Diagrams. 258pp. 5⅜ x 8.
S68 Paperbound **$1.50**

THE WORKS OF ARCHIMEDES, edited by T. L. Heath. All the known works of the great Greek mathematician, including the recently discovered Method of Archimedes. Contains: On Sphere and Cylinder, Measurement of a Circle, Spirals, Conoids, Spheroids, etc. Definitive edition of greatest mathematical intellect of ancient world. 186 page study by Heath discusses Archimedes and history of Greek mathematics. 563pp. 5⅜ x 8.   S9 Paperbound **$2.00**

COLLECTED WORKS OF BERNARD RIEMANN. Important sourcebook, first to contain complete text of 1892 "Werke" and the 1902 supplement, unabridged. 31 monographs, 3 complete lecture courses, 15 miscellaneous papers which have been of enormous importance in relativity, topology, theory of complex variables, other areas of mathematics. Edited by R. Dedekind, H. Weber, M. Noether, W. Wirtinger. German text; English introduction by Hans Lewy. 690pp. 5⅜ x 8.   S226 Paperbound **$2.85**

THE THIRTEEN BOOKS OF EUCLID'S ELEMENTS, edited by Sir Thomas Heath. Definitive edition of one of very greatest classics of Western world. Complete translation of Heiberg text, plus spurious Book XIV. 150 page introduction on Greek, Medieval mathematics, Euclid, texts, commentators, etc. Elaborate critical apparatus parallels text, analyzing each definition, postulate, proposition, covering textual matters, refutations, supports, extrapolations, etc. This is the full Euclid. Unabridged reproduction of Cambridge U. 2nd edition. 3 volumes. 995 figures. 1426pp. 5⅜ x 8.   S88, 89, 90, 3 volume set, paperbound **$6.00**

AN INTRODUCTION TO GEOMETRY OF N DIMENSIONS, D. M. Y. Sommerville. Presupposes no previous knowledge of field. Only book in English devoted exclusively to higher dimensional geometry. Discusses fundamental ideas of incidence, parallelism, perpendicularity, angles between linear space, enumerative geometry, analytical geometry from projective and metric views, polytopes, elementary ideas in analysis situs, content of hyperspacial figures. 60 diagrams. 196pp. 5⅜ x 8.   S494 Paperbound **$1.50**

ELEMENTS OF NON-EUCLIDEAN GEOMETRY, D. M. Y. Sommerville. Unique in proceeding step-by-step. Requires only good knowledge of high-school geometry and algebra, to grasp elementary hyperbolic, elliptic, analytic non-Euclidean Geometries; space curvature and its implications; radical axes; homopethic centres and systems of circles; parataxy and parallelism; Gauss' proof of defect area theorem; much more, with exceptional clarity. 126 problems at chapter ends. 133 figures. xvi + 274pp. 5⅜ x 8.   S460 Paperbound **$1.50**

THE FOUNDATIONS OF EUCLIDEAN GEOMETRY, H. G. Forder. First connected, rigorous account in light of modern analysis, establishing propositions without recourse to empiricism, without multiplying hypotheses. Based on tools of 19th and 20th century mathematicians, who made it possible to remedy gaps and complexities, recognize problems not earlier discerned. Begins with important relationship of number systems in geometrical figures. Considers classes, relations, linear order, natural numbers, axioms for magnitudes, groups, quasi-fields, fields, non-Archimedian systems, the axiom system (at length), particular axioms (two chapters on the Parallel Axioms), constructions, congruence, similarity, etc. Lists: axioms employed, constructions, symbols in frequent use. 295pp. 5⅜ x 8.   S481 Paperbound **$2.00**

CALCULUS, FUNCTION THEORY (REAL AND COMPLEX), FOURIER THEORY

FIVE VOLUME "THEORY OF FUNCTIONS" SET BY KONRAD KNOPP. Provides complete, readily followed account of theory of functions. Proofs given concisely, yet without sacrifice of completeness or rigor. These volumes used as texts by such universities as M.I.T., Chicago, N.Y. City College, many others. "Excellent introduction . . . remarkably readable, concise, clear, rigorous," J. of the American Statistical Association.

ELEMENTS OF THE THEORY OF FUNCTIONS, Konrad Knopp. Provides background for further volumes in this set, or texts on similar level. Partial contents: Foundations, system of complex numbers and Gaussian plane of numbers, Riemann sphere of numbers, mapping by linear functions, normal forms, the logarithm, cyclometric functions, binomial series. "Not only for the young student, but also for the student who knows all about what is in it," Mathematical Journal. 140pp. 5⅜ x 8.   S154 Paperbound **$1.35**

THEORY OF FUNCTIONS, PART I, Konrad Knopp. With volume II, provides coverage of basic concepts and theorems. Partial contents: numbers and points, functions of a complex variable, integral of a continuous function, Cauchy's intergral theorem, Cauchy's integral formulae, series with variable terms, expansion and analytic function in a power series, analytic continuation and complete definition of analytic functions, Laurent expansion, types of singularities. vii + 146pp. 5⅜ x 8.   S156 Paperbound **$1.35**

THEORY OF FUNCTIONS, PART II, Konrad Knopp. Application and further development of general theory, special topics. Single valued functions, entire, Weierstrass. Meromorphic functions: Mittag-Leffler. Periodic functions. Multiple valued functions. Riemann surfaces. Algebraic functions. Analytical configurations, Riemann surface. x + 150pp. 5⅜ x 8.   S157 Paperbound **$1.35**

PROBLEM BOOK IN THE THEORY OF FUNCTIONS, VOLUME I, Konrad Knopp. Problems in elementary theory, for use with Knopp's "Theory of Functions," or any other text. Arranged according to increasing difficulty. Fundamental concepts, sequences of numbers and infinite series, complex variable, integral theorems, development in series, conformal mapping. Answers. viii + 126pp. 5⅜ x 8.　　　　　　　　　　　　　　S 158 **Paperbound $1.35**

PROBLEM BOOK IN THE THEORY OF FUNCTIONS, VOLUME II, Konrad Knopp. Advanced theory of functions, to be used with Knopp's "Theory of Functions," or comparable text. Singularities, entire and meromorphic functions, periodic, analytic, continuation, multiple-valued functions, Riemann surfaces, conformal mapping. Includes section of elementary problems. "The difficult task of selecting . . . problems just within the reach of the beginner is here masterfully accomplished," AM. MATH. SOC. Answers. 138pp. 5⅜ x 8.
S159 Paperbound **$1.35**

ADVANCED CALCULUS, E. B. Wilson. Still recognized as one of most comprehensive, useful texts. Immense amount of well-represented, fundamental material, including chapters on vector functions, ordinary differential equations, special functions, calculus of variations, etc., which are excellent introductions to these areas. Requires only one year of calculus. Over 1300 exercises cover both pure math and applications to engineering and physical problems. Ideal reference, refresher. 54 page introductory review. ix + 566pp. 5⅜ x 8.
S504 Paperbound **$2.45**

LECTURES ON THE THEORY OF ELLIPTIC FUNCTIONS, H. Hancock. Reissue of only book in English with so extensive a coverage, especially of Abel, Jacobi, Legendre, Weierstrass, Hermite, Liouville, and Riemann. Unusual fullness of treatment, plus applications as well as theory in discussing universe of elliptic integrals, originating in works of Abel and Jacobi. Use is made of Riemann to provide most general theory. 40-page table of formulas. 76 figures. xxiii + 498pp. 5⅜ x 8.　　　　　　　　　　　　S483 Paperbound **$2.55**

THEORY OF FUNCTIONALS AND OF INTEGRAL AND INTEGRO-DIFFERENTIAL EQUATIONS, Vito Volterra. Unabridged republication of only English translation. General theory of functions depending on continuous set of values of another function. Based on author's concept of transition from finite number of variables to a continually infinite number. Includes much material on calculus of variations. Begins with fundamentals, examines generalization of analytic functions, functional derivative equations, applications, other directions of theory, etc. New introduction by G. C. Evans. Biography, criticism of Volterra's work by E. Whittaker. xxxx + 226pp. 5⅜ x 8.　　　　　　　　　　　S502 Paperbound **$1.75**

AN INTRODUCTION TO FOURIER METHODS AND THE LAPLACE TRANSFORMATION, Philip Franklin. Concentrates on essentials, gives broad view, suitable for most applications. Requires only knowledge of calculus. Covers complex qualities with methods of computing elementary functions for complex values of argument and finding approximations by charts; Fourier series; harmonic anaylsis; much more. Methods are related to physical problems of heat flow, vibrations, electrical transmission, electromagnetic radiation, etc. 828 problems, answers. Formerly entitled "Fourier Methods." x + 289pp. 5⅜ x 8.
S452 Paperbound **$1.75**

THE ANALYTICAL THEORY OF HEAT, Joseph Fourier. This book, which revolutionized mathematical physics, has been used by generations of mathematicians and physicists interested in heat or application of Fourier integral. Covers cause and reflection of rays of heat, radiant heating, heating of closed spaces, use of trigonometric series in theory of heat, Fourier integral, etc. Translated by Alexander Freeman. 20 figures. xxii + 466pp. 5⅜ x 8.
S93 Paperbound **$2.00**

ELLIPTIC INTEGRALS, H. Hancock. Invaluable in work involving differential equations with cubics, quatrics under root sign, where elementary calculus methods are inadequate. Practical solutions to problems in mathematics, engineering, physics; differential equations requiring integration of Lamé's, Briot's, or Bouquet's equations; determination of arc of ellipse, hyperbola, lemiscate; solutions of problems in elastics; motion of a projectile under resistance varying as the cube of the velocity; pendulums; more. Exposition in accordance with Legendre-Jacobi theory. Rigorous discussion of Legendre transformations. 20 figures. 5 place table. 104pp. 5⅜ x 8.　　　　　　　　　　　　　S484 Paperbound **$1.25**

THE TAYLOR SERIES, AN INTRODUCTION TO THE THEORY OF FUNCTIONS OF A COMPLEX VARIABLE, P. Dienes. Uses Taylor series to approach theory of functions, using ordinary calculus only, except in last 2 chapters. Starts with introduction to real variable and complex algebra, derives properties of infinite series, complex differentiation, integration, etc. Covers biuniform mapping, overconvergence and gap theorems, Taylor series on its circle of convergence, etc. Unabridged corrected reissue of first edition. 186 examples, many fully worked out. 67 figures. xii + 555pp. 5⅜ x 8.　　　　　　S391 Paperbound **$2.75**

LINEAR INTEGRAL EQUATIONS, W. V. Lovitt. Systematic survey of general theory, with some application to differential equations, calculus of variations, problems of math, physics. Includes: integral equation of 2nd kind by successive substitutions; Fredholm's equation as ratio of 2 integral series in lambda, applications of the Fredholm theory, Hilbert-Schmidt theory of symmetric kernels, application, etc. Neumann, Dirichlet, vibratory problems. ix + 253pp. 5⅜ x 8.
S175 Clothbound **$3.50**
S176 Paperbound **$1.60**

DOVER SCIENCE BOOKS

DICTIONARY OF CONFORMAL REPRESENTATIONS, H. Kober. Developed by British Admiralty to solve Laplace's equation in 2 dimensions. Scores of geometrical forms and transformations for electrical engineers, Joukowski aerofoil for aerodynamics, Schwartz-Christoffel transformations for hydro-dynamics, transcendental functions. Contents classified according to analytical functions describing transformations with corresponding regions. Glossary. Topological index. 447 diagrams. 6⅛ x 9¼.   .S160 Paperbound **$2.00**

ELEMENTS OF THE THEORY OF REAL FUNCTIONS, J. E. Littlewood. Based on lectures at Trinity College, Cambridge, this book has proved extremely successful in introducing graduate students to modern theory of functions. Offers full and concise coverage of classes and cardinal numbers, well ordered series, other types of series, and elements of the theory of sets of points. 3rd revised edition. vii + 71pp. 5⅜ x 8.   S171 Clothbound **$2.85**
                                                                                S172 Paperbound **$1.25**

INFINITE SEQUENCES AND SERIES, Konrad Knopp. 1st publication in any language. Excellent introduction to 2 topics of modern mathematics, designed to give student background to penetrate further alone. Sequences and sets, real and complex numbers, etc. Functions of a real and complex variable. Sequences and series. Infinite series. Convergent power series. Expansion of elementary functions. Numerical evaluation of series. v + 186pp. 5⅜ x 8.
                                                                                S152 Clothbound **$3.50**
                                                                                S153 Paperbound **$1.75**

THE THEORY AND FUNCTIONS OF A REAL VARIABLE AND THE THEORY OF FOURIER'S SERIES, E. W .Hobson. One of the best introductions to set theory and various aspects of functions and Fourier's series. Requires only a good background in calculus. Exhaustive coverage of: metric and descriptive properties of sets of points; transfinite numbers and order types; functions of a real variable; the Riemann and Lebesgue integrals; sequences and series of numbers; power-series; functions representable by series sequences of continuous functions; trigonometrical series; representation of functions by Fourier's series; and much more. "The best possible guide," Nature. Vol. I: 88 detailed examples, 10 figures. Index. xv + 736pp. Vol. II: 117 detailed examples, 13 figures. x + 780pp. 6⅛ x 9¼.
                                                          Vol. I: S387 Paperbound **$3.00**
                                                          Vol. II: S388 Paperbound **$3.00**

ALMOST PERIODIC FUNCTIONS, A. S. Besicovitch. Unique and important summary by a well known mathematician covers in detail the two stages of development in Bohr's theory of almost periodic functions: (1) as a generalization of pure periodicity, with results and proofs; (2) the work done by Stepanof, Wiener, Weyl, and Bohr in generalizing the theory. xi + 180pp. 5⅜ x 8.   S18 Paperbound **$1.75**

INTRODUCTION TO THE THEORY OF FOURIER'S SERIES AND INTEGRALS, H. S. Carslaw. 3rd revised edition, an outgrowth of author's courses at Cambridge. Historical introduction, rational, irrational numbers, infinite sequences and series, functions of a single variable, definite integral, Fourier series, and similar topics. Appendices discuss practical harmonic analysis, periodogram analysis, Lebesgue's theory. 84 examples. xiii + 368pp. 5⅜ x 8.
                                                                                S48 Paperbound **$2.00**

SYMBOLIC LOGIC

THE ELEMENTS OF MATHEMATICAL LOGIC, Paul Rosenbloom. First publication in any language. For mathematically mature readers with no training in symbolic logic. Development of lectures given at Lund Univ., Sweden, 1948. Partial contents: Logic of classes, fundamental theorems, Boolean algebra, logic of propositions, of propositional functions, expressive languages, combinatory logics, development of math within an object language, paradoxes, theorems of Post, Goedel, Church, and similar topics. iv + 214pp. 5⅜ x 8.
                                                                                S227 Paperbound **$1.45**

INTRODUCTION TO SYMBOLIC LOGIC AND ITS APPLICATION, R. Carnap. Clear, comprehensive, rigorous, by perhaps greatest living master. Symbolic languages analyzed, one constructed. Applications to math (axiom systems for set theory, real, natural numbers), topology (Dedekind, Cantor continuity explanations), physics (general analysis of determination, causality, space-time topology), biology (axiom system for basic concepts). "A masterpiece," Zentralblatt für Mathematik und Ihre Grenzgebiete. Over 300 exercises. 5 figures. xvi + 241pp. 5⅜ x 8.   S453 Paperbound **$1.85**

AN INTRODUCTION TO SYMBOLIC LOGIC, Susanne K. Langer. Probably clearest book for the philosopher, scientist, layman—no special knowledge of math required. Starts with simplest symbols, goes on to give remarkable grasp of Boole-Schroeder, Russell-Whitehead systems, clearly, quickly. Partial Contents: Forms, Generalization, Classes, Deductive System of Classes, Algebra of Logic, Assumptions of Principia Mathematica, Logistics, Proofs of Theorems, etc. "Clearest . . . simplest introduction . . . the intelligent non-mathematician should have no difficulty," MATHEMATICS GAZETTE. Revised, expanded 2nd edition. Truth-value tables. 368pp. 5⅜ 8.   S164 Paperbound **$1.75**

13

CATALOGUE OF

TRIGONOMETRICAL SERIES, Antoni Zygmund. On modern advanced level. Contains carefully organized analyses of trigonometric, orthogonal, Fourier systems of functions, with clear adequate descriptions of summability of Fourier series, proximation theory, conjugate series, convergence, divergence of Fourier series. Especially valuable for Russian, Eastern European coverage. 329pp. 5⅜ x 8.					S290 Paperbound **$1.50**

THE LAWS OF THOUGHT, George Boole. This book founded symbolic logic some 100 years ago. It is the 1st significant attempt to apply logic to all aspects of human endeavour. Partial contents: derivation of laws, signs and laws, interpretations, eliminations, conditions of a perfect method, analysis, Aristotelian logic, probability, and similar topics. xvii + 424pp. 5⅜ x 8.					S28 Paperbound **$2.00**

SYMBOLIC LOGIC, C. I. Lewis, C. H. Langford. 2nd revised edition of probably most cited book in symbolic logic. Wide coverage of entire field; one of fullest treatments of paradoxes; plus much material not available elsewhere. Basic to volume is distinction between logic of extensions and intensions. Considerable emphasis on converse substitution, while matrix system presents supposition of variety of non-Aristotelian logics. Especially valuable sections on strict limitations, existence theorems. Partial contents: Boole-Schroeder algebra; truth value systems, the matrix method; implication and deductibility; general theory of propositions; etc. "Most valuable," Times, London. 506pp. 5⅜ x 8.	S170 Paperbound **$2.00**

GROUP THEORY AND LINEAR ALGEBRA, SETS, ETC.

LECTURES ON THE ICOSAHEDRON AND THE SOLUTION OF EQUATIONS OF THE FIFTH DEGREE, Felix Klein. Solution of quintics in terms of rotations of regular icosahedron around its axes of symmetry. A classic, indispensable source for those interested in higher algebra, geometry, crystallography. Considerable explanatory material included. 230 footnotes, mostly bibliography. "Classical monograph . . . detailed, readable book," Math. Gazette. 2nd edition. xvi + 289pp. 5⅜ x 8.					S314 Paperbound **$1.85**

INTRODUCTION TO THE THEORY OF GROUPS OF FINITE ORDER, R. Carmichael. Examines fundamental theorems and their applications. Beginning with sets, systems, permutations, etc., progresses in easy stages through important types of groups: Abelian, prime power, permutation, etc. Except 1 chapter where matrices are desirable, no higher math is needed. 783 exercises, problems. xvi + 447pp. 5⅜ x 8.			S299 Clothbound **$3.95**
S300 Paperbound **$2.00**

THEORY OF GROUPS OF FINITE ORDER, W. Burnside. First published some 40 years ago, still one of clearest introductions. Partial contents: permutations, groups independent of representation, composition series of a group, isomorphism of a group with itself, Abelian groups, prime power groups, permutation groups, invariants of groups of linear substitution, graphical representation, etc. "Clear and detailed discussion . . . numerous problems which are instructive," Design News. xxiv + 512pp. 5⅜ x 8.	S38 Paperbound **$2.45**

COMPUTATIONAL METHODS OF LINEAR ALGEBRA, V. N. Faddeeva, translated by C. D. Benster. 1st English translation of unique, valuable work, only one in English presenting systematic exposition of most important methods of linear algebra—classical, contemporary. Details of deriving numerical solutions of problems in mathematical physics. Theory and practice. Includes survey of necessary background, most important methods of solution, for exact, iterative groups. One of most valuable features is 23 tables, triple checked for accuracy, unavailable elsewhere. Translator's note. x + 252pp. 5⅜ x 8.	S424 Paperbound **$1.95**

THE CONTINUUM AND OTHER TYPES OF SERIAL ORDER, E. V. Huntington. This famous book gives a systematic elementary account of the modern theory of the continuum as a type of serial order. Based on the Cantor-Dedekind ordinal theory, which requires no technical knowledge of higher mathematics, it offers an easily followed analysis of ordered classes, discrete and dense series, continuous series, Cantor's transfinite numbers. "Admirable introduction to the rigorous theory of the continuum . . . reading easy," Science Progress. 2nd edition. viii + 82pp. 5⅜ x 8.					S129 Clothbound **$2.75**
S130 Paperbound **$1.00**

THEORY OF SETS, E. Kamke. Clearest, amplest introduction in English, well suited for independent study. Subdivisions of main theory, such as theory of sets of points, are discussed, but emphasis is on general theory. Partial contents: rudiments of set theory, arbitrary sets, their cardinal numbers, ordered sets, their order types, well-ordered sets, their cardinal numbers. vii + 144pp. 5⅜ x 8.					S141 Paperbound **$1.35**

CONTRIBUTIONS TO THE FOUNDING OF THE THEORY OF TRANSFINITE NUMBERS, Georg Cantor. These papers founded a new branch of mathematics. The famous articles of 1895-7 are translated, with an 82-page introduction by P. E. B. Jourdain dealing with Cantor, the background of his discoveries, their results, future possibilities. ix + 211pp. 5⅜ x 8.
S45 Paperbound **$1.25**

DOVER SCIENCE BOOKS

NUMERICAL AND GRAPHICAL METHODS, TABLES

JACOBIAN ELLIPTIC FUNCTION TABLES, L. M. Milne-Thomson. Easy-to-follow, practical, not only useful numerical tables, but complete elementary sketch of application of elliptic functions. Covers description of principle properties; complete elliptic integrals; Fourier series, expansions; periods, zeros, poles, residues, formulas for special values of argument; cubic, quartic polynomials; pendulum problem; etc. Tables, graphs form body of book: Graph, 5 figure table of elliptic function sn (u m); cn (u m); dn (u m). 8 figure table of complete elliptic integrals K, K′, E, E′, nome q. 7 figure table of Jacobian zeta-function Z(u). 3 figures. xi + 123pp. 5⅜ x 8. **S194 Paperbound $1.35**

TABLES OF FUNCTIONS WITH FORMULAE AND CURVES, E. Jahnke, F. Emde. Most comprehensive 1-volume English text collection of tables, formulae, curves of transcendent functions. 4th corrected edition, new 76-page section giving tables, formulae for elementary functions not in other English editions. Partial contents: sine, cosine, logarithmic integral; error integral; elliptic integrals; theta functions; Legendre, Bessel, Riemann, Mathieu, hypergeometric functions; etc. "Out-of-the-way functions for which we know no other source." Scientific Computing Service, Ltd. 212 figures. 400pp. 5⅝ x 8⅜. **S133 Paperbound $2.00**

MATHEMATICAL TABLES, H. B. Dwight. Covers in one volume almost every function of importance in applied mathematics, engineering, physical sciences. Three extremely fine tables of the three trig functions, inverses, to 1000th of radian; natural, common logs; squares, cubes; hyperbolic functions, inverses; $(a^2 + b^2)$ exp. ½a; complete elliptical integrals of 1st, 2nd kind; sine, cosine integrals; exponential integrals; $Ei(x)$ and $Ei(-x)$; binomial coefficients; factorials to 250; surface zonal harmonics, first derivatives; Bernoulli, Euler numbers, their logs to base of 10; Gamma function; normal probability integral; over 60pp. Bessel functions; Riemann zeta function. Each table with formulae generally used, sources of more extensive tables, interpolation data, etc. Over half have columns of differences, to facilitate interpolation. viii + 231pp. 5⅜ x 8. **S445 Paperbound $1.75**

PRACTICAL ANALYSIS, GRAPHICAL AND NUMERICAL METHODS, F. A. Willers. Immensely practical hand-book for engineers. How to interpolate, use various methods of numerical differentiation and integration, determine roots of a single algebraic equation, system of linear equations, use empirical formulas, integrate differential equations, etc. Hundreds of short-cuts for arriving at numerical solutions. Special section on American calculating machines, by T. W. Simpson. Translation by R. T. Beyer. 132 illustrations. 422pp. 5⅜ x 8. **S273 Paperbound $2.00**

NUMERICAL SOLUTIONS OF DIFFERENTIAL EQUATIONS, H. Levy, E. A. Baggott. Comprehensive collection of methods for solving ordinary differential equations of first and higher order. 2 requirements: practical, easy to grasp; more rapid than school methods. Partial contents: graphical integration of differential equations, graphical methods for detailed solution. Numerical solution. Simultaneous equations and equations of 2nd and higher orders. "Should be in the hands of all in research and applied mathematics, teaching," Nature. 21 figures. viii + 238pp. 5⅜ x 8. **S168 Paperbound $1.75**

NUMERICAL INTEGRATION OF DIFFERENTIAL EQUATIONS, Bennet, Milne, Bateman. Unabridged republication of original prepared for National Research Council. New methods of integration by 3 leading mathematicians: "The Interpolational Polynomial," "Successive Approximation," A. A. Bennett, "Step-by-step Methods of Integration," W. W. Milne. "Methods for Partial Differential Equations," H. Bateman. Methods for partial differential equations, solution of differential equations to non-integral values of a parameter will interest mathematicians, physicists. 288 footnotes, mostly bibliographical. 235 item classified bibliography. 108pp. 5⅜ x 8. **S305 Paperbound $1.35**